ı) 3

SYMBOLS, OUR UNIVERSAL LANGUAGE

SYMBOLS.

DRAGON BENEFICENT -
SPIRIT OF ALL KNOWLEDGE

Our Universal Language

Eva C. Hangen

Professor Emeritus English Literature and Language
University of Wichita

Author: A CONCORDANCE OF THE POETICAL WORKS
OF SIR THOMAS WYATT

Illustrations by Sally Gorum Braht

Wichita, Kansas, 1962

TO THOSE NOBLE MEN AND WOMEN

OF ALL TIME AND ALL PLACE

WHO HOLD IN ESTEEM, AND HELP PERPETUATE

THE TRUE VALUES OF GREAT BOOKS AND INSPIRATIONAL ART;

WHO REVEL IN THE GLORIOUS BEAUTIES AND WONDERMENT OF NATURE;

AND WHO CHERISH THE DELIGHTS OF SIMPLE LIVING.

PREFACE

For out of olde feldes, as men seith,

Cometh al this newe corn from yeer to yere;

And out of olde bokes, in good feith,

Cometh al this newe science that men lere.

Parlement of Foules, lines 22-25
Geoffrey Chaucer,

Symbols form connections with the past which we cannot afford culturally to lose. Many have come from the far past — antiquity, Chaucer's "olde feldes." Time and locality altered somewhat their implications and significations, yet the glamor of the romance, the myths, legends, and stories which lead us to their origin remains intact, enriching the literary realms of creativity and fancies.

Fully aware of the great challenge involved in an attempt to compile into one volume the numberless traditional symbolisms, together with origin and meaning, it is with diffidence that I present to my readers SYMBOLS — OUR UNIVERSAL LANGUAGE. The "felde" is a large one, and I ask only to be accepted as a pioneer. Urgency of friends in educational, commercial, cultural and religious circles, who have given testimony that such a compendium would be a valuable asset in their specific areas of interest has spurred me on and afforded me a pleasant, and I hope, fruitful pastime in my years of retirement.

During my reading experiences as a student, and in the years following as a teacher of English Literature, I kept faithfully a listing of what to me at the time were vague-meaning symbols and out-of-the-past mythological allusions for which I could find no one encyclopediac reference book giving me satisfactory enlightenment.

With this list as a starting point, I began a search for materials helpful to my project of gathering together facts for a comprehensive, wideencompassing compendium of traditional symbolisms. The information I needed was scattered, yet the required reading fascinating. I was first led to the Ancients (in translation), to books on mythology, religions of the world, bestiaries and fables, heraldry, art and architecture, the Bible, and many others. Valuable, also, were technical books on plants, minerals, and

3

animal life, as were general reference works — dictionaries, encyclopedias, especially those dealing with the customary practices of the various schools of religious thought.

Helpful, also, in substantiating what I had learned through reading, was close hand examination of real objects: markings on old coins and rings; crests, chevrons, insignia, armorial devices, helmets, shields, government seals, emblems, family coats of arms, gargoyles, fountains, gravestones, stained glass windows, tapestries, paintings and other works of art. Word derivations, likewise, often provided a clue for establishment of origins.

Most pleasurable, and exceedingly desirable for verification purposes, were the excursions to far-away places, with visits to ancient temples, and shrines of the Orient and Middle East, Catacombs of Rome, old European cemeteries, tombs and archaeological collections in Egypt; cathedrals, museums, libraries, art displays, and famous architectural structures of Europe and our own Americas.

From the huge mass of information I had collected from these various sources, the basis of selection as to what to include and what to reject was at times problematical. There was often the close kinship of the commonly defined symbol with the psychologist's or sociologist's charms, taboos, mores, superstitions. There was the near-semblance to personifications and metaphors of literary writings. My line of demarcation is not absolute. I have included attributes and significations of pagan divinities, mythological heroes, Old Testament patriarchs, and patron saints. In justification for their inclusion, I have followed the opinions of recent literary authorities who maintain that the phenomena which these characters, real or mythical, personify have remained the same for such a great length of time that they may rightfully be thought of as symbols. I have also included emblematic state flowers, birds, trees, and animals, in that they, too, through their continued usage as symbolisms by creative writers and artists may rightfully be classed as symbols.

Not included in SYMBOLS — OUR UNIVERSAL LANGUAGE, though they do speak one language over the greater areas of the world, are symbols used as *signs* in a technical sense, objective, having fixed denotation, such as symbols in mathematics, phonetic symbols of dictionaries, symbols for musical terms. Omitted, likewise, are symbols which hold special meanings for isolated groups having handbooks with explanations of significations applicable only to each particular group — e.g. manuals of fraternal organizations, Girl Scouts, educational honorary societies.

It is my sincere hope that in presenting SYMBOLS — OUR UNIVERSAL LANGUAGE to my readers that it will in a small measure fulfill the purposes which gave the book its inception: to aid in the preservation of the precious heritage of the traditional symbolisms which surround us; to add enrichment, understanding, and sensitivity to our readings, and interpretation to our study of the arts; to bring about a closer spiritual kinship among churchmen of different faiths, through deeper understanding of the inward feelings embedded in the outward form of the symbols exhibited in the architecture, the rituals and embellishments of their fellow worshipers; to provide useful information for artisans in the various fields of activity — architects, designers, florists, printers. At the close of the compilation, there is a listing of numerous occupational groups which have a chosen patron. This convenient list comes for the convenience of designers of medals, trophies, trademarks, and emblems who have need for a ready reference work of this type.

The drawings in the early pages of the book are representative of the numerous categories of symbolic figures, descriptions of which are given in the alphabetical listings of the book, where number designation corresponds to the number under the drawing. The list of illustrations is limited, yet reflective of the many, many objects or shapes employed as bases for traditional symbols. We are told that for the cross, alone, some 400 different representations appear.

Arrangement of headwords is in alphabetical order. Occasional use of cross-references obviates repetition of descriptive details. Biblical references unless otherwise stated are from the Authorized King James version.

In addition to the acknowledgments appearing on the final pages of the book, I wish to extend thanks of lasting gratitude to the many friends and former colleagues who have followed my undertakings with personal interest; to staff members of Wichita Public Library who have generously placed for my needs all of the resources of the library; to members of the staff of Morrison Library at the University of Wichita, who have made special concessions that I might have free use of all of the facilities of the library; to Sally Gorum Braht who in the attractive, meaningful illustrations has thrown full-force her skill as an artist and her keen understanding of the underlying symbolism hidden in the objective forms she has drawn.

I wish, also, to include my acknowledgment of the fine workmanship and earnest cooperation of the publishers, McCormick-Armstrong, Inc., to Bill Jackson, designer of the book, and more especially my thanks to Mr. W. J. van Wormer, who with intelligence and dispatch has handled with careful detail the matters of printing.

1843 N. Lorraine

Wichita, Kansas

The author

Eva C. Hangen

PLATE I. DEITIES — REMEMBERED FOR THEIR ATTRIBUTES

1. Poseidon

2. Pallas Athene

3. Apollo

4. Osiris

5. Hercules

6. Artemis

7. Dionysus

8. Atlas

9. Hera

10. Medusa's Head

11. Zeus

PLATE II. MONSTERS OF FABLE AND FANCY

1. Griffin

2. Antelope

3. Dragon

4. Sphinx

5. Sea-horse

6. Chimera

7. Apis

8. Unicorn

9. Pegasus

10. Garuda

11. Centaur

PLATE III. SYMBOLS FROM STORIES AND BELIEFS

1. Winged Sun-disc

2. Phoenix

3. Bodhi Tree

4. Ganesha

5. Lion

6. Sag

7. Dolphin

8. The Sun

9. Harpy

10. Thunder Bird

11. Anubis

9

PLATE IV. FAMILIAR FIGURES AND FORMS

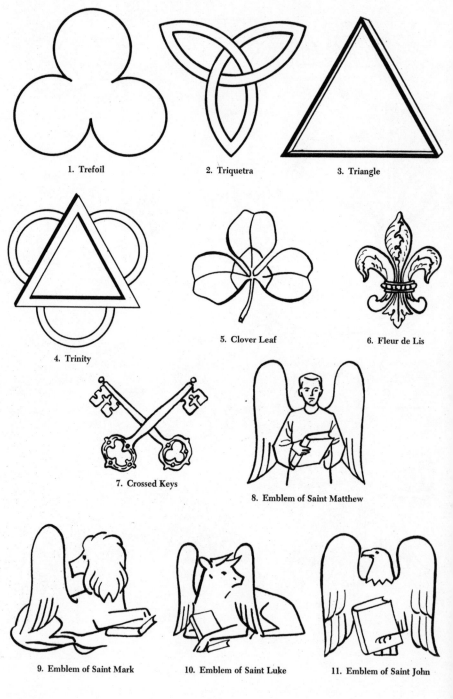

1. Trefoil

2. Triquetra

3. Triangle

4. Trinity

5. Clover Leaf

6. Fleur de Lis

7. Crossed Keys

8. Emblem of Saint Matthew

9. Emblem of Saint Mark

10. Emblem of Saint Luke

11. Emblem of Saint John

PLATE V. SYMBOLS OF DEVOTION

1. Cross and Crown

2. All-seeing Eye

3. The Hand of God

4. Fish

5. Butterfly

6. Agnus Dei

7. Pelican

8. Conventional Rose

9. Peacock

10. Menorah

11. Altar Cross

12. Chi-Rho

11

PLATE VI. CROSSES LEAD THE WAY

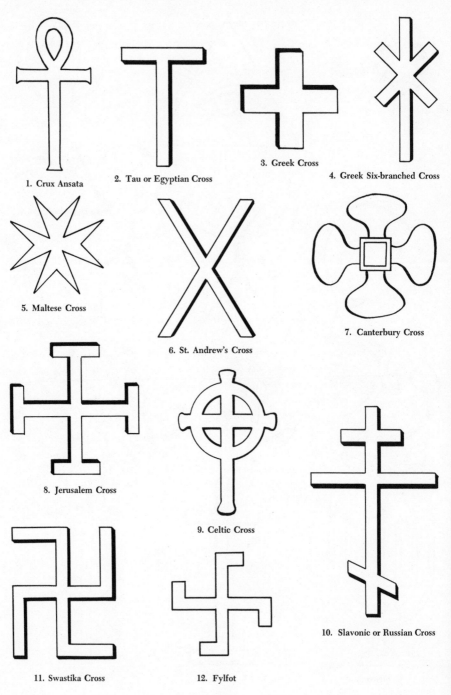

1. Crux Ansata

2. Tau or Egyptian Cross

3. Greek Cross

4. Greek Six-branched Cross

5. Maltese Cross

6. St. Andrew's Cross

7. Canterbury Cross

8. Jerusalem Cross

9. Celtic Cross

10. Slavonic or Russian Cross

11. Swastika Cross

12. Fylfot

PLATE VII. THE THIRTEEN CRUCIFIXION SYMBOLS

1. Whipping Post

2. Lance

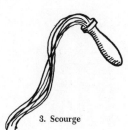

3. Scourge

4. Crown of Thorns

5. Nails

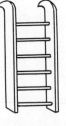

6. Ladder

7. Veronica's Napkin

8. Seamless Garment

9. Sponge

10. Reed

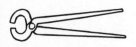

11. Pincers

12. Latin Cross of Suffering

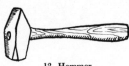

13. Hammer

13

PLATE VIII. SYMBOLS OF CEREMONY

1. Crosier

2. Chasuble

3. Alb

4. Cassock

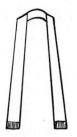

5. Stole

6. Mitre

7. Biretta

8. Amice

9. Buckler

10. Wheel of the Law

11. Ark

14

PLATE IX. OBJECTS OF SYMBOLIC SIGNIFICANCE

1. Beehive

2. Bugle Horn

3. Scales

4. Battle Axe

5. Simitar

6. Hourglass

7. Horseshoe

8. Anchor

9. Escallop

10. Conch

11. Palmer's Staff

15

PLATE X. OBJECTS SACRED AND MEANINGFUL

1. Censer

2. Ciborium

3. Open Bible

4. Ampulla

5. The Seven Flames

6. Lyre

7. Shofar

8. Easter Lily

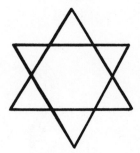

9. Star of David

10. The Chalice

11. Bell

12. The Cup and the Cross

16

PLATE XI. LIVING CREATURES CONTRIBUTE SYMBOLS

1. Goat

2. Fox

3. Cat

4. Hare

5. Bear

6. Lynx

7. Leopard

8. Sheep

9. Scarab

10. Pair of Fishes

11. Bee

12. Bat

PLATE XII. BIRDS AND FOWLS TELL THEIR STORIES

1. Owl

2. Bluebird

3. Cock

4. Falcon

5. Stork

6. Raven

7. Crane

8. Dove

9. Ostrich

10. Swallow

11. Swan

PLATE XIII. SYMBOLISMS OF THE OCCUPATIONS

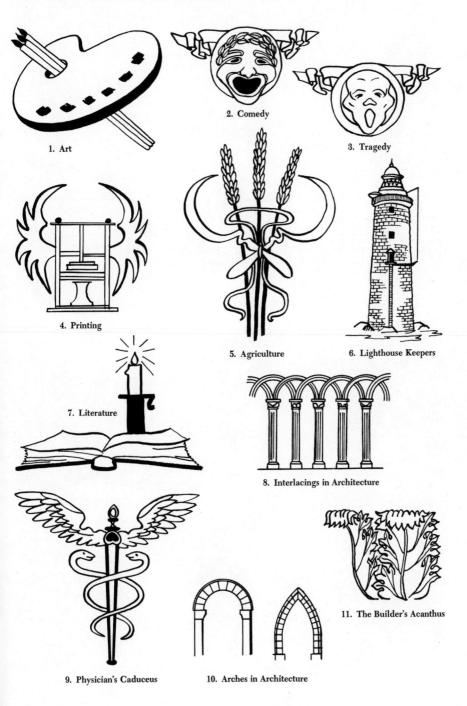

1. Art

2. Comedy

3. Tragedy

4. Printing

5. Agriculture

6. Lighthouse Keepers

7. Literature

8. Interlacings in Architecture

9. Physician's Caduceus

10. Arches in Architecture

11. The Builder's Acanthus

PLATE XIV. NATURE ADDS HER SYMBOLS

1. Acorn

2. Lotus

3. Grapes

4. Thistle

5. Pomegranate

6. Daisy

7. Pansy

8. Rosebud

9. Hyacinth

10. Peony

11. Passion Flower

12. Sunflower

PLATE XV. EACH MONTH A NEW FLOWER

1. Carnation — January

2. Violet — February

3. Jonquil — March

4. Sweet Pea — April

5. Lily of the Valley — May

6. Rose — June

7. Larkspur — July

8. Gladiolus — August

9. Aster — September

10. Calendula — October

11. Chrysanthemum — November

12. Narcissus — December

21

PLATE XVI. TREASURED SYMBOLISMS OF SENTIMENT

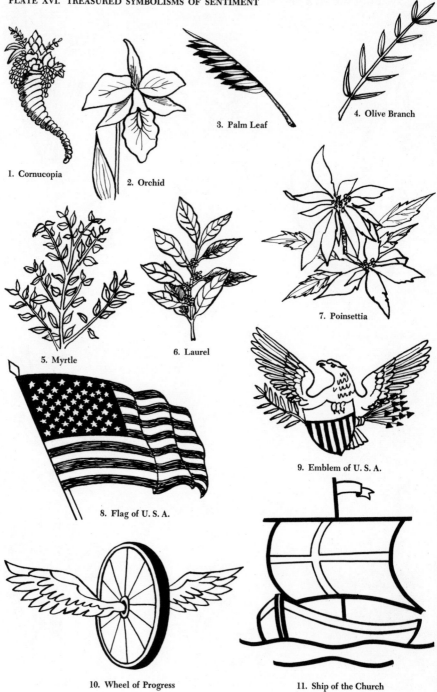

1. Cornucopia

2. Orchid

3. Palm Leaf

4. Olive Branch

5. Myrtle

6. Laurel

7. Poinsettia

8. Flag of U. S. A.

9. Emblem of U. S. A.

10. Wheel of Progress

11. Ship of the Church

AARON

In church symbolism, *ecclesiastical leadership,* from the story in Exodus, Chapters 28 and 29. He was the first Jewish high priest, and in art is pictured wearing the prescribed vestment of his office. His attributes are a censer and a flowering rod.

AARON'S ROD

Tall flowering autumn plant, signifying *encouragement,* in that it brightens the fall months with its profusion of flowers. In architecture, the term applies to an ornamental small column or post with sprouting leaves as a decoration. From an allusion to Aaron's experience in Numbers 17:8.

ABRAHAM

Exalted father. First of the patriarchs and father of the Hebrews. Genesis, Chapter 11.

ABRAXAS

Deity invented by pre-Christian Gnostics with body of a human, head of a cock, legs of serpents, and armed with mace and buckler. Symbol of *the mind, the word.*

ACACIA

Friendship, Platonic love, from the fragrance of the plant's many clustered flowers; *fecundity* from its pinnate leaves; *immortality* from the hardness and durability of the wood.

In Biblical symbolism, when the Egyptian variety is shown afire, the *call of Moses* is implied. National flower of Australia.

ACANTHUS

The flower, with its beautiful spiny leaves, signifies *art, heaven, gardens of heaven,* and with this denotation has been carried over into the field of architecture, as a widely used ornamentation pattern, particularly in capitals of Corinthian column. Illustration p. 19:11.

ACHATES

In literary allusion, *faithful friend,* from Achates' inseparable companionship with Aeneas in Vergil's *Aeneid.*

ACHILLES

Strength, valor, beauty, from the physical features of this young Greek hero of Homer's *Iliad.*

ACONITE

As for the common monk's hood, symbolizes *remorse, revenge, illicit love,* in association with the poisoning nature of the plant.

ACORN

Independence and *strength,* symbol, also, of the sturdy oak tree of which the acorn is the nutty fruit. Illustration p. 20:1.

ACRISIUS

In Greek mythology, king of Argos, slain by Perseus. Signifies *darkness, bitterness.*

ACTAEON

In classical mythology, a huntsman who was changed into a stag by the goddess Diana whom he had spied upon while at her bath. *False allegiance.*

ADAM

Human frailty, original sin. From his characterization in Genesis Chapters I to V. His attributes — old, yet sturdy man girded with fig leaves.

ADAMANT

In Biblical symbolism denotes *obstinacy, hardness of heart, unyieldingness.* Ezekiel 3:9; Zechariah 7:12.

ADAMASTO

In Zoroaster's *Oracle,* as one of the nine spirits of intelligence, signifies *conflict, violence.*

ADDEPHAGIA

Symbol of *good cheer,* from this rosy, buxom Roman goddess pictured in epicurean surroundings, smiling contentedly.

ADDER

In Biblical literature, *deadly malice, hidden evil.* Psalm 140:3; Proverbs 23:32.

ADDER'S TOOTH

(See dog-toothed violet.)

ADONIS

In classical mythology, a young hunter of great beauty who was deeply loved by Venus. While young, he met death from an attack of a wild boar, and from this legend have sprung the traditional symbols, *youthful beauty, early death.*

ADONIS

A flower of the crowfoot family, with symbols, *change, brief-blossoming.* It takes its name from the Adonis legend, where it is said the red drops of blood, following his attack by a wild boar, were transformed into the red blossoms of this flower.

SAINT ADRIAN

Patron saint of *brewers* and of *foot soldiers.* His special day is September 8.

AEGIS

In ancient Greek story, the breastplate of Pallas Athene, made from the skin of the goat which had suckled Zeus. From this legend, the symbols *productive power,* or *the great nutritive principle of nature.*

AEOLUS

In the *Odyssey,* Greek god of the *winds.*

AGATE

This gem has many symbolisms, *strength, long life, prosperity, health, wealth, mastery, serenity,* all easily drawn from its physical characteristics. In early times reputed to guard against danger, and bring victory to the wearer; hence *security, supremacy.* Young boys even to this day bid for the agate as a good luck omen in a game of marbles.

Birthday stone for June.

SAINT AGATHA

Patron saint of Catania, Italy, where on her special saint's day, February 5th, an annual festival is held in commemoration of her death from imprisonment and torture by the Emperors in A.D. 251. Her attributes, a *palm branch for victory,* and a *salver bearing two breasts,* in allusion to the method of her martyrdom for her refusal to deny Christ.

AGERATUM

A modest lavender-blue flower symbolizing *longevity,* in association with the Greek derivative word meaning *ageless.*

AGLDE

In Zoroaster's *Oracle,* as one of the nine spirits of intelligence, signifies *recovery* and *health.*

AGLOIA

In Greek mythology, as one of the three Graces — daughters of Zeus and Eurynome — *splendor.*

SAINT AGNES

Child saint of Salerno and Rome, who at thirteen consecrated her life to Christianity. Patron saint of *young girls.* Her attribute is the *lamb led by a cord.* The faggots of the stakes at her execution failed to burn, and the prefect had her beheaded when she refused to marry his son who would have forced her to give up her religious beliefs. Her special dates, January 20, 21, now known as Saint Agnes Eve are now celebrated with all sorts of magic charms and games. See John Keats, "Eve of Saint Agnes."

AGNI

Early Hindu fire-god. Of mysterious birth and threefold form: fire on earth, lightning, and the sun. Depicted in art with three heads, symbolizing the *triple birth;* three legs, the *three fires of ritual.* While seven arms represent his *seven rays of light.*

AGNUS DEI

One of the earliest and most beautiful symbols of the *Son of God,* representations of which were found in the catacombs of Rome. When lamb is reclined, the meaning is, *suffering;* when holding a banner, *victory over death.* Illustration p. 11:6.

AGRICULTURE

Among the many emblems of agriculture, the one pictured p. 19:13, is the most popular, coming to us from Mediaeval times.

AHRIMAN (also called AHURA MAZDA)

The *evil spirit* in the doctrine of Zoroaster, and the original creator of *all that is evil.*

AIDES

(See Pluto.)

AIDOS

In early Greek religion, divinity of *modesty, selfconsciousness.*

AILOS

In Greek mythology, steward of the *winds,* denoting in modern literary allusions *mobility, variability.*

AIRPLANE or AIRSHIP

One of the many modern symbols for *commerce, travel.*

AISLE

In early church architecture, aisle usually meant center aisle, and from this location we get the signification, *the way that leads to the Throne.*

AJAX

A leading Greek hero in the Trojan War of Homer's *Iliad,* from whom we get the symbol, *offensive presumption, gigantic strength and courage.*

ALABASTER

Purity in that it, as one variety of gypsum, is usually white and translucent.

ALB

A full length vestment of officiants of the Eucharist in many liturgical Christian churches, originating in the robe of mockery Herod put upon the Christ at the crucifixion. Presently, it symbolizes *chastity, purity, innocence, the eternal joy of the redeemed.* Illustration, p. 14:13.

ALBATROSS

Signifies *distant seas,* or *long voyage,* in that this large wandering bird is capable of enduring long flights. It is a sailor's omen. See S. T. Coleridge, "The Ancient Mariner."

ALCESTIS

Symbol of *sacrifice* drawn from this noble woman, wife of Admetis, King of Thessaly, who in Greek legend died voluntarily to save the life of her husband.

27

ALCMENE

In Greek mythology, wife of Amphitryon, and mother of the great hero Hercules. She is hailed as *the dawn.*

SAINT ALEXIS

Patron saint of *pilgrims* and of *beggars.* His attributes are a *ladder* held in his arms, a *palm branch* and a *cross.* Near him a beggar with a dish. His special day, July 17.

ALGAE

A seaweed symbolizing *long life* or *thoughts from afar,* from the fact that the part above water may be attached to a holdfast some distance down in the depth of the sea. In Japan, popularly used in New Year Festivals, and sent as a special message with gifts to friends.

ALI

In Norse literature, symbol of *bravery.* Son of Odin and Rind, known for his courage and excellence in marksmanship.

ALL-SEEING EYE

Symbol of the *watchfulness* of God, who sees all. Illustration p. 11:2.

ALMOND

The flower symbolizes *youth, constancy, hope,* and, in Christian symbolism, *divine approval* or *favor.* Numbers 17:1-8. From this reference it became one of the symbols of the Virgin.

The symbol of *constancy* can be traced to the legend of shipwrecked Demophon. A princess whom he was to marry pined away to death because of her lost lover, and, as a symbol of her constancy, the gods transformed her body into a flowering almond.

The tree, is regarded as a symbol of *spring,* with the idea of *wakefulness,* in that its blossoms are among the first among those of all trees. This meaning may also have been determined from the Hebrew name for almond *skeked,* to waken or watch. Tradition has it, that the rod of Aaron was a branch of the almond tree.

ALMS-BOWL

(See also dish.) In Buddhist religion, signifies *begging.*

ALMS BOX

As a church receptacle, *charity, benevolence.*

ALOE

Symbolizes *sorrow, contempt, bitterness,* from the physical characteristics of the juice of the leaves.

In Biblical symbolism, coupled with myrrh (Song of Solomon 4:14), it denotes *sweet smelling.* In this reference, the aloe is a large tree which exudes a fragrant gum.

ALPHA AND OMEGA

End of earthly life and beginning of a heavenly one is the interpretation of these two Greek letters widely used in Christian symbolism, and found on early tombs and sarcophaguses.

SAINT ALPHEGE

Archbishop of Canterbury, whose special day is April 19. His attributes in art: *bishop's robe, mitre, crosier,* and *chasuble* adorned with costly stones.

ALTAR

The altar in most branches of the Christian church merits the central focus of the building. Symbols ascribed are: *the throne of God, devotion, worship, thanksgiving, sanctuary of refuge, Christ's sacrificial death, His presence.* When located in the east portion of the sanctuary, there is an additional meaning, *the sun of righteousness.* When table-shaped, there is a reminder of the Lord's table in the upper room in Jerusalem where the Last Supper was instituted.

When shaped like a tomb, the intent is to keep alive the holy ordinance of the Lord's Supper. Figures of altars seen on the tombs of martyrs in the catacombs of Rome.

A person kneeling before the altar signifies *prayer, faith.*

There is a special significance attached to reading the gospel from the north end of the altar. In early centuries the barbarians lived in the north, the cold regions. This act shows the desire of the church to convert the barbarians to Christianity.

ALTAR CLOTH

A symbol of the *shroud of Christ* at the crucifixion. Symbolic materials, markings, and colors have variable meanings for congregations of differing faiths. The altar cross, a Latin cross with three steps at the base, signifies *faith, hope,* and *love.* Illustration p. 11:11.

ALYSSUM

The symbol for this small perennial plant is *innocence,* from its clusters of dainty, fragrant blossoms.

AMARANTH

The foliage of this imaginary flower "that never fades," signifies *incorruptibility*.

The flowers of the living plant called amaranth denote *affectation*, drawn from their likeness of color and shape to the crest of a cock's head.

AMARYLLIS

The flower symbolizes *beauty, nobleness, gentility* in association with Amaryllis, who, in classical pastoral poetry is a *shepherd's sweetheart*.

AMAZON

Fearless, gigantic, from Greek myth of a fabulous group of females who warred against the masculine leaders. One example of their hard-heartedness and cruelty was that they destroyed the right breast of their children to prevent it from getting in the way of the bowstring, as they were being trained for battle.

AMBER

This resinous mineral symbolizes *joy after sorrow*, in reference to the surprising results when the fossilized mass has been polished into a form of high brilliance.

AMBO

In early Christian church, a large pulpit signifying the *Word of God*.

SAINT AMBROSE

His special day is December 7. Patron saint of *beekeepers, bakers of honeybread, wax refiners, domestic animals, geese*. Also, in more recent times, patron of *betrothed couples*. His most outstanding attribute is a *beehive* and *book*. Legends relate that as an infant a swarm of bees alighted on his mouth, thus foretelling his future eloquence.

AMEN-RE

In early Egyptian religion, king of the gods. He was consort of Mut, the sky goddess, and father of Khonsu, chief deity of Thebes. He is symbol of the *reproductive forces in life*. In art pictured in cap with two plumes.

AMETHYST

This beautiful purple or bluish-violet gem symbolizes *deep love, truth unto death, sincerity.*

In church hierarchy the stone symbolizes *humility, earthly sufferings.* Widely used as an ornament of crowns and rings of church orders. Legend has it that the possessor of an amethyst is protected against the evils of strong drink.

AMICE

As a liturgical vestment, it symbolizes the *helmet of salvation,* originating with the form of cloth with which Christ was blindfolded at the crucifixion. Illustration p. 14:8.

It consists of an oblong cloth, always white, usually linen, worn earlier on the head, but more modernly about the neck and shoulders under the alb and chasuble.

AMPHION

In Greek mythology, characterized as a great singer and musician. He built the walls of Thebes by charming the stones into position with his skilful playing of the lyre; hence, in literary allusion a *charmer.*

AMPHITRITE

Wife of Poseidon and goddess of the *sea.* In literary allusion she is a *generous hostess,* stemming from her attentive care of the water creature.

AMPULLA

Symbol of *consecration.* Name given to the cruet or vase which contains the holy oil in church sacraments, or the wine and water at Mass. Illustration p. 16:4.

AMUN

Human-headed god of Egyptian Thebes with home in the Temple of Karnah. The name implies *hidden.*

ANAIDEIA

Greek divinity of *vice* and *virtues,* signifying *shamelessness.*

ANA PURNA

Hindu god of *plenty*. From legend we get the story that in time of starvation she saved her people by distributing milk and rice. It is the belief that those who have eaten even a small portion of the food found in her temple will forever be void of starvation.

ANCHOR

Has long been used as a Christian symbol of *faith, steadfastness,* and *hope* grounded in Hebrews 6:19, "Which hope we have as an anchor of the soul, both sure and steadfast." Freely used as a Christian symbol in the catacombs, the crescent-form base, or an angling fish suspended from the cross-bars, aiding as a disguise of the simple form of the cross. When the anchor is combined with a heart and cross, the meaning is *love, devotion, tranquility, anchoring the soul in faith and love.* The anchor is a commonly used symbol of mariners implying *safety, security,* in dangers of shipwreck. Occasionally one sees an anchor with dolphin intertwined, rare symbol for *Christ.* Illustration p. 15:8.

ANDREW, THE APOSTLE

Patron saint of *Scotland.* Likewise of *fishermen, fishmongers, sailors.* His attribute is a simple transverse cross, and his special day, November 30. The cross is suggestive of his martyrdom by the Roman governor of Patrae where the apostle had grown successful in converting people to the Christian faith. Illustration of Saint Andrew's cross, p. 12:6.

ANDROMEDA

Wife of Perseus, in Greek legend a personification of *the dawn.* She was an Ethiopian princess, rescued by Perseus from a cliff where she had been chained to be devoured by a monster. After her death, she was changed into a constellation representing the figure of a woman in chains.

ANEMONE, (Also called windflower)

Symbolizes *love, early death.* Favorite flower of Venus, goddess of beauty and love. From the story of Venus and Adonis comes the *early death* signification.

In Gothic story, the anemone is the Easter Resurrection flower. Christ's blood fell upon it at Calvary, giving it a touch of red. Its tri-lobed leaf is suggestive of the *Trinity.*

ANGEL

Signifies *purity, messenger or herald of God, the Annunciation, the Nativity.*

Dependent upon attitude or positions, angels reflect various symbols in Christendom:

Holding a scepter, *divine authority.*

Holding a sword upright, *justice.*

Holding a flaming sword, *guardianship,* or *judgment.*

Holding a censer, *heavenly adoration.*

Holding a lily, *purity, annunciation.*

Holding a branch with three white flowers, *mercy.*

Holding a trumpet, *proclaiming preachers of the Gospel.* From Revelation 14:6.

Kneeling with head upturned and hands clasped, *intercession, prayer.*

Kneeling before a triangle, *The Trinity, the Holy Family, adoration.*

Singing, the *Nativity of Christ, Christmas festivities.*

ANGELICA

An herb of *inspiration.*

ANKH

A T-shaped cross surmounted by a loop, from Egyptian symbolism meaning *life, prosperity.* Also called *crux ansata.,* symbol of *immortality.* Illustration p. 12:1.

SAINT ANNA

Tradition has it that she was the mother of the Virgin Mary. In art, pictured with green mantle and red dress, symbolizing *divine love, immortality.* When pictured with the Holy Family, she holds a book. Her special day is July 26. Patron of *cabinet makers.*

SAINT ANSANUS

Known as the apostle of Siena, and adopted as patron saint of that city. His special day is December 1. In art, pictured as a youth, richly clothed, before a fountain indicative of the place where his head fell when he was executed because of his great success in gaining converts through his preaching of the gospel.

SAINT ANSELM

Archbishop of Canterbury. His special day, April 21. His attribute, the model of a ship which, in art, he holds in his hands, as the Virgin with the Holy Infant appears before him.

ANT

From habits of the insect, together with Biblical allusions, (Proverbs 6:6-8 and 33:24, 25), these symbolisms: *Providence, thrift, industry, resourcefulness, forethought, prudence, community spirit.* Often made use of in modern emblems of industrial or social organizations.

ANTAEUS

Strength, invincibleness. In Greek mythology a giant wrestler who could not be overpowered while he touched the earth. Hercules discovering his source of strength, lifted Antaeus from the ground and succeeded in crushing him to death.

ANTELOPE (Same as for gazelle)

Emblematic animal of the state of Nebraska. The illustration, p. 8:2 is a representation of an early Roman mythical antelope, which in literary allusion signifies a *struggle.*

SAINT ANTHONY, ABBOT

Patron of *pork butchers* and *basketmakers,* known widely for his combats against the hosts of evil, and as a symbol of *triumph over sin.* He lived to be 105 years old. His special day, January 17. Among his many attributes are a crutch, and a hog with bell around its neck.

SAINT ANTHONY OF PADUA

Patron saint of Padua, and of Portugal. His special day, June 13. Pictured with kneeling ass, from an old legend of a heretic who refused to believe the presence of Christ in the Eucharist, unless his ass would leave the stable and kneel before the Sacrament table. Legend tells us that Saint Anthony witnessed the fulfilment of this episode.

ANTIGONE

Daughter of Oedipus and Jocasta, symbol of *faithfulness* and *nobility,* in Greek legend. Heroine in *Oedipus at Colonus,* by Sophocles.

ANUBIS

In early religion of Egypt, a god of the nether world. He presided over the *tombs* and *conducted souls to their homes in an unseen world*. Pictured with the head of a jackal, wolf, or dog, and, hanging from a pole, the skin of a newly killed ox. Illustration p. 9:11.

ANVIL

Early depicted as symbol of *martyrdom*. In art, the attribute of Saint Eligius, patron saint of *goldsmiths* and all *metal workers*. In modern commercial art, emblem of *mechanics* or *manufacturing*.

APE

This animal symbolizes all of the wiles of Satan: *sin, lust, greed, sloth, malice, cunningness, levity, cruelty* and *fraud*.

APHRODITE

(See Venus.)

APIS (SERAPIS)

The sacred bull of Egypt recognized as a god, the reincarnation of the soul of Osiris. Known as the *runner*. The bull was allowed to live no more than 25 years, then drowned in one of the sacred wells of the Nile. Greatly mourned by the people until a new animal with these markings of the original Apis appeared: black coat, white triangular spot on the forehead; spot like a half moon on his right side, and under his tongue a knot like a scarab, and on his back an eagle. Illustration p. 8:7.

APOLLO (PHOEBUS)

Represented in art and classical literature more frequently than any other deity. Son of Zeus and Leto, brother of Artemis. He is god of *music, poetry, archery, healing*. Among his attributes are: the *lyre*, the *bow*, the *laurel wreath*, the *wolf, swan, raven, stag* and *dolphin*. Illustration p. 7:3.

SAINT APOLLONIA OF ALEXANDER

A deaconess, patron of *dentists*. Her attributes are the palm of martyrdom, and a pair of pincers holding a tooth. Her special day is February 29. Arrested for preaching the Christian gospel in Alexandria, and for failure to bow to the gods of the city, she was bound to a column and her teeth extracted with a pincers. Later she was martyred.

APPLE

The tree symbolizes *fruitfulness, useful beauty.* The blossom signifies *good luck.* With this meaning, an appropriate flower for brides, and it is not unusual for a sprig to find its way into the wedding bouquet. In 1897 made the adopted flower of Michigan, and in 1901 approved as state flower of Arkansas. The word *apple* and *evil* in Latin are identical (malum) out of which similarity has grown the legend that the tree of good and evil in the Garden of Eve was an apple tree.

The fruit of the apple has many symbolic meanings, dependent upon its association with other objects, or in whose hands it is held. In Christian art one finds these depictions:

In the hand of the Infant Jesus, *redemption, salvation.*

In the hand of the mature Christ, *fruit of salvation.*

In the hands of the Virgin Mary, *Christ's mission on earth for the redemption of mankind.*

In the hand of Adam, *sin, discord.*

Sodom's apple, *sinful lust.*

Golden apples of Hesperides, *wisdom.*

APRON

In Free Masonry, the white apron of lambskin, *purity of life and conduct.*

APSE

In early Christian church architecture, *God's richest beauty,* and whether it was found in choir loft, transept, or niche, it always received foremost attention from the decorator.

AQUAMARINE

A bluish-green transparent beryl stone, signifying *serenity,* in that the color is suggestive of the tint of quiet seawater; and *courage* from the quality of the gem.

Together, with the bloodstone, is emblematic birthstone for March.

AQUARIUS

The *water-bearer.* Sign of the zodiac for January.

ARACHNE

In Greek mythology, daughter of Idmon of Colophon in Lydia. She vied with Athene in weaving, and was transformed by her into a spider when the latter found the girl's skills in weaving. From this episode have arisen the symbols of Arachne, *presumption, ambition.*

ARAI

A Greek divinity presiding over *curses.*

ARBORVITAE

Sacrifice, vaguely associated with the rite of burnt offering. The tree exudes a resinous oil, in early use as an incense burned as an offering to some deity.

ARBUTUS (mayflower)

Stands for *hardihood, better days to come, noble and unselfish deeds.* After the first winter sufferings of the Puritans in Plymouth, they were heartened by the early appearance of the mayflowers.

Since 1918 the trailing arbutus has been the state flower of Massachusetts, and since 1901 the emblematic flower of Nova Scotia.

ARCH

Rich in symbolism in church architecture, the pointed arch denoting *aspiration and growth in the spiritual life, and triumph.* Arches joining pillars and walls serve in the imagination as a reminder of Christ and the Sacraments by which God and man are joined together. Arches in these positions, also, symbolize the beneficence of God and the hospitality of men of the Christian faith.

The rounder form of arch suggests *authority* and *dependability* because of the huge or rugged character of buildings into which this type is projected. Illustrations p. 19:10.

The Gothic form which is high and pointed suggests *depth of feeling.* Broken arch symbol of *untimely death.*

ARCHANGELS

Because of their functionings, these angels signify *guardianship, communication and revelation of God to men.*

ARCHER

Purpose, aim, from zodiacal sign, Saggitarius, for November.

ARCHIMAGO

In Spenser's *Faerie Queene,* signifies *hypocrisy.*

ARES

Son of Zeus and Hera. God of *war* with steeds Deimos (panic) and Phobos (fear).

ARETE

Greek goddess of *virtue, excellence* who led Hercules to a life of hardship and toil, rather than to seek riches, ease and love, promised him by Arete's sister, Kakia.

ARETHUSA

A woodnymph of Diana who in Vergil's *Ecologue* 10:1 is addressed as a divinity of *poetical inspiration*. To shield her from the pursuit of Alpheus, the river god, Artemis transformed her into a stream which ran under the sea and emerged in Sicily as a fountain.

ARGENT

Archaic word for silver, symbolical of *faith, and purity,* and reflects this meaning when argent fields serve as a background for flags or shields.

ARGO

In Greek mythology the vessel in which Jason set sail in search of the golden fleece. Out of the story attending the Argonauts on this expedition has grown the symbol of the *earth as a parent, which contains in itself the germs of all living things.*

ARGUS

Son of Zeus and Niobe, in Greek legend a *watchful guardian,* famed as having one hundred eyes which, after he was slain by Hermes, were transferred to the tail of the peacock.

ARIADNE

In Greek mythology goddess of *spring, vegetation* and of *the dawn.* She was daughter of King Minos of Crete. Abandoned by her lover, Theseus, on the Isle of Naxos, she was found there by Dionysus who made her his wife.

ARIEL

Symbolic name for Jerusalem, *strong city,* referred to in Isaiah 29:1,2,7. In poetical use, signifies *guardian spirit.* In Pope's *Rape of the Lock,* the sylph who protected Belinda.

ARIES

The ram, appears in the sign of the zodiac for the month of March.

ARK

From the ark of the covenant in Old Testament narrative, *salvation, divine presence, divine law,* and the church as a *refuge for all humanity.* In modern representations an ark with attending anchor signifies *steadfast hope, a well-spent life.* Illustration p. 14:11.

ARM

When pictured as a symbol of the church, means *protection, strength, defense.* From Psalms 10:15 and Ezra 30:21, signifying *power.*

SAINT ARNOLD

Earnest preacher against clerical riches. Patron saint of *brewers.* Special day, July 18.

ARROW

In ancient times symbol of *authority.* Of more recent denotation *speed, directness, keenness, power held in reserve.*

Arrows from cupid's bow, *a message of love.*

On seal of United States of America, *protection, preparedness for military service, readiness for war.* The arrows are feathered and turned upward in a flying position, further signification of *readiness in war.*

In church symbolism, the arrow is a symbol of *Saint Thomas,* the weapon of his martyrdom.

In art, attribute of Saint Ursula and Saint Sebastian, who were at the mercy of torturers using arrows, and Saint Giles who saved a hind which had been shot by arrows.

ARROWROOT

Cleansing power from lore of American Indians who claimed that the starchy substance of the plant had magic power of healing for wounds inflicted by poisoned arrows.

ART

A palette, brush, and a maulstick form a well-known symbol for *art* and *artists.* Illustration p. 19:1.

ARTEMIS

Huntress and *mistress of wild life,* daughter of Zeus and Leto, and sister of Apollo. In art, equipped for hunting and followed by one or more dogs. Pictured on p. 7:6 with the *bow,* one of her attributes.

ARTEMIS LEAF

From Chinese symbolism, *good luck.*

ASGAARD

In Norse mythology, abode of the gods where palaces are of silver and villages of gold.

ASHES

Represent *grief, mourning, frailty, hoplessness.* When used in burial rites, dust and ashes symbolize the *shortness of earthly life.* In church rites of placing ashes on the forehead on Ash Wednesday (first day of Lent), they symbolize *humility, penitence,* and *grief.*

ASHUR

Assyrian god of *war.*

ASP

Ancient Egyptian symbol of *royalty* when used to adorn the headdress. A winged asp or the head of an asp ready to strike, symbolizes *defense, protection,* or *life itself.*

ASPARAGUS

From the multiple of stalks that spring up from a single root, a *strengthener of the sense of responsibilities.*

ASPEN TREE

Symbol of *fear* associated with the legend that the cross of Crucifixion was made of aspen wood, and when the tree realized its purpose, the leaves began to tremble with horror and have never ceased. A second legend relates that the aspen was the only tree which refused to bow in sorrow of the Crucifixion, and because of this obstinacy the leaves were fated to eternal trembling.

ASPERGES

Symbol of *purification* in the religious rite of sprinkling altar, clergy, and people with holy water. A ceremony having its roots in the Latin phrasing of Psalm 51:7, "Asperges me, Domine, hyssope."

ASPHODEL

Favorite flower of poets both ancient and mediaeval. In Greek mythology it is spoken of as the flower that grew in the underworld, often connected with Persephone, queen of Hades, who is sometimes pictured wearing a garland of asphodels. The flower is the symbol of *death*.

ASS

Seen in the catacombs in a fresco, this animal represents *heresy*, or *Satan*. In India it symbolizes *humility, austerity*. Generally in literature the significance is *patience* or *stupidity*, and on the other hand, *willingness to serve*. When pictured in Nativity scenes, the implication is that the least and humblest of animal creatures were present at the birth, as the ass appears beside the ox and sheep. The fact that these animals recognized the Child as the Son of God fulfilled the prophecy in Isaiah 1:3.

ASTARTE

Named Ashtoreth in the Bible, a Semitic goddess of *nature, reproduction, fertility*. Pictured with the head of a bull or of a cow.

ASTER

This flower signifies *garden of light*. The name is derived from a Greek word meaning *star;* hence the association of *light*. One variety of asters, the Christmas starwort symbolizes the *Nativity*, and is popular as a Christmas flower. Illustration, p. 21:9.

ATALANTA

Beautiful Greek heroine, the *dawn maiden* and renowned *swift-footed huntress*. In the Calydonian races she offered to marry any one who could out-run her. Stopping to pick up three golden apples, she lost the race to Hippomenes. Later the two were turned into lions.

ATARGATIS

Syrian *nature* goddess usually described as the *moon* or *fish* goddess. In legends she typifies the *power of destiny*.

ATEN

Egyptian *sungod* whose emblem appears often on ancient ruins, as a sundisc with long rays terminating in hands.

ATHENE, PALLAS

Greek goddess of *wisdom,* the *industries,* and *war.* She sprang out of the head of Zeus, her father, full grown, clothed in glittering armor, holding a spear and chanting a song of victory. Patroness of *domestic arts* and *crafts.* Inventress of the *plow.* In art, she is generally seated among one of her many attributes — a griffin, snake, horse, and most often, an *owl,* the attribute with which she is pictured on p. 7:2.

ATHENESIC

Among North American Indians, the *moon* goddess.

ATLAS

The bearer of great burdens, symbol of *strength.* Pictured as bearing the world on his shoulders. In Homer, a Titan, brother of Prometheus, described as "one who keeps the tall pillars which hold heaven and earth asunder." He had great wisdom and a knowledge of astronomy. In later life he was transformed into a lofty mountain. Illustration p. 7:8.

ATROPOS

Eldest of the three Fates. The *inflexible,* bearer of the shears with which she cuts off the thread of life, sending another soul on its way to the dark Kingdom of Hades.

ATTAR OF ROSES

Signifies *elegance,* reflective of the fragrance of the perfume made from the damask rose.

ATUM

Re, Egyptian god of the *sun* as it approaches the horizon toward evening.

SAINT AUGUSTINE OF CANTERBURY

Apostle to the First Primate of England. In art he is seen baptising King Ethelbert of Kent. Special day, May 26.

SAINT AUGUSTINE OF HIPPO

Noted for his learning. He spent most of his life in Africa, where at Hippo he died at the age of 76. His attributes are a *book* and *flaming heart* sometimes pierced by an arrow, suggestive of his flaming piety. His special day, August 28.

AUM (ON)

Secret name for God among early Hebrews.

AUREOLE

A halo of white, gold or blue surrounding or emanating from the three persons of the Trinity, the Madonna, or the Virgin and Child. It may be of different shapes, elongated, a circle, quatrefoil, or elliptical, or surrounding the entire body of Christ. Symbol of *celestial glory, supreme power.*

AURORA

Rosy-fingered Aurora, Roman goddess of the *dawn* (Greek Eos). She is represented rising from the ocean in a chariot, attended by the Hours, her fingers dripping with dew, opening the flowers.

AUTOMOBILE

In modern picture language the symbol of *travel.*

AUXO

In Greek myth one of the beautiful daughters of Zeus and Themis; goddess of *growth, stimulation of plant life,* and was responsible for the *change of seasons.*

AWL

In art, *attribute of Saint Benignus.*

AXE

A headsman's axe symbolizes *execution;* a double-bladed battle axe, *power, war, sacrifice.* In ancient Greece the axe was a symbol of *thunder* and *lightning.* In Christian art it is an attribute of Saint Matthew. In the United States the axe or hatchet has become an emblematic ornament for Washington's birthday festivities, reminder of the boy's honesty in the story, now become legendary, of his chopping down a small cherry tree. Illustration p. 15:4.

AZALEA

Symbol of *abundance, stately beauty, living fire,* from the vivid colorings and profusion of blossoms. From Chinese lore comes the symbol of *devotion* and *brotherly love,* from an old folk tale where a young boy in search of a lost brother lies down exhausted after a fruitless attempt. As he wept tears of blood, these tears developed into beautiful azalea flowers.

B.

BABOON
Ancient Egyptian religious symbol of *wisdom hailing the dawn* when the animal poses with arms extended.

BACCHUS
(See, also Dionysus) Greek god of *wine* and *revelry*. Often represented with a crown of grapes or ivy leaves with leopard or panther at his side. Less spiritual than Dionysus. His attendants were satyrs and bacchantes.

BACHELOR'S BUTTON
(See cornflower.)

BADGER
Emblematic animal for the state of Wisconsin.

BAG
A money-bag in church symbolism, stands for the *treachery* of Judas, Matthew 26:15. Three money-bags form one of the emblems of Saint Matthew, the tax gatherer.

In modern symbolic language money-bags signify *wealth, greed,* or *commerce* and *banking*.

BALANCE
(See, also scales.) In Biblical symbolism *just standard, true measure.* Job 31:6; Daniel 5:27.

BALDUR
Son of Odin, who in Norse mythology, represents *light, peace, eloquence,* and *wisdom*. Pictured often with a mistletoe branch, in recollection of his death from a stray shot of mistletoe shaft by blind Hothr. His attributes are *brightness* and *beauty*.

BALL
From Japanese art, *pearl of wisdom*. In modern symbolism suggests *rejection* (black ball). Ball and chain, symbol of *enslavement*. Three golden balls, *triple perfection,* associated with the arms of the Medici family of Italy. Emblem of *pawnbrokers*.

44

BALSAM

Consolation from the effectiveness of an exuding fragrance. Sometimes called the Virgin's tree, often appearing in pictures of the Sorrowing Virgin.

BALTHAZAR

In Biblical literature, implies *consecrated wealth*, from the reference to him as one of the three Magi.

BAMBOO

A cherished New Year's decorative element in China and Japan with the special message of *happiness, long life, good luck*. Other symbolisms arising from physical characteristics of bamboo:

Family loyalty, many stalks of the plant radiate from the parent stem.

Resilience, and *strength through yielding*, in that if bent by the wind, it will again straighten itself out.

Open heartedness, from its hollow stem.

Endurance, since its leaves remain green when those of other plants and trees wither away.

BANANA

The tree signifies *continuing life* from its power to propagate itself from the same root.

BANNER

In general, symbol of *victory, triumph*, or *protection*. In church symbolism, *victory over sin* or *death*.

BANYAN TREE

From the peculiar growth of the tree wherein the branches bending to the earth take root, we have these symbolisms, *expanding knowledge, close union of the physical and spiritual man*.

BAPTISM

A religious rite denoting *divine initiation into the family of the redeemed*. Matthew 20:22; Romans 6:3,4.

There are many attributes: a *fish, two fishes crossed*, the *Head of Christ and two fishes*, a *cross, escallop shell*.

45

SAINT BARBARA

Patron saint of *architects, builders, artillerymen, armorers, gunsmiths, firefighters, fireworksmakers,* and *miners.* Protectress in thunderstorms. Her festival day is December 4. She is the only female saint who bears the sacramental chalice and host. Her chief attribute is a tower with three windows. Daughter of a heathen father who kept her carefully guarded in a tower while he was away from home. Disobeying his orders, in having three windows installed in the tower, instead of only two, he dragged her to the prefect who had her beheaded for her insistence on symbolizing the Holy Trinity in the number of windows she demanded.

SAINT BARNABAS, THE APOSTLE

His special day is June 11. His attributes, a pilgrim's robe, staff and wallet, and the gospel of Saint Matthew in his hand.

BARN

Rare symbol of the *Silver Age of the world* ruled over by Jupiter, and the introduction of *agriculture* by Saturn.

SAINT BARTHOLEMEW, THE APOSTLE

Patron saint of *tailors, bookbinders, butchers, corn chandlers, dyers, glovers, furriers, leatherworkers, shoemakers, tanners, plasterers, vine growers,* and of Florentine salt and cheese merchants. His special day, March 4. While preaching in Armenia, he was seized by heathen, flayed alive, and then killed with a large knife of peculiar shape, which instrument has become his chief attribute. Occasionally there is added a human skin thrown over his arm.

BASIL

Aromatic herb, in India sacred to both the gods, Vishnu and Krishna.

BASILISK

In Greek legend, a horrible monster, half snake and half cock whose breath or even look was fatal. In early Christian symbolism, *the devil* or *antichrist.*

BASIN

In church symbolism, the *humility of Christ's love and the estimate of true greatness in His Kingdom.* John 13:5. When pictured with a pitcher above it, the implication is the act of *Pilate washing his hands,* in his maintaining that Christ was innocent.

Basin and towel, symbolize *Christ's ministry of service.*

BASKET

Filled with flowers or fruit signifies *opportunity, reward, fruitfulness, plenty, victory, success,* and in Christian symbolism the *first fruits of the church.*

BAST

A lion-headed or cat-headed goddess of early Egyptian religion reflecting the *life-producing power of the sun.*

BAT

Symbols, in general, from the color or the movements while flying, are, *night, death, black magic, misfortune.* Illustration p. 17:12. Since early ages, the bat, in China and Japan has stood for *good-fortune, joy, happiness, prosperity, riches, peace, love of virtue.* In Chinese art, five bats surrounding a human being stand for *longevity.*

BATTERY

In modern commercial art, *electricity.*

BATTLE-AXE

(See axe.) Illustration p. 15:4.

BAY

As for laurel, in ancient Greece, bay signified *merit, reward, victory,* in crowning-services for victors. Later, *joy, peace, glory,* are added significations. Homes of early Christians were adorned with bay in commemoration of the Nativity.

BAYBERRY CANDLES

Following an old tradition, these candles symbolize good *luck, prosperity,* when lighted Christmas Eve to burn until New Year's.

BEADS

Signify *memory* from the Middle English *bede,* meaning prayer, in conjunction with their use in retaining a count in the recitation of the rosary.

BEAMS

In church architecture, in that they tie portions of the building together, they betoken the members of the congregation tied together to *defend their common faith.*

BEAR

As a wild animal, symbolizes *cruelty, ferocity, strength, endurance.* Illustration p. 17:5.

In Old Testament narrative, a bear stands for a *fierce, destructive, powerful enemy,* from its appearance as one of the four beasts in the vision of Daniel. Daniel 7:5.

BEAST

Wild beasts symbolize *untamed power, human depravity, the passions.* The beast in Revelations 13:11-18 is a symbol of the *anti-Christ.*

Beasts of burden, camel, ass, donkey often in pictures stand for *primitive transportation* and *early commerce.*

BEAVER

From its swift actions in building dams to protect underwater lodges, *industry.* The animal, likewise, reflects this meaning as we see it as one of the eight predominating symbols on Northwest American Totem Poles.

BED

In modern picture language, *sleep, illness.*

BEDE THE VENERABLE

Patron of *students,* with special day, May 27.

BEE

Because of its work habits, the bee is a widely used symbol of *activity, thrift, orderly life, organization, happiness through prosperity.* Legend has it that the bee never sleeps. Illustration p. 17:11. In Japanese art, bees swarming in a house symbolize *prosperity.*

BEECH

Symbolizing *victor, honor, fame,* a wreath of beech leaves was presented to the winner of Pythian games of strength before the time that Apollo had adopted the laurel as his own tree.

BEEHIVE

Signifies *industry, cooperation, well being.* Illustration p. 15:1. In Christian symbolism of more recent years, the beehive aptly suggests the *organization of numerous persons who work for the good of all.* Seen in many pictures of the saints as an attribute signifying *eloquence.*

48

BEETLE

(See scarab.)

BEFANA

Signifies *benefaction*, from the legendary female figure who brings gifts to the good children of Italy on Epiphany, in commemoration of the gifts of the Magi.

BEGGAR

In modern day picture language, *indigence*.

BELL

Joy, warning, alarm. The church bell symbolizes the *call of worship above all other activities.* The old Philadelphia United States of America Liberty bell, with its plainly visible crack, signifies *freedom, liberty.* The school bell, early symbol of *learning.* In Buddhism, the bell, as one of the eight symbols, stands for *law.* Illustration p. 16:11.

BELLEROPHON

A mythical Corinthian, *the killer,* who slew the Chimera with the help of Pegasus.

BELLONA

Murderous Roman goddess of *war*, sister of Mars, driver of his chariot, and protectress of his safety.

BELLOWS

In commercial art, symbol of *mechanics*.

SAINT BENEDICT

Patron of *schoolchildren* and *coppersmiths.* His festival day is June 12. Founder of the Benedict order. Writer of the basic rules that have served as a guide for most Western monasteries. Easily recognizable in art for his attractive attributes: *a raven,* the bird he fed when he was a hermit; a *broken cup,* a *luminous ladder,* a *dove.*

SAINT BERNARD

Twelfth Century abbot, known for his mystic writings, *the Meditations.* Shown in art with three mitres at his feet, in reference to three bishoprics he refused. His special day, August 20.

SAINT BERNARDINO OF SIENA

Patron of wool-weavers. His attributes, a tablet or sun inscribed with IHS, or a heart. His special day, May 20.

BERYL

Gem of *happiness, good luck,* and *cooperation.*

BES

Egyptian god of *recreation, feasting,* and of the *feminine arts.* Strangler and devourer of lions, boars, antelopes, and serpents. Patron and *protector of children, inspirer of joy,* but enemy of noxious beasts. Represented as an ugly dwarf with large head and protruding tongue, and clothed in a cat's skin.

BETEN

In Japanese art and literature one of the seven gods of *luck.*

BHISHMAPITAMA

Hindu god of *strength.*

BIA

Greek personification of *violence,* daughter of Pallas and the river god, Styx.

BIBLE

Symbol of the *Word of God.* Illustration p. 16:3.

Closed, the signification is, *Saint Matthias chosen to take the place of Judas,* the betrayer.

Open, with sword, Saint Paul *(sword of the spirit).*

With a fish, Saint Simon, traveling companion of Saint Jude on his missionary journeys *(fishers of men).*

BILLOWS

In Biblical art and literature, *overwhelming trials,* Psalms 42:7; Jonah 2:3.

BINDWEED

From the small white flower often hidden by leaves, *humility.*

BIRCH

Since 1947 emblematic tree of New Hampshire.

Birch rod, in early United States signified *punishment*, in that the bog-birch twigs made useful flogging sticks.

BIRDS

More especially in early Christian symbolism, birds had many useful significations. In general, they stood for *winged souls*, the *faithful*, the *spiritual* as opposed to the material.

A bird escaping from a cage meant *liberation of soul* from the earthly prison of the body. Favorite religious pictures show the Christ Child holding a bird in hand or one tied to a string. Another favorite is the picture of Saint Francis of Assisi preaching to the birds.

BIRETTA

With smock, the symbol of *artists*. Illustration p. 14:7. Symbolic colors are distinguishing features of clergymen's birettas. That of the pope, *white;* of a cardinal, *scarlet;* of a bishop, *purple;* all others, *black.*

BIRTHSTONES

See gems.

BISHAMON

One of the seven Japanese gods of *good luck.*

BITTER ROOT

By legislative act of 1875 became the emblematic flower of Montana.

BLACK

(See, also, liturgical colors.) From Old Testament allusions, Job 30:30; and 2:6, and from the knowledge that black absorbs all colors, and thus buries the light, have come these symbolisms: *affliction, anguish, humiliation, darkness, death, despair, night, sin, wickedness, mourning, sorrow, penitence.*

BLACKBIRD

From its tireless song and dark feathers, artists of Christian subjects have painted the bird as a symbol of the *darkness of sin,* and also as *attractive temptations of the world.* The blackbird repeatedly appears with Saint Benedict who fought valorously against the temptations of the flesh.

BLACK-EYED SUSAN

Adopted by legislative act in 1918 as the emblematic flower of Maryland.

SAINT BLAISE

Patron saint of *wild animals* who welcomed him rather than attacked when he retired to a cave in the mountains for meditation. Also patron saint of *physicians, wax-chandlers, weavers,* and *woolcombers.* His attribute, a comb, reflective of his martyrdom by Emperor Licinius of Armenia who tortured him with iron combs tearing his flesh, and then had him beheaded.

BLARNEY STONE

Symbol of *eloquence,* from the traditional saying that those who kiss the stone in Ireland's Blarney Castle will become proficient in use of blarney.

BLEEDING HEARTS

This heart-shaped, deep pink flower reflects *wistful tenderness, sympathy, condolence, faithfulness in misfortune,* a most expressive sickroom plant.

BLOOD

In Old Testament symbolism, *slaughter, depth of pain,* Isaiah 34:3; Ezekiel 32:6. In New Testament signification, *Christ's Passion, essential life, atonement, the human soul,* and from Matthew 27:27,28, *redemption.*

BLOODSTONE

From the sprinkling of red spots as of blood, *courage.* With the aquamarine, the birthstone of March.

BLUE

In blazonry signifies *vigilance, perseverance, justice.* Azure blue symbolizes *truth, constancy, loyalty, fidelity, sincerity, divine truth and eternity, godliness, heaven,* and is one of the Virgin's colors.

The ancient Israelites bade their brides wear a blue ribbon on the shoulders of their fringed robes, which ribbons symbolized *purity, fidelity, love,* and it is said that from this practice has arisen the custom that modern brides wear something *blue* as a part of their wedding clothing.

BLUEBIRD

From its soft warblings and delicate lifting of wings while perching, *happiness, joy.* Illustration p. 18:2.

Emblematic bird of Missouri and New York. The mountain bluebird was adopted as the emblematic bird of both Idaho and Nevada in 1931.

BLUEBONNET

A species of lupine, adopted as state flower of Texas in 1901.

BLUET

One of the Virgin's flowers, and as such signifies *humility.*

BOAR

As associated with the Norse myth of Frey and Freya, symbol of *courage* and *fertility.* Since early times, the boar's head has played a popular part in the Christmas festivities of many countries.

BOAT

Signifies *venture,* and in Biblical symbolism, *security* (the ark of Noah). The sailboat in Christian art frequently appears as an attribute of Saint Peter, the fisherman, and of Saint Jude the Apostle because of his many missionary journeys by water.

BOBWHITE

Adopted by Rhode Island in 1931 as state bird, and by Oklahoma in 1932.

BODHI TREE

Tree under which Buddha received his superior enlightenment from which has grown the symbol, *spiritual refreshment.* Illustration p. 9:3.

BONA DEA (same as Fauna)

Roman goddess of *chastity,* and of *fruitfulness,* both of earth and of women. In art often represented with crown of vine leaves, a serpent under her foot, or with cock beside her.

SAINT BONAVENTURA

Cardinal and great scholar of the Franciscan Order. His special day, July 14. Sometimes pictured with angel bearing him the sacramental wafer.

SAINT BONIFACE

Patron of *brewers* and *tailors*. His special day, June 5. Pictured with axe thrust in the root of a tree.

BOOK

In general signification *education, scholarship, the Gospel.* Open book, *perfect knowledge,* or with religious denotations *divine intelligence, Word of God.*

 With candle, symbol of *literature.*

 Two books, from Chinese art, *wisdom, learning.*

 Pictured in the hands of Evangelists or Apostles, the *gospels.*

 In the hands of Doctors, *learning.*

BORAGE

Rough, hairy blue-flowered herb of Europe signifies *courage.*

BOREAS

In Greek mythology, god of the *North Wind,* son of Aeolus and Aurora. In literature the *north wind* personified.

BO TREE

(See, also bodhi tree.) Name given by Buddhists of India and Ceylon to the pipal or sacred wild fig (ficus religiosa). It was the tree beneath which the Buddha attained perfect knowledge, and now bears the symbolic meaning *heavenly light.* Usually a bo tree is planted on graves of the monks of Kandy, Ceylon. Illustration p. 9:3.

BOUGH (or BRANCH)

With green leaves, the sign of *friendliness, hospitality, protection,* from the fact that boughs or branches extend out from a central area.

BOUQUET

An expression of sentiment, *tribute to the living, sweet thoughts,* from the fragrance of most flowers.

BOW

From the bow of Ulysses signifies *test of strength.* Bow and arrow, an old-time symbolism from India, meaning *power of will* in association with Shiva, noted huntsman who accomplished celebrated deeds through skill in marksmanship and straight thinking.

BOWING

An attitude, reflecting *deference* and *respect for fellow man*. As a sanctuary ritual, signifies *reverence* and *humble respect* for God, the Father; Christ, the Son; or the Virgin Mother.

BOWL

Together with a cross in Christian symbolism, *service*. In Vedic myth, emblem of Kali who holds in her left hand a bowl and a lotus flower, symbolizing *abundance* and *eternal generation*.

BOX

In modern picture language signifies a *treasure;* when closed, implies *secrecy*.

BRAGI

Norse god of *poetry* and *eloquence, wisdom*. Patron saint of *poets* and *harpists*.

BRAHMA

In Hindu religion, *creator of the universe*, and, with Vishnu and Shiva, one of the Hindu Trinity. Usually shown with four heads, signifying the scope of his intelligence. Images of him may be found in temples of other gods, but he has neither temples nor altars strictly his own.

BRAMBLE

Believed to be the burning bush in Exodus 3:2, in Biblical symbolism signifies *riches which kill the soul*.

Also a symbol of *purity* of the Virgin who was not consumed by the lusts of the world.

BRANCH

(See bough.)

BRASS

As for copper, in Biblical symbolism indicates *strength, hardness, firmness, obstinate resistance*.

BREAD

In general, the significance is *staff of life*.

Special meaning in France, *goodness*.

As a substance in the rite of Holy Communion, *the body of Christ*.

Bread and salt in Russia conveys *hospitality*.

BREASTS

Symbols of motherhood and its attending attributes of *love, devotion, nourishment, protection.*

Two breasts on a platter are an attribute of Saint Agatha who, before her martyrdom, suffered agonies through a mutilation of her breasts.

BREASTPLATE

In Biblical symbolism, *righteousness as a defense*, Ephesians 6:14. The symbol of the tribe of Levi in the beautiful bronze door of the Baptistry in Florence.

BRIAREUS

In literature signifies *many-handed,* from the monster in Greek myth having one hundred arms. Featured in many Greek stories as a *giant of the sea,* or the *inventor of warships.*

BRIARS

From their physical characteristics comes the symbol, *major sins.*

BRIDE

In Christian symbolism, stands for the *church,* the *soul.* From Ephesians 5:32, bride and groom represent *Christ and the church.* In modern picture art, a bride symbolizes *happiness, adoration.*

BRIDLE

Signifies the *law,* in meaning an outgrowth of the Biblical idea of *moral restraint* in Psalm 32:9.

BRIMSTONE

Torment, desolation, utter destruction, from Job 18:15, and Revelation 14:10.

BRISEIS

One of the impersonations of *the dawn,* captive of Achilles during the Trojan War.

BROCADE

In Japan, a roll of brocade symbolizes *splendor.*

BROCCOLI

Signifies *tranquility.* No traceable origin, perhaps associated with a sleep-producing substance within the leaf.

BROOM

From its slender stalks and small leaves, *humility*, but from thorny variety of the plant, *tenacity*. The household gadget implies *victory, dominance*. From Japanese folklore comes the implication of the witch's broom, *vanishment of evil*.

BROWN

In early monastic life, *penitence, grief, barrenness, poverty, renunciation*.

BROWN THRASHER

State emblematic bird of Georgia, having been adopted in 1928 at the selection of children of the schools.

BRUSH

With palette and maulstick, emblem of the *artist*. With brushes thrust into the thumb hole of the palette, *painting*.

BRUSSELS SPROUTS

Light-heartedness, gaiety, said to be associated with the quick growth of the numberless little rosettes around the lower axils of the stem.

BUBASTIS

(See Ubasti.)

BUCKEYE (horse chestnut)

Adopted as Ohio's emblematic state tree in 1953. The seed (not as a symbol, but a superstition), when carried on the person of an individual serves as a protective charm.

BUCKLER

In Biblical symbolism, signifies *divine defense*, Psalm 18:2, 30. Illustration p. 14:9.

BUCKTHORN

Tradition has it that the crown placed upon the head of Christ at the crucifixion was of buckthorne; hence the symbolism, *pain, suffering*.

BUDDHA

Religious teacher of the Buddhists, who received enlightenment in meditation under a bo tree. Looked upon by his followers, not as a symbol, but as a deity.

BUDDHIST SYMBOLS IN CHINA
1. Lotus flower, *purity out of the unclean.*
2. Covered vase, *a reliquary.*
3. Conch shell, *talisman of mariners.*
4. Two fishes, *domestic faith and happiness.*
5. Umbrella, *official authority.*
6. Canopy, *sovereign rank.*
7. Bell or *wheel of the law.*
8. Knot of *longevity.*

BUDS

Buds of flowers suggest *promise for the future.*
Partly open, they symbolize *vitality.* Illustration of rosebud, p. 20:8.

BUFFALO

The water buffalo stands for *serenity, contentment,* and often, in art, additional stress is given to this meaning when a boy is seated on the animal playing a flute or reading a book. The American buffalo was officially adopted as the emblematic animal of Kansas in 1955.

BUFONITE (or toadstone)

The stone signifies both *health* and *witchcraft,* associated with its serving as a charm by persons of superstition who wear it as an antidote to poison or other harmful potions.

BUGLE HORN

Symbol of a *call to action.* Illustration p. 15:2.

BUILDER'S RULE

From church architecture, *spiritual building.*

BULL

A winged bull, with early Assyrians, symbolized *protection, beneficent genius.*
Symbol of the tribe of Manassah in the bronze door of the Baptistry of Florence.

Zodiacal sign for April, signifying *creative force, lordship.* One of the four animals — horse, elephant, lion honored by the Buddhists, honored because he helped Buddha when in the guise of an humble man, he plowed the fields. Also, in India sacred to Shiva, who held in respect the animal for his power to protect those elements which of need should be preserved.

BULRUSH

A symbol of *salvation* in association with the Old Testament narrative of safety of Moses, hidden as a child among thickly clustered rushes.

BUNNY

The symbol of *hope* and *life* ascribed to the Christian Easter bunny, seemingly, had its origin in ancient Egypt where the hare was used as a symbol for the spring festival that inaugurated a new year of hope and life.

BUNTING

As for the lark, the bunting symbolizes *joy, happiness,* from its brilliant, soft, sweet song.

The emblematic bird of the state of Colorado.

BUSH

A burning bush signifies *delivery from bondage,* referring to the Old Testament episode of the call of Moses to deliver the Israelites from the bondage of the Egyptians.

In religious decorative art, a burning bush is representative of the *Virgin,* or of *God, Himself.*

BUSKIN

In literature this half-boot, thicksoled foot covering, stands for *tragedy,* or *tragic drama.* Classical actors of tragedy wore the buskin.

BUTTERFLY

A beautiful Christian Easter symbolism of the *resurrection.* In its earliest stages, a caterpillar depicting *life;* next the chrysalis as *death,* and lastly, the butterfiy signifying *the resurrection of all mankind,* the *new life.* Illustration p. 11:5. In modern symbolism, a yellow butterfly implies *pleasure,* even *frivolity.*

In Chinese and Japanese art, a flight of black butterflies signifies *melancholy.*

C.

CABBAGE

Disentanglement, said to have gained this symbolism from an ancient Roman fable in which cabbages were purported to have sprung from the divine beads of perspiration which formed on Jupiter's brow as he struggled to think out a difficult problem.

CABLE

Symbol of *strength.*

CACTUS

Protection, associated with the thick coat of thorns which shield the waxy white flowers.

The Hepal cactus is national flower of Mexico; the Saguaro, since 1931 the emblematic state flower of Arizona, after having been adopted by the territorial government in 1901.

CADMUS

In Greek mythology a young prince, having slain a dragon, was compelled by the immortal gods to sow the monster's teeth. From this planting, a crop of Spartan giants sprang up who immediately began fighting among themselves until only five were left. These men with Cadmus founded Thebes.

CADUCEUS

Wand of Mercury entwined by snakes, symbol of the *doctor's profession.* This wand produced sleep, the *great healer.* From this early signification have arisen numerous others. As an emblem of *commerce and industry,* the rod stands for *power;* the serpents, *wisdom,* and the wings *diligence and activity.* In this emblem, there are but two serpents. In its earliest form, the caduceus was the distinctive mark of heralds and ambassadors — a mere rod ending with two short prongs, perhaps an olive branch with two small shoots. To test it, Mercury threw it between two quarreling snakes, who immediately wound themselves around it. This so pleased Mercury, that he allowed the snakes to remain. Illustration, p. 19:9.

CALDRON

A steaming caldron signifies *witchcraft, black magic, martyrdom.*

In art, attribute of Saint John the Evangelist, from the legend that under the Domitian ruler he was thrown into a caldron of boiling oil, but miraculously preserved.

CALENDULA (see, also, marigold)

The flower symbolizes *disquietude, jealousy,* associated with the mythical story that a host of jealous wood nymphs striving to gain the esteem of Apollo made such a loud disturbance that Diana transformed them into yellow marigolds or calendulas. Illustration, p. 21:10.

CALF

From Old Testament narrative comes the denotation *mammon, god of unrighteousness* in reference to an idol raised by the children of Israel. Exodus, Chapter 33.

In modern symbolism (thought of as a *golden* calf) *material gain, idolatry.*

The winged calf signifies *sacrifice,* symbol of Saint Luke, the Evangelist.

CALLA, or CALLA LILY

Popular as an Easter flower, and, as the center of a memorial spray signifies, *hope of a new life, resurrection, promise of immortality.*

CALLIOPE

In Greek mythology, chief of the nine muses, presiding over *eloquence, heroic poetry.*

CALYPSO

From African folklore, *gaiety, lightheartedness.*

CAMEL

In the Orient, sign of *royalty, dignity.* In general, *endurance, resistance,* from natural characteristics of the animal. Of recent years, popular as an addition to picture art of Christmas scenes.

CAMELLIA

Flower of *contentment, domesticity, chastity.* State emblematic flower of Alabama.

CAMOMILE (also chamomile)

In Middle Ages called the Virgin's flower, and from this association have sprung the symbols, *patience, humility.* From natural characteristics of the plant we get *courage in adversity.* It has medicinal values.

In Norse mythology, symbol of *Balder the Beautiful.*

CAMPANULA (also Canterbury bell)

Adulation, from showy, red-blue, bell-shaped flowers.

CANDELABRUM

A seven branched menorah, from olden times, sign for Judaism with traditional meaning, *light of God and Torah.* In later times there is the symbolism of *creation of the universe in seven days,* the middle branch standing for the Sabbath.

In Christian symbolism the seven branches represent the seven gifts of the spirit, *wisdom, understanding, counsel, strength, knowledge, piety, peace.*

CANDLE

The candle, from the material of which it is made (wax) and from the uses that it serves (shedding light) offers multitudinous opportunities for effective symbolisms in the home, in affairs of state, in religions of the world, and, in social festivities, besides having possibilities for emblem construction in the fields of commercial advertisement.

In general symbolic depiction there are these significations, *increasing knowledge, information, inquiry.* A candle and book, *literature, learning.*

In church symbolism, the meaning is conveyed, as a rule, through the number of candles or the position in connection with some other object.

With only one lighted candle on the altar, *Christ, the light of the world.*

Two on the altar, *the divine and human nature of Christ.*

Three, arranged as a triangle, *the Holy Trinity.*

Four, when placed at the corners of a table or desk, *the four Evangelists* — Matthew, Mark, Luke, and John.

Five candles, rare, but used in some specialized ceremonies, *the five wounds of the Crucifixion.*

Six candles, six attributes of the Creator — *wisdom, majesty, power, love, mercy,* and *justice.* Some say they signify the six days of creation, or, the six hours on the cross.

Seven candles, the seven sacraments — *baptism, confirmation, the Eucharist, penance, extreme unction, holy orders,* and *matrimony:* also, may signify, as of the Menorah — *wisdom, understanding, counsel, strength, knowledge, piety, peace,* the seven gifts of the Holy Spirit.

Eight candles — in the Christmas festival of Saint Lucia the candles placed into a wreath of holly, signify the *eight Beatitudes.*

In Christian art, a candlestick with a host wafer above it, symbolizes *the Eucharist.*

CANDRA

Early Hindu *moon-god* pictured with four arms, in a chariot drawn by a number of horses harnessed abreast.

CANNON, or CANNON BALLS

Symbols of *war*.

CANOPY

One of the eight Buddhist symbols, with the meaning, *sovereign rank*. The canopy still reflects that meaning, in general, *symbolism*.

CAP

The Phrygian cap, almost conical in shape denotes *liberty, independence*.

CAPE JASMINE

(See gardenia.)

CAPRICORNUS

The *goat* in the December sign of the zodiac.

CAR (CHARIOT)

Interesting in art are the pictures of the various animals which draw the chariots of gods of Greek, Roman, or Norse mythological divinities. A list follows:

Asses — Silenus
Bears — The firmament
Cats — Freya
Cocks — Night
Deer — Artemis
Dogs — Hephaistos
Dolphin — Amphrite, Aphrodite, Galatea, Poseidon, Tetys
Doves — Aphrodite
Dragons — Medea
Eagles — Zeus
Elephants — Chronos (Kronos)
Goats — Pan, Thor
Horses — Phoebus, Apollo, Death, Luna, Ares, Night, Pluto, the Sun
Lions — Cybele
Lizards — Hermes
Owls — Pallas Athene
Oxen — Saturn

Panthers — Dionysus
Peacocks — Hera
Rams — Hermes
Sea horses — Poseidon
Serpents — Demeter, Ceres
Sparrows — Venus
Storks — Hermes
Swans — Aphrodite
Tigers — Dionysus
Unicorn — Chastity
Whales — Oceanus
Wolves — Ares

CARBUNCLE

In Christian symbolism *Christ's Passion* or *Martyrdom*, a meaning emanating from the deep-red colors of the stone. When five of these gems appear as an embellishment of a cross, they stand for the five wounds of the Crucifixion. In the Middle Ages, the stone was held as a great protection against battle wounds, or dangers in trips on land and sea. Also as a cure for hemorrhages and for inflammatory diseases, and to calm anger and discord.

CARDINAL

Popular emblematic bird, having been adopted by Kentucky in 1926; by Illinois, in 1929; by Indiana, Ohio, and North Carolina in 1933.

CARDINAL VIRTUES

Four in number, *justice, prudence, temperance, fortitude,* pre-eminent from among the ancients.

CARNATION

Flower of *endurance, love, fidelity,* emblem of Mother's Day in forty countries of the world. The carnation was chosen by Miss Anna Jason of Philadelphia because it was her mother's favorite flower. The white carnation worn on this day (second Sunday in May in the United States) indicates that the mother of the wearer is *deceased;* while a flower of color signifies a *living mother.* Illustration p. 21:1.

From an old Flemish legend, a pink carnation is a symbol of *marriage.* The bride on her wedding day wears a concealed flower for which the groom must make a search.

Since 1904 the red carnation has been the state emblematic flower of Ohio.

CARNELIAN

Gem of *good luck, dignity,* and *power.* An especially lucky stone for Moslems.

CARP

Voracity, perseverance, endurance, fortitude, energy, ability to surmount difficulties, the latter meaning derived from the habits of the fish in leaping cataracts, and in swimming rapids to reach headwaters in which to spawn.

SAINT CASIMOR

Patron saint of *tailors* with special day, March 4. Pictured crowned, holding a lily, or praying at a church door at night.

CASSANDRA

In Greek legend a *prophetess,* daughter of Priam and Hecuba. Apollo, who gave her the gift of prophecy, afterwards, in anger, decreed that no one should believe in her prophecies, and *Cassandra* now refers to any *prophet of evil who is not believed.*

SAINT CASSIAN OF IMOLA

Patron of *schoolmasters.* Special day, August 13. Pictured in art with a stiletto in the heart.

CASSOCK

From Mediaeval times, in church vestment, signifies *devotion to Christ and the church.* The black color of the garment stands for the *law of the Old Testament* and the white surplice, *purity, and the gospel.* According to some authorities the interpretation is that the white (gospel) covers the blackness of sin. Illustration, p. 14:4.

CASSOWARY

As for the phoenix, symbolizes a *re-birth.*

CASTLE

In art, a castle denotes *safety, impregnableness,* and *romance.*

CAT

From the variance in moods or habits of activity, symbols are: *domesticity, ease, laziness, spitefulness, cruelty, self indulgence, lust.* Illustration p. 17:3.

In Egypt the cat is a sacred animal associated with Bastet, the sun-goddess.

The cat as *black magic* or *misfortune* goes back to Scandinavia where the cat was an attribute of Frey, goddess of beauty and love. After the Christianization of Scandinavia, the church declared Freya to be a witch, and thereafter the cat became the *attribute of witches.*

CATERPILLAR

As one stage of the development of a butterfly, a caterpillar signifies *Life.* Jeremiah 51:14 gives us, *devastating enemies.*

SAINT CATHERINE OF ALEXANDRIA

Patron saint of *philosophers* and *schools of learning,* of *students, spinsters, saddlers,* and *rope-makers.* Protectress against diseases of the tongue. Her special day, November 25. Her chief attribute, a spiked wheel, a device which Maximin II used in torturing her when she refused to be his wife. She was saved by a flame from heaven, but was later beheaded.

SAINT CATHERINE OF SIENA

Patron saint of *maidens,* the greatest female saint of the Dominican Order. Shown bearing the stigmata imprinted on her hands. Her attributes a crown of thorns, a lily, and a wedding ring. She was reputed as having had a mystic marriage with Christ. Her special day, April 30.

CATTLE

Pictured grazing in green pastures signify *agriculture.* Fat cattle, *prosperity.*

SAINT CECELIA

Patron saint of *music* and *musicians,* inventress of the *organ.* In picture, she is portrayed listening to music, singing, or playing some instrument. A favorite Saint in literature. Sometimes shown with three wounds in her neck from three attempts of the governor of Rome to slay her for refusing to cease preaching the gospel of Christ. Said to be so close to Heaven that she could hear the singing of angels. Her day, November 23.

CEDAR

Constancy, in that the branches are changeless through all seasons. *Virtue, beauty,* and *majesty* from its stately form. From its long life expectancy, *longevity, steadfast faith.*

CELENO

In Zoroaster's *Oracle,* one of the nine spirits of intelligence. Stands for *dullness, slowness.*

CENSER

In general the censer signifies *worship, adoration, prayer.* In Old Testament symbolism, the *pleas of the worshiper that his prayers may be acceptable to God;* in New Testament significations, the smoke of the incense represents the *prayers of the faithful ascending to Heaven.* Illustration p. 16:1.

CENTAUR

Race of monsters who united the head and body of man and horse. They symbolize the two natures of man, *as torn between good and evil.* Illustration p. 8:11.

CERBERUS (KERBERUS)

The three-headed, snaky-haired, sleepless watchdog of Hell in early Egyptian religion. In literature, a personification of *drouth, darkness, the underworld;* or symbol of a *vigilant custodian* or *guardian.*

CERES

In Roman mythology, daughter of Opa and Saturn. Goddess of *agriculture, all growing things, and sprouting seeds.* Always depicted fully draped, with ears of corn and poppies or other products in her hands.

CHAIN

Symbol of *strength, security, legal control.*

Chains, in plural form of the word, depicts *punishment, slavery, hopeless misfortune.*

CHAIR

An empty chair in legend signifies *hope that never dies,* from ancient Jewish belief that a vacant chair is for the coming of the Messiah.

A rare marker in ancient cemeteries in memory of a deceased loved one.

CHALICE

Faith, redemption, sacrifice, suffering, the *Eucharist,* all these symbolisms radiating from the cup of the Last Supper. Chalice and cross in Christian decorative art, reveals *Christ in Gethsemane.* Illustration p. 16:10.

Chalice with Communion wafer emerging, the *Eucharist,* or *Bread of Life, faith.*

A chalice, with serpent, is the emblem for *Saint John.*

CHALK
In masonry, a piece of chalk, charcoal or clay is the mark of an *apprentice.*

CHAMELEON
Changeableness, fickleness, inconstancy, symbols drawn from the peculiar ability this small reptile has to change its color.

CHAMOMILE
(See camomile.)

CHARCOAL
From Japan, the signification *prosperity, changelessness.* In masonry, with chalk, and clay, sign of *apprenticeship.*

CHARGER
(See dish, platter.)

CHARG KUO-LAO
In Taoism one of the seven immortals, meaning *the magic power.*

CHARIOT
(See car.)

SAINT CHARLEMAGNE THE GREAT
Venerated as saint in Germany and the Netherlands. His special day, January 18. Pictured in armor with ermine mantle. Embroidered on his robe, are three crowns, an orb, and a cross.

CHARON
In Greek mythology, son of Erebus and Nyx. He ferries the souls of the dead over the river Styx into Hades.

CHASUBLE
In liturgical vestment signifies *charity, protection, that which covers all.* It is the outer garment with which the celebrant of the Mass is vested. It had its beginning in the garment Pilate ordered to be placed on Christ as "The King of Kings." Illustration p. 14:2.

CHERRY

The tree, in the United States since the days of George Washington, has assumed a symbolism of *truthfulness,* from his admission that he had chopped down the cherry tree, with the statement "I cannot tell a lie." Cherry branches signify *manly virtue, chivalry.*

The fruit denotes *increase* from the number of stems that radiate from a central point. In Christian symbolism, the implication is *Fruit of Paradise, delights of the Blessed, sweetness of character.*

In Japan, the blossom (though the adopted national flower is the chrysanthemum), is still the flower of the people. It signifies, for them, *the beauty of spring,* or a *woman's outstanding beauty.*

CHERUB (and CHERUBIM)

In general symbolism, *eternal youth, loving service,* and in Biblical significations, *divine attendants.*

CHESS BOARD AND PIECES

Stand for the *game of life.*

CHEST

A chest reinforced with metal bands is an old time symbol for *banking,* and if closed implies *secrecy.*

CHESTNUT

In church symbolism, *chastity,* in that its husk is surrounded by thorns, but the fruit is unharmed by them. In general symbolism, the chestnut means *success* in association with its productiveness.

CHICK

When emerging from the shell, a popular emblem for *Easter Day* with underlying implications of *newly born, rebirth.*

CHICKADEE

The crested chickadee adopted as the state emblematic bird of Maine in 1927; and of Massachusetts in 1941. The Carolina chickadee became the adopted state bird of North Carolina in 1931.

CHICKEN

In the United States, the chicken symbolizes *endurance, pluck,* from the legend of the Blue Hen of the Revolutionary War where Delaware soldiers had as mascots fighting cocks, offspring of hens of a bluish color.

CHILD

An infant boy, unclothed, has long served as a popular symbol for the *New Year*.

CHIMERA

In Greek mythology, a hideous fire-breathing she-monster, having the body of a goat, the head of a lion, and tail of a dragon, with implications of *drought, darkness,* and the *underworld.* Sacred beast to Artemis as *generator, preserver.* Illustration p. 8:6.

CHIMNEY

In commercial art, a series of factory chimneys indicate *power, industry, commerce.*

In pictured art of the Christmas season, a chimney reflects the *joy of giving.*

CHIN-LIN

In Taoism, a gentle, one-horned beast signifying *happiness* and *good-omen.*

CHI RHO

Illustration p. 11:12. A widely used monogram made up of the first two letters of *Christ* in the Greek alphabet. It is seen with numerous combinations.

Surrounded by a circular aureole, it signifies *the glory of the risen and ascended Christ.*

With rays of light streaming from behind it, and placed high in a church, *Jesus enthroned in Heaven.*

When put together with cross and shepherd's crook, *Christ's pastoral mission and His death.*

CHISEL AND MALLET

Emblem of sculpture. Occasionally used to denote *the effect of education on the human mind.*

SAINT CHLODULF OF METZ

Patron of *nailmakers.* His attribute, the robe of a Benedictine monk with royal insignia, holding in his hand large nails. His special day, June 8.

CHLORIS

Ancient Greek goddess of *flowers*.

SAINT CHRISTINA

Patron saint of Venice, with special festival, July 24. Her attributes arrows, millstone, crown, and palm. She tramples on a pagan.

CHRISTMAS ROSE (or STARWORT)

Species of the aster family with white or purplish flowers symbol of *unselfish love*, and the *Nativity of our Lord*. Appropriate for the Christmas season in that it blooms late, and that its colors signify *purity* or *royalty*.

CHRISTMAS TREE

In the United States, preferably an evergreen, holding a central place in Christmas festivities with symbol of, *the Great Giver*.

CHRISTOGRAM

Distinctive monogram of Chi-Rho, in wide use for embellishment of church linens, wood carvings, and decorations for books and other printed documents. The monogram signifies the *Divine Saviour as a member of the Trinity*. Illustration of Chi-Rho, p. 11:12.

SAINT CHRISTOPHER

Patron of *protection*, especially that of *travelers*, and *sailors, navigators*. His special day is July 25. In art, pictured as wading waters with the Infant Christ on his shoulders, a scene taken from a legend wherein the saint received a call from a child to carry him across the turbulent river. In his hand, a palm tree staff which legend asserts Christ asked him to plant, that it might bear flowers and fruit. He was tortured and beheaded for his faith, and, as he was being led to his martyrdom, he prayed that all who saw him and trusted in God might be saved from fire, storm, and earthquake. Modern travelers are frequently seen wearing a Christopher ornament, as a reminder of the Saint's concern for their protection during their journeys.

CHRYSANTHEMUM

Denotes *regal beauty*, from its physical characteristics; *constancy, reliability*, in that it withstands the first frosts of autumn. The smaller variety suggests *modesty, dignity*.

The chrysanthemum is the national flower of Japan where it signifies *scholarliness*. In Chinese art, *prosperity, spiritual realities*. Illustration p. 21:11.

CHRYSOLITE or PERIDOT

A gem dedicated to Simeon of New Testament narrative, signifying *good tidings*. The peridot, with the sardonyz, is birthstone for August.

CHRYSOPRASE

Apple-green color variety of chalcedony, symbolizes *acrimony*. By some authorities held to be the emblematic gem for the month of December.

CHUNG-LI CH'NAN

In Taoism one of the seven immortals, signifying the *resurrection*.

CHURCH

For description of the symbolic church year, see *year*.

CHURCH BELL

Regardless of location, whether in tower or in the church yard acclaims the *priority of worship over both work and play*.

CHURCH SPIRE

An important symbolic figure in church architecture, as a reminder of *things above, things heavenly*, or *aspirations*.

CIBORIUM

The vessel which holds the Eucharist wafers, signifying *consecration*. Illustration p. 16:2.

CICADA

The symbol, as for a locust, grasshopper or katydid, from the sounds of the notes uttered, *loquacity, garrulity, worldly grandeur*.

CIRCE

In the Odyssey, an island sorceress who feasted the mariners, and then turned them into beasts. Widely featured in literary allusion to convey *enchantment, female wiles*.

CIRCLE

A popular symbolic figure with numerous implications in both secular and ecclesiastical areas, among them: *completeness, eternity, perfection, infinity, continuity, changelessness, light, health, peace, achievement, victory, having neither beginning nor end*, the *Infinite One;* also *unbroken harmony* and *endless friendship*.

The significations for special occasions or the circle in combination with other objects:

Circle of fire, *monastic chastity, magic, inviolability.*

As a wedding ring, *continuing devotion and love.*

Between the arms of a cross (Celtic cross), when used as a grave marker, *eternity victory.*

Three interwoven circles, in Christian symbolism, the *Holy Trinity.*

Four circles when linked to a fifth and larger one, the *words of wisdom.*

A triangle within a circle, *life unending.*

In architecture, circular form of church, *God's perfection, without beginning or end.*

Circle made by serpent swallowing its tail, *God the Creator is constantly absorbing His own output.*

In Mexico, two serpents entwined into a ring, *time without end.*

In China, a circle separating two serpents, the *two Principles claiming the universe.*

SAINT CLARA OF ASSISI

Patron of *embroiderers.* Nurse and companion of Saint Francis of Assisi of the Saint Francis Order, but later she founded her own Order, that of the Order of Poor Clares, which provided care and education for underprivileged girls. Her special day is November 4. Her attribute, a *ciborium.*

CLARISSA

In Spenser's Faerie Queene, symbol of *faith, hope, charity.*

CLAY

In church symbolism, *clinging trouble,* Psalm 40:2; Romans 9:21. In modern symbolism, the sign of an *apprentice.*

CLEMATIS

In general flower symbolism, *hardihood.* When a blossom is woven into a bridal bouquet, the signification is *affection.*

In church symbolism, the purple flower symbolizes the *Passion of Christ, suffering.* The five petals stand for the *five wounds,* and the spearshaped leaves *martyrdom.*

SAINT CLEMENT OF ROME

Patron of *hatters*, with special day, November 23. Often pictured with a lamb which led him to the waters of a spring when his Christian converts were famishing from thirst. His outstanding attribute an *anchor*, from the myth that during the reign of Roman Emperor Trajan, the saint had been banished for his failure to give up Christian preaching. His enemies tied an anchor around his neck and hurled him into the sea.

CLIO (also CLEIO)

In Greek mythology, known as the *muse of history* among the eight others. In art, represented with a laurel wreath and a book and stylus, to indicate her readiness to record events of the immortal gods.

CLOCK

Used as a symbol of *time*, usually *quick passing of time*, or the fact that each moment brings one nearer to one's eternal home.

CLOTHO (KLOTHO)

In Greek mythology, the youngest of the Three Fates. She *spins the thread of life* in which both bright and dark lines are intermingled.

SAINT CLOTILDA

Patroness of Tours, France. In pictures, holds a shield profusely emblazoned with fleur-de-lis, and small model of a church. Her festive day, June 3.

CLOUDS

Symbol of *mystery, sanctity, providence*. In church symbolism, *Jehovah*, or, with rays of light extending, *dimness of our knowledge of God*. With hand emerging, *Divine Omnipotence*.

CLOVER

Three-leaved as for shamrock, the *Holy Trinity*. The leaf was used by Saint Patrick of Ireland with this symbolic interpretation in his evangelism campaign. Now the emblem of Ireland. Illustration, p. 10:5.

Four leaved is symbol of *good luck, good wishes*.

The red clover blossom adopted as state emblematic flower of Vermont, in 1894.

CLUB

Weapon of *brutality*. Man with a club indicates *strength, labor*.

CLYTEMNESTRA

Half sister of Helen of Troy and wife of Agamemnon, referred to as *the dawn* in the sun-myths of the Trojan War.

COALS

Burning coals depict *ordeal by fire.*

COAT

In Christian symbolism, a seamless coat stands for the *Passion,* in reference to the garment for which lots were cast at the Crucifixion. Coat of camel's hair, *attribute of Saint John the Baptist.* Coat with three stones, *attribute of Saint Stephen,* first Christian martyr.

COBRA

(Same as for serpent.)

COBWEB

Denotes *human frailty,* from physical aspects of the web.

COCK

From natural characteristics of the fowl, *defiance, exultation, watchfulness, victory.* Illustration p. 18:3.

In Christian symbolism, one of the indications of Christ's *Passion,* stemming from Peter's denial and repentance.

Crowing cock, *faithful preachers.*

Cock with palm near or in his bill, *reward obtained.*

When a part of church architecture, *victory* or *resurrection.*

As seen on ancient tombs, *resurrection.*

On towers, the *office of preaching.*

On lamps with monogram of Christ above, *Christ the Light.*

Fighting cocks, man's *readiness to combat his faults and imperfections.*

On French flags, *supremacy, vigilance.*

As attribute of Abraxas, the *supreme spirit.*

COCKATRICE

Fabulous serpent with a deadly glance, said to have been hatched by a reptile from the egg of a cock. Symbol of *Satan, evil.*

COCKLE

Symbolizes *wickedness* as it strives to invade the field of the church. Job 31:40.

COCOANUT

The fruit symbolizes *fertility, abundance,* from its many uses — oil, food, fibrous thatch, etc.

CODFISH

Productiveness, from its many uses as food, and as oils, and from the rapid reproductiveness of the fish.

COGWHEEL

In early times symbolized *fate.* Later, a popular emblem for *mechanics* or *industry.*

COIN

From an early signification in China, *riches, tribute.* A new coin is said to bring *good luck.*

COLLAR

Well-known personification of the *clergy.*

COLORS

(See liturgical colors.) (See, also symbolism of each different color in proper alphabetical listing in this book.)

COLUMBINE

General signification, *innocence.* In Biblical symbolism, *Holy Spirit,* an association of the "Holy Spirit descending as a dove." The Latin form *columba* means *dove,* and the columbine, in form, much resembles a white dove.

The seven petals of the flower are said to signify the seven gifts of the Spirit, Isaiah 11:2. In the Middle Ages, one of the Virgin's flowers, it was also called the *"Love of Mary."*

In 1899 by act of the legislature of Colorado, the white and lavender mountain columbine was made state flower. Here the colors signify: blue, *for the skies;* snow, *viewed on the mountains the year around,* and the yellow of the centers, the *gold interests of the state in 1858.*

COLUMN

General symbolic meaning, *strength, support.*

In church architecture the number of columns determines the significance:

Twelve columns represent, the *twelve apostles.*

Eight, the *eight Beatitudes,* Matthew 5:5-11.

Four, *stability.*

Two, *strength and beauty.*

One lone column, *Christ's Passion,* as one of the thirteen symbols of the Passion.

A broken column, early used as a gravestone, denotes *unfinished life work, death.*

COMEDY

From the ancient Greeks has come this symbolic figure for comedy — a human mask with an expression of mirth. See illustration p. 19:2.

COMET

From visible aspects of this astronomical body, we get the symbolic terms, *brilliant career.*

From Japan comes the signification of *famine, calamity, war.*

COMMERCE

There are many symbolic representations, among them, an *airplane,* an *automobile,* a *beast of burden,* a *globe,* a *railway train,* a *ship,* *telephone or telegraph poles,* a *truck,* a *typewriter,* a *money-bag,* *flying Mercury,* or the *head of Mercury.*

COMPASS

Symbol of *guidance.* Also used emblematically for *astronomy, geometry, science, architecture.* A compass and square, denotes *skilled craftsmanship.*

CONCH SHELL

(See shell.) Illustration p. 15:10.

CONDOR

This huge vulture, on Ecuador's seal and coins denotes *strength.*

CONE

(See pine cone.)

CONSENTES (same as Pan)

In Roman mythology, son of Mercury and Penelope. He is the god of *shepherds,* the *universe,* and personification of *nature;* also strongly devoted to *music* and *the dance.*

CONVOLVULUS

Symbolism of this twining plant, as for the morning glory, *humility,* in that the flower is often hidden under the leaves.

COPE

The richest and most magnificent piece of ecclesiastical vestment, the colors of which are in strict keeping with the colors of the church season. The symbolic meaning is *dignity, purity, innocence.*

COPESTONE

In architecture, signifies *completion.*

COPPER

In church symbolism, same as for brass, *firmness, hardness, strength.*

CORAL

Signifies *protection against evil,* an outgrowth from its early use as a charm against the evil eye.

With the amethyst and emerald, makes the third emblematic jewel in the crown of Pope John XXIII, as a symbol of *protection.*

CORD

Symbolizes, in general, *execution.* In ecclesiastical vestment, *chastity, temperance, self-restraint.*

CORN

As an element of consecration, corn symbolizes nourishment; wine, *refreshment,* and oil of joy, *health, plenty, peace.*

Corn in shock, symbol of *harvest, abundance.* Popular emblematic object of Thanksgiving Day.

CORNERSTONE

Symbolizing *foundation.* In church structure, by some authorities, *Christ, the Foundation,* from Ephesians 2:20; by others, *Saint Peter the Apostle,* Matthew 16:18.

CORNFLOWER (bachelor's button)

From its blue color signifies *devotion.* In the tri-color of Flander's Field, the cornflower is the *blue;* the poppy, *red;* the daisy, the *white.* The cornflower made the national flower of Germany in 1871.

CORNUCOPIA

Signifies *plenty, prosperity, lavish productivity, abundance.* These implications have been handed down from Classical mythology where Amalthea's horn became filled with whatever fruits the possessor desired. Illustration, p. 22:1.

CORONET

(See crown.)

CORONIS

In Greek mythology, maiden of the *dawn,* mother of Aesculapius. She figures prominently in the Sun and Dawn myths, where she (the dawn) is wooed and won by Apollo (the Sun), but she proves untrue. A white raven reports the tryst, and Apollo, with an arrow, pierces her heart. He then relents, and, in vain, tries to restore her to life.

CORYDON

A shepherd in Theocritus's *Idyls* and Vergil's *Ecologues,* basis for the conventional name for a *rustic young swain* in modern pastorals.

SAINTS COSMAS AND DAMIAN

Twin brothers, patron saints of *medicine* and *surgery,* of *barbers,* and *apothecaries.* Later adopted as patron saints of the famous Medici family of Italy. Their special day, September 27.

COSMOS

Popular fall flower, signifying *modesty,* associated with the fact that the weight of the flower may cause its head to bend, bowing, so to speak, on its slender stem.

COTTON

The blossom signifies *happiness, well-being,* from the assumed feelings it reflects as the stalks move rhythmically in gentle winds.

COTTONWOOD

The state emblematic tree of the state of Kansas, adopted as such in 1937, because of its *hardiness,* suggestive of the characteristic trait of the pioneer settlers of the territory.

COW

Symbol of *procreation.* In ancient Egypt, the animal sacred to, and symbol of the goddess Hathor (Isis), wife and sister of Osiris and mother of Horus. Hathor who was thought of as the goddess of procreation and mother of the race, was usually represented with a cow's horn on her head.

In Greece, a similar symbolism is attached to the association of the cow with Hera, wife of Zeus.

COWSLIP

Flower of early spring, with symbolism, *youth, gaiety, dalliance.*

CRAB

Symbol of *aggressiveness, peevishness,* from habits of the small marine creature. A crab is now an easily recognizable emblem for the disease, *cancer.* In the zodiac, the sign of June.

CRANE

Vigilance, symbol drawn from an old fable wherein the bird is pictured with a stone in its claw, held there that if by chance it fell asleep, the stone in dropping would awaken it. Added to the symbol of *vigilance,* from the Middle Ages we get, *loyalty, good life,* good *works, prudence, happiness.* Illustration, p. 18:7.

From Japan, comes *longevity, good fortune, conjugal fidelity.* Here, in olden times, the crane was widely venerated, and nobody was allowed to kill a crane without an order from the emperor.

In pictures, a crane standing on a turtle expresses a wish of *good fortune and long life.* A flight of cranes is representative of *many, many good wishes.*

In machinery, a crane, in commercial art, stands for *mechanics, manufacturing.*

CRATOS

In Greek mythology, son of Pallas Athene and the river god, Styx. In literature, a personification of *force*, in association with his strength in carrying out the revenge of Zeus upon Prometheus.

CRESCENT

Symbol of Artemis (Diana), in connection with her station as goddess of night. From this early denotation, there have arisen for the crescent moon, the symbolisms *sleep, womanhood, growing brightness.*

SAINT CRESCENTIA

Patron saint of *nurses*, with special day, June 15.

CRESS

From the winter cress of this hardy plant, there is this symbolic attachment, *old age*, the life of a man after passing through spring, summer, and autumn.

CRESSET

In church symbolism, the *gospel light held aloft by Christ or His followers.*

CRIMSON

Symbol of *love*.

SAINT CRISPIN

Patron of *shoemakers* and *cobblers*. His special day, October 25.

CROCODILE

From early Egyptian legend, the symbolisms *ferocity*, and *spirit of evil*. Later, in Egyptian myth, *reason, understanding.* Also *hypocrisy*, and *disinclination.*

The epithet, crocodile tears, stems from the fact that the reptile sheds tears over the prey which it has just devoured.

CROCUS

One of the favorite flowers of Juno, reflecting the symbolisms, *joy, mirth,* and *charity,* from the welcome given its early spring appearance.

CRONUS (KRONUS)

In Greek mythology, a Titan, son of Uranus and Gaea, who dethroned his father, and in turn was dethroned by his son, Zeus. Known as god of the *harvests*, and divinity of *time*. Pictured as an old man carrying a scythe, symbolical of *time, primal cause.*

CROOK

In Biblical symbolism the shepherd's crook or staff denotes *Divine leading, sovereignty, power.*

CROSIER, also CROZIER

When used as a symbol of pastoral office, in church symbolism signifies *leadership, authority.* The crook at the top suggests the responsibility of drawing people into the fold of Christ, while the pointed lower end indicates the duty of spurring the faithful to greater Christian service. This symbolic meaning early pertained only to the office of archbishop, but has expanded to include all religious leaders, having, also the added significance of *guidance, correction, ministration.* Illustration p. 14:1.

CROSS

A comprehensive interpretation of the cross is that it is the symbol of the Christian faith, the love of God for sinful man, and a triumphant hope for a life yet to come. We are told that there exist more than four hundred different representations of the cross as to shape, or combination with other figures. In this study, only the most commonly recognizable forms, with the special significations, have been included. See illustrations, p. 12.

CROW

One interpretation of this bird as a symbol is, as for the owl, *wisdom.* From its natural habits, *piracy, scavenger.* It often stands for *filial piety,* in that it is said when a crow becomes infirm it is cared for by its young. In Asia, the symbolism is *hospitality;* in Japan, a croaking crow signifies *misfortune.*

CROWN

In general, *sovereignty, reward, honor, victory, royalty, excellence.* In Christian symbolism there are special interpretations:

A king's crown, *the Lord's victory over sin and death, and His rulership over men.*

Crown of thorns, Christ's ministry of *redemption,* His *suffering, humiliation.* Illustration, p. 13:4.

Reed and crown, *Christ's Passion.*

Other secular interpretations:

Crown of acorns — *abundance of the earth.*
Crown of cypress — *death, mortality.*
Crown of elm and grapevine leaves — *benevolence.*
Crown of ebony — *Pluto.*
Crown of fennel — *Faunus.*
Crown of figs — *Melpomene or Pan.*
Crown of flowers — *spring.*
Crown of iron — *tyranny.*
Crown of ivy and laurel — *poetry.*
Crown of ivy, olive, or mulberry — *Mercury.*
Crown of laurel — *triumphal honors, peace, victory.*
Crown of myrtle — *minor difficulties.*
Crown of roses — *love, virtue.*
Crown of red and white roses — *virginity.*
Crown of stars — *justice.*
Crown of wheat ears — *abundance, agriculture.*
Crown of grape leaves — *Bacchus.*

Two crowns, in certain wedding ceremonies when held over heads of bride and groom by the "best man" — *equality and virtue.*

CRUCIFIX

In Western churches, a representation of Christ upon a Latin cross. In earlier forms He is shown clothed, crowned, and reigning in His threefold character — Prophet, Priest, and King. With the advent of mediaeval asceticism, the figure of the suffering Christ appeared on the cross, not so much a symbol of *suffering* but as a reminder of the *Passion of Christ.*

CRUCIFIXION

The thirteen symbols: See thirteen, and for illustrations, p. 13.

CRUTCH

A symbol of *misfortune, temporary handicap.*

CRUX ANSATA

Symbol of *immortality.* Illustration p. 12:1.

CRYSTAL

As a setting in jewelry or for other ornamentations, *purity, simplicity.*

CUBE

A symbolical geometrical figure signifying *truth, firmness, moral rectitude, stability.*

CUCKOO

Symbol of *egoism, selfishness, usurpation, infidelity,* implications developed in Europe from the practice of the bird in laying its eggs in the nest of others. In India, bird of Kama, Hindu god of love.

CUP

Christian symbol of Christ's ministry of *redemption,* and the bitter pain he bore for the salvation of mankind.

In modern interpretation, a cup symbolizes *temperance, friendship.* In mythology, special attribute for: Bacchus, Hygeia, Aesculapius.

CUPID

In Roman mythology, god of love, son of Venus and Mars. Lover of the nymph Psyche, and noted for his golden bow and arrows which he used wantonly. Pictured as a naked, winged young boy with bow, arrows and quivers. In different positions, he denotes different symbolisms:

Cupid holding a key — *power.*
Cupid quenching a torch — *lost love.*
Cupid balanced on Fortuna's wheel — *good luck.*
Cupid fallen from Fortuna's wheel — *bad luck.*
Cupid taking steady aim in Valentine Day festivities — an *appeal for affection.*

SAINT CUTHBERT

Patron of *shepherds* and *seafarers.* His attribute, the crowned head of Oswald held fast in his hands. His special day, March 20.

CYBELE

Greek goddess of nature, identified with Roman Rhea. Accompanied by a train of attendants, she frequented mountain forests, and wild-moving streams. The famous fountain of Cybele in Madrid emphasizes her chief attributes as wearing a high, turreted crown. She holds the reins of two mammoth lions who draw her four-wheeled chariot.

CYCLAMEN

The white flower, called the *bleeding nun,* was early dedicated to the Virgin Mary, symbolizing *bleeding sorrow* because of the red spot at the heart of the flower.

The crimson flower signifies *voluptousness, bitterness, Christ's Passion;* also *carnal passion.*

CYCLOPS

In Greek mythology, a race of massive giants having only one eye, and that in the middle of the forehead. They were builders of city walls and breeders of cattle. As smiths of Zeus, they forged the thunderbolts.

CYMBALS

Musical instrument composed of two half-global parts, having a sharp ringing sound when played. One of the symbols of the *dance.*

CYNTHIA

In Greek mythology goddess of the *moon* and the *chase.* A favorite character in English poetical allusions. In art, represented as a beautiful maiden, clad in short hunting dress, armed with a bow, a quiver full of arrows at her side, and a crescent on her head. Same as Artemis.

CYNTHIUS

In Greek mythology, one of the names given to Apollo, god of the sun, and of fine arts.

CYPRESS

General symbolic implication *mourning, mortality.* Even in pagan times associated with *death,* and the tree still may be found in ancient cemeteries beside the tombs of both pagans and Christians. Its natural physical characteristics readily explain the symbolism *mortality* for it has a deep-green foliage, and when it has once been cut down, it does not again spring up from the old roots.

CYTHEREA

The name given to Venus, goddess of *love, beauty and laughter.* In fable, the girdle of Cytherea brought love to the wearer.

D.

DAEDALUS

This character from Greek mythology, is a symbol of *cunning worker, contriver*. He invented an early flying device wherewith he and his son escaped from prison. Icarus flew too near the sun, and, overcome with heat, he fell into the sea, but the ingenious father made his way back to Sicily.

DAFFODIL

Flower of *benevolence, joy, untiring devotion, prosperity*, and symbol of Wales.

DAGGER

Symbol of *danger, treachery*, when pictured in the hand of a muscled arm.

DAGON

In early Babylonian religion, god of *earth* and *agriculture*. He is mentioned many times in the Old Testament, referred to in his earlier days as the *fish god*.

DAHLIA

Flower of *good cheer*, in association with its showy, highly-colored blooms.

DAIKOKU

One of the seven Japanese gods of luck, symbolizing *wealth* and *happiness*.

DAISY

In language of the flowers, generally, symbolic of *youth, innocence*, in association with the meaning of the word *day's eye*, from which the later spelling was derived. Illustration p. 20:6.

In Christian religion, the symbolism early became, *humility, innocence of the Divine Child*. In later centuries it appeared in paintings where formerly the white lily had been used to depict innocence.

With the violet and lily is one of the three national flowers of Italy. Also, with the red poppy, and the blue "bachelor's button," is flower of the Flander's Field patriotic combination.

86

DALMATIC

Traditional outer vestment of deacons and certain prelates of the Western World church, symbol of *joy, salvation, justice.* Its shape — the form of a cross — refers to the *Passion of Christ.*

SAINT DAMIAN

(See Saint Cosmas.)

DANAE

Symbol of *earth,* from the Greek legend of her having been washed to the Island of Seriphus after she and her son had been put afloat by her father, angered at her secret marriage with Zeus.

DANDELION

Flower of varying symbolisms. In the Gothic period, *bitterness, grief, sorrows of the Virgin,* the *Passion of Christ,* associated with the bitter, sour juice of the plant.

From the color and shape of the flower, it symbolizes the *sun,* and *wisdom.* The ripened dandelion with its many seeds afloat is held to be an indication of a *gossiper.* Also symbol of *fertility.*

DANIEL

In Biblical allusions, *judgment, efficacy of prayer,* from Daniel 6:16-23.

DAPHNE

The *dawn,* from Sanskrit *Dahana.* There is a pathetic story of Daphne in Greek mythology of her pleas to the gods to be changed into a laurel tree to escape the love of Apollo. Her request was granted, and, in that disguise, in literature, she becomes the personification of *morning dew.*

DARKNESS

Stands for *perplexity, distress, failure, ignorance,* and in Biblical symbolism, *spiritual darkness, unbelief.*

DART

Same symbolism as for arrow. In Biblical implication, *sharp and sudden temptation.* Ephesians 6:16.

DATE PALM TREE

From the terminal crown of its large fan or feather-shaped leaves, the symbolic signification is *triumph, victory, success,* and often in Christian symbolism, *resurrection.*

DAVID'S SHIELD
(See hexagon.)

DAWN
In Christian art, pictures of the dawn reflect the *Advent of Christ.*

DEER (DOE, STAG)
In general symbolism, *fleetness.* From Japan, the implication *longevity.*

DEIANEIRA
In Greek mythology, wife of Hercules, personification of *the daylight.*

DELPHINIUM
With larkspur, member of the crowfoot family, signifying *continuing well-being,* in that the leaves do not drop off until new ones have gained a good start. Also represents *fickleness,* from the fact that the petals, though beautiful while the flower is freshly cut, wither away readily.

DEMETER
Greek goddess of *agriculture,* the *guardian of marriage,* and the *fruitfulness of mankind.* Identified with Ceres by the Romans.

DEMONS
Of all shapes, signify *punishment.*

DEW
In symbolism of Christian religion, *morning, divine blessing, revival, refreshment.* Hosea 14:5.

DIADEM
(See crown.)

DIAMOND
Most precious of stones, symbol of *light, innocence, purity, life, joy.*

When seen in a ring, the diamond suggests *invulnerable constancy,* not from the hardness of the stone, but from an ancient belief that gods could not resist the prayers of anyone carrying a diamond. Symbolic birthstone for April.

DIANA

Roman goddess of the moon, the chase, the woods, and helper of women in childbirth. Her famous shrines were in the woods, and there she had as associates Egeria, a water nymph, and Virbius, a wood nymph.

DIANTHUS (garden pink)

During the Middle Ages, accepted as one of the flowers of the Virgin with the symbolism of the *Holy Spirit*.

DICE

Signify *chance, fortune, debauchery, gambling*. In church picture language, three dice symbolize *Christ's Passion*, in association with the casting of lots at the Crucifixion.

DIDO

Queen of Carthage who killed herself for the love of AEneas. She has become a symbol of *tragedy*.

DIKE

In Greek mythology, daughter of Zeus and Themis, goddess of *good faith, truth, justice*.

DILL

An European herb, the anise of the Bible, signifies *cleansing power*. In the Middle Ages used by magicians in casting spells against witchcraft.

DIOMEDES

Symbol of *bravery*, as one of the bravest of the Greeks in the Trojan War, became king of Thrace. In legend we are told that he fed his horses on human flesh, and, to punish him for this inhumane practice, Hercules had him slaughtered and fed to his own horses.

DIONE

In Greek mythology, mother of Aphrodite, known as goddess of *beauty, love, laughter*, and of *moisture*.

DIONYSUS (see, also BACCHUS)

Son of Zeus and Semele, god of *fertility of plant life*, especially the grapevine. God of *wealth, revelry*, and *wine*, and youthful god of *inspiration*. His attributes easily recognizable — a crown of vine-leaves, and a leopard by his side. Illustration p. 7:7.

89

DIS

Roman god of the *underworld* identified with Pluto by the Greeks.

DISH

Meaning *martyrdom*, when associated with Salome, Matthew 14:6-12, who demanded that the head of John the Baptist be brought to her on a charger. When used as an alms-bowl, a dish, *symbol of begging* goes bāck to Saint Alexis, patron saint of pilgrims and beggars.

DISK

Ancient Egyptian symbol of the *sun as protector of life*, hence often used with modern interpretation as *eternal life*. In Buddhism the disk with radiating lines is the basis for the "Wheel of the Law."

DISTAFF

Symbolizes *industry, authority, domain*. As an emblem of *manufacturing*, the meaning has stemmed from Klotho (Clotho), the spinner from among the three Fates in Greek mythology.

DOE

Female of any species of deer, antelope, or hare, signifies *fleetness;* in Japan, *longevity*.

DOG

Friend of man, signifies *fidelity, guardianship, protection, sagacity, flattery*. Rare, in church symbolism, but from Exodus 22:31, *ungodly person, contempt, impurity*. When pictured as a dog biting his tail, the allusion is to Satan who goaded Judas on, and rested not until Christ hung on the cross.

DOGWOOD

The mass of flowers in early spring is an attraction of much beauty, as is the foliage, turning red, in the autumn. In Christian significations, the blossom suggests the *Cross of Christ* from the one long bract, and two shorter ones in suggestion of the central pole and arms of the Latin cross. In Victorian days in England, dogwood denoted *indifference*. If a young man sent a tulip as a declaration of love to the young lady he adored, she might reply with a dogwood blossom to convey her *indifference* to his appeal.

By act of General Assembly on March 6, 1918, the blossom became the official emblematic flower of Virginia. In North Carolina, the adoption was in 1941. Flowering dogwood is also the symbolic flower of British Columbia.

DOLPHIN

As seen in literary allusion, the dolphin signifies *swiftness, persistency, diligence,* from natural physical characteristics of the fish.

In religious symbolism, there are different interpretations; the one taken from the drawings on the walls of the catacombs, *Christ and His Resurrection,* and the other a depiction of Peter as a *fisher of men's souls.* Sometimes, in Christian art, a dolphin coiled about an anchor denotes a *swift bearer of souls to heaven, after a life well anchored in Christ on earth.* Illustration p. 9:7.

SAINT DOMINIC

Thirteenth century preaching friar, founder of the Dominican Order. His special attributes a lily, for purity, and a rosary, in that he earnestly inspired devotion of the rosary. It is said that a star appeared on his forehead when he was baptized.

DOMINOES

From China, come the symbolisms, *scholarship, learning.*

DOOR

An open door suggests *hospitality, good cheer.* In Christian symbolism *opportunity for service.* First Corinthians 16:9.
In church architecture, when the door is decorated with angels or saints, the implication is the *Glorified Christ.*

SAINT DOROTHEA

Patroness of *brides, mid wives, gardeners,* and *brewers.* Often in art seen offering a basket of fruit and flowers to the Virgin. She was condemned to execution for her faith. Her festive day is February 3.

DOVE (see, also, turtledove)

The dove, from its obvious natural characteristics and habits — color, graceful descending movements, care of its young, and from the numerous scriptural references to the bird, has taken on many symbolic denotations: *peace, gentleness, meekness, timidity, purity, soul, sacrifice, Christian love.* In Greek mythology, Aphrodite, goddess of love and beauty, chose doves as the conductors of her chariot. From pagan times, we get the symbolisms, *constancy, conjugal affections,* and *contentment.* In Biblical denotations, the position of the bird, in flight or at rest, together with the object surrounding it, gives rise to the symbolisms:

Dove ascending – *resurrection.*

Dove descending – *God and the Holy Spirit,* especially a white dove with nimbus encircled head.

The dove in *baptismal scenes* is usually descending with outstretched wings, and with light rays extending from its beak.

Dove with olive branch in its beak – *peace and good tidings, or deliverance of the soul from death.*

Dove coming down from the starry heavens – *inspiration, spiritual guidance.*

Seven doves, sometimes surrounding a circle – the gifts of the Holy Spirit, which are, *wisdom, understanding, counsel, might, knowledge, piety,* and the *fear of the Lord.*

Dove of David, signifies *peace.*

A black dove in Egypt – *widowhood.*

Markings on early gravestones – *soul at rest.*

Twelve doves – *the twelve apostles.*

Dove with ring around its neck – *encircling sweetness of the Divine Word.*

Two wings of a dove – *love of God and love of man.*

Illustration of dove, p. 18:8.

DRAGON

The dragon, in both secular and ecclesiastical symbolism, offers many implications – *sin, idolatry, despotism, ignorance, enemy of truth,* the *devil,* also *pestilence.* Illustration, p. 8:3.

In China, a representation of a dragon has many meanings including those of the *emblem of the emperor, guardian of the heavens, success, beneficence.* He is the Chinese farmer's patron saint who brings rain in times of drought. In Japanese art, a dragon piercing the clouds over Fugiyama denotes *prosperity, success.*

Dragon the Beneficent, in classical mythology, signifies *custodian of the House of Life,* the *Reconciler* and *Deliverer,* and the *Spirit of all Knowledge.*

DRAGON FLY

As an emblem in Japan, signifies *victory.* Dragon's teeth, suggest *warfare* and *dissension,* in association with the myth of Cadmus who sowed dragon's teeth from which armed soldiers sprang up.

DRAWBRIDGE

Ancient symbol of *defense*.

DRYADS

In Greek mythology, a special group of tree nymphs, serving as guardians over *vegetation*.

DUCK

When carved over the door of a church, though seldom seen in modern-built structures, serves as a reminder that one should *enter quietly* and *pray in silence.*

From Japan comes the symbolic implication of a pair of mandarin ducks reflecting *conjugal fidelity, happiness, immunity from worry,* and *long life.*

DUNCE CAP

Symbol of *ignorance*.

DURGA

Hindu goddess of *blood, war, sacrifice.* One of the consorts of Shiva.

DUST AND ASHES

Following Hebrew representations, symbols of *death, deep mourning.*

In burial rites — a *return of the physical elements of the body to their original form of composition.*

EAGLE

From the various poses and flight movements of the eagle have come countless symbolic significations. It appears as a heraldic device in ancient Persia, Assyria, Egypt, and the Roman legions. Later, also, in Germany, Austria, Prussia, and the French Empire. For early American Indians, an eagle with outstretched wings meant *speed, wisdom.* In church symbolism, the eagle is the attribute of Saint John the Evangelist because his Gospel writings are said to soar on eagle's wings from beginning to end. The ascending eagle denotes the *Ascension of Christ,* while the descending bird signifies the *Holy Spirit.* Perched on high mountain points, the eagle stands for *kingship, dominion, superiority.* In flight, *freedom, liberty, speed.* In Greek myths, the eagle is the bird of Zeus. Illustration p. 22:9.

Since 1782 the bald eagle has reigned as the emblematic national bird of the United States. Pictured with wings aloft, and bearing a shield with thirteen stripes, the eagle stands for *protection, liberty, justice, courage.* On the United States seal, he holds in one claw thirteen arrows, in the other an olive branch with thirteen leaves or with thirteen berries.

EAR

When accompanied by a knife, in Christian symbolism, an ear represents the *betrayal of Christ,* or the *Passion,* in reference to John 18:10.

An elongated ear lobe in figures of Buddha signifies *aristocratic birth.*

EARTH

A handful of earth is said to imply *mortality, death.* In Christian symbolism the earth, or globe, upon which a cross is planted is a symbol of the church which feeds mankind with *spiritual faith,* and offers him *shelter.*

EASTER LILY

See lily. Illustration p. 16:8.

EBISU

In Japan one of the seven gods of *good luck.*

ECHO

In Greek mythology, a nymph who pined away for the love of Narcissus until nothing was left but her voice; hence *sympathetic appreciation.*

EGG

From early pagan lore, the egg has become the symbolic representation of many related meanings — *creation, fertility, life force in nature, immortality.* Christians readily accepted these implications, adding *hope* and *resurrection* as the egg, for them became a favored symbol for Easter observances. Eggs symbolized *vitality* as an ingredient of the Shrove Tuesday pancake of the early Middle European observance of that day.

EIGHT

In Biblical symbolism, the number eight has taken on the signification of *perfection* and *completion* in that the visible world was made in seven days and the invisible kingdom of grace followed as an added benefaction.

In church architecture, eight columns are representative of the *eight Beatitudes.* An octagonal baptistry or baptismal font signifies *rebirth, regeneration.*

In Buddhist symbolism the number eight is of great significance. Here we find: The eight-fold path of Buddha with these principles:

1. Right faith.
2. Right resolve.
3. Right speech.
4. Right action.
5. Right living
6. Right effort.
7. Right thought.
8. Right self-concentration.

Also the eight Buddhist symbols derived from objects:

1. The lotus flower — *purity out of the unclean.*
2. Covered vase — a *reliquary.*
3. Conch shell — *talisman of mariners.*
4. Two fishes — *domestic faith and happiness.*
5. Umbrella — *official authority.*
6. Canopy — *sovereign rank.*
7. Bell or wheel — the *law.*
8. Knot — longevity.

EIRENE

In Greek mythology the most cheerful of the three daughters of Zeus and Themis, known as the *guardian goddess of songs and festivities*, the *proponent of peace*, and *stimulator of plant life*.

ELDER FLOWER

Of the honeysuckle family, the elder tree in church symbolism signifies *zeal*.

ELECTRA

In Homeric writings, personification of *vengeance*. Daughter of Agamemnon and sister of Orestes.

ELEPHANT

In general symbolism, *superhuman power, sagacity, self-restraint, patient endurance*. In different countries, and when pictured with other objects the interpretations vary:

For early Brahmas, the signification is *royal splendor*, the white elephant bestowing *earthly blessings*, and bringing down *abundant rains* from heaven.

In India, still, the animal is symbol of *patient endurance*, and *self-restraint*.

With a tower on his back — *prudence*.

Lifting his trunk to the sun in midday, *piety*.

From the fact that an elephant will drink no more water than he needs, *temperance*.

A miniature elephant, *good luck*.

In U.S.A. the elephant is the emblematic figure for the *Republican Party*.

ELEVEN

In Christian symbolism, eleven heads on a wheat stalk signify the fact that eleven apostles produced good fruit for their Lord, while one of the twelve did not.

SAINT ELIGIUS OF NOYON

Patron of *farriers, gold and silversmiths*, and all metal workers. His attributes a hammer, anvil, and horseshoe. His festival day, December 1.

SAINT ELISABETH OF HUNGARY

Patroness of *bakers, beggars,* and *confraternities engaged in good works, Sisters of Mercy, charitable organizations,* and *lacemakers.* Her attribute is an apron full of roses, or a basket full of food for the needy. Her festival day, November 19.

ELM

In Christian symbolism, from its habits of growth, and the spread of branches the elm is indicative of the strength gained through continued study of the Scriptures, and the *dignity of life.*

The American elm tree became emblematic in Nebraska in 1937; in Massachusetts in 1941, and in North Dakota in 1947.

ELYSIAN FIELDS

Signify *ideal delight, happiness, paradise,* associated with classical mythological allusions describing the fields as the place where the good dwell after death. The location in these earlier times was in the Western Ocean.

EMERALD

In Christian symbolism, gem of *hope in immortality, exalted faith, tranquil peace, victory over trial and sin, resurrection, vigor of Christian piety as opposed to infidelity.*

In general, these implications have expanded to include *love* and *success,* and the gem is supposed to bestow *wealth* and *eloquence* upon the wearer. With the amethyst and coral, the emerald is one of the gems in the crown of Pope John XXIII.

EMPUSA

In Greek mythology, a destructive monster of the underworld, with one foot of brass, the other that of an ass. Had a tremendous appetite for human flesh.

EMU

Frequently pictured as an emblematic figure for Australia, in badges, signs, or advertisements of Australian products, but the emu has not had official adoption.

ENDYMION

In Greek mythology, a young man of great beauty, beloved by the moon goddess, Selene, who through her magic power threw Endymion into a sleep in order that he might not be conscious of her caresses. In literature, he is the personification of *beauty*.

ENTRANCE

In church architecture, an open glass front of the structure expresses the unity of man and nature, or extends to the passer-by a welcome.

EOS

Greek goddess of the *dawn, rouser* of the sleeping sun, awakener of the morning breeze, and bestower of the dew. She was the daughter of Hyperion; sister of Helios and Selene. In pictures seen running or flying, with streaming hair and garments. Same as Roman Aurora.

EPHOD

Vestment garment of the High Priest of the Hebrews, with historical beginnings recorded in Exodus Chapters XXVIII and XXIX. A short tunic, richly embroidered, worn over the outer robe and fastened with a girdle. A similar, less ornate ephod of linen is the mark of the priesthood.

SAINT ERASMUS OF GAETA

Patron saint of *sailors*. Pictured holding a windlass around which his entrails are wound, as a sign of his brutal martyrdom. His special day, June 2.

ERATO

In classical mythology one of the nine muses, daughter of Zeus and Mnemosyne. She presided over the *lyric,* and all other *amatory poetry.* Her attribute is a zither or lyre, and she wears a crown of myrtle and roses.

EREBUS

In Greek mythology, *god of darkness,* son of Chaos and Night. He rules over the souls of babes and lovers, and of brave soldiers killed in battle. He dethroned and supplanted Chaos, then married his own mother, and the two produced the gigantic egg from which Eros, god of love, emerged to create the earth.

ERINYS

(See EUMENIDES.)

ERIS

In Greek mythology, *goddess of strife*, same as Discordia. Daughter of Night; sister of Ares and of Parsimony and Death; mother of misery, famine, war, contest, and slaughter.

She was the bestower of the apple of Discord given to Aphrodite by Paris as a prize of beauty. Her attributes are a spear, and a serpent, a wolf and a lamb in company.

ERMINE

This small animal symbolizes *purity*, from its white fur, and from the legend that it preferred death to impurity. The fur signifies *royalty, aristocracy*.

EROS (same as Cupid)

In Greek mythology, winged boy with arrows and quiver, son of Chaos, hatched from the egg of Night, god of *sexual love*. In philosophy, Eros is the cosmic force of *attraction*. In the statue of Eros before a fountain in London, the implication stresses Lord Shaftesbury's wide love for humanity.

EROSIA

In Zoroaster's *Oracle* Erosia stands for *love* and *enjoyment* as one of the nine spirits of intelligence.

ESCALLOP SHELL (see, also shell)

In Christian picture language represents a *pilgrimage*. Illustration, p. 15:9.

EUCHARIST

A sacramental rite in most Christian churches in which bread, or bread and wine, are consecrated by an official representative of the church body, and shared by the people as a thanksgiving to God. Among the significations are: *sacrifice, union of heaven and earth, resurrection, spiritual union with one God*. Among the attributes are: a chalice, grapes, vine with grapes, bread and wine.

EUMENIDES

In Greek mythology, goddess of *vengeance*, one of the snaky-haired women who hunted out evil-doers and tormented them to madness. She is known, also, as Erinys, or as one of the Furies.

EUNOMIA

Greek goddess of *order*, and *stimulation of plant life*. One of the beautiful daughters of Zeus and Themis.

SAINT EUPHEMIA OF CHALCEDONIA

Maiden of Asia Minor of the third century, persecuted for her faith and eventually beheaded. Her special day, September 16. The epithet "of good report" has arisen from her virtues.

EUPHROSYNE

In Greek mythology, one of the three graces, standing for *good cheer, longing*. She was the daughter of Zeus and Eurynome.

EURIPIDES

See Orpheus.

EUROPA

Daughter of Agenor, king of Phoenicia, known as the "broad spreading light" in the sun and dawn myths. Zeus, in the form of a white bull carried her away from her birthplace, swimming with her to Crete. Here she bore Zeus three sons.

SAINT EUSTACE — OF ROME

Patron saint of *huntsmen*. His special day, September 20. Represented in art as a soldier or knight on horseback. His most usual attribute, a stag with crucifix between its horns, from the legend that while hunting, he saw a white stag with a cross of bright light between its horns.

EUTERPE

In Greek mythology, *delight*, one of the nine muses, daughter of Zeus and Mnemosyne. She presided over *flute music*. Her attributes a flute and crown of flowers.

EVERGREEN

An evergreen tree, non-deciduous, popular as a Christmas decorative tree, signifies *eternal life, everlasting love*.

EWER

In general symbolism, *refreshment*. In Christian implication when pictured with a towel, is symbolic of *Christ's ministry of service*. John 13:5.

EYE

In general, the human eye signifies *watchfulness, vigilance, intelligence,* and *love, insight, perception*. With other meanings:

Eye of Odin — search for *truth, wisdom*.

In church architecture or ornamentation, the all-seeing eye set within a triangle surrounded by a circle and radiating rays of light — *holiness of the Triune God*, God the Father, symbol of *power, majesty, omnipotence*. Illustration p. 11:2.

On U.S.A. seal or back of dollar bill — the *ever-watchful providence or omniscience of God*.

In Egypt, two eyes of Horus, one black, one white — *night* and *day*.

F.

FALCON

Emblematic bird of *hunting* in association with the popular sport of falconry of the Middle Ages. Illustration p. 18:4.

In Christian symbolism a wild falcon stands for a *wicked man, evil thought and deed;* the tame bird, on the other hand signifies the *converted man,* one *brave* and *alert.*

FAMA

In classical mythology, attendant of Jupiter, hundred-tongued goddess of *fame.* Pictured as a winged woman in the act of crowning with laurel a person chosen for some service of distinction.

FAN

In general symbolism, *coquetry, fickleness.* In Japan, the type of fan, or the use to which it is put determines the significance:

A fan, half open, an *unfolding life.*

Attached to a bamboo stem and carried in the hand, *madness.*

A folding fan, extended in full, *expanding fortune.*

A flat fan carried by a man of authority, indicates *power to act.*

The fan may bear decorations of varied designs, but never the figure of a woman.

FASCES

In ancient Rome, fasces consisted of a bundle of rods, usually of elm or birch bound together with red thongs. Each carried an axe in the center, the iron of which projected. When borne before a magistrate, the fasces signified *authority* — the rods representing *power to scourge,* and the axe, *power to behead a malefactor.*

FATES

In Greek mythology, the three goddesses who control the destinies of men: Clotho (Klotho) the spinner who *spins the thread of life;* Lachesis, disposer of lots, who determines *life-length;* Atropos, the inflexible one, who *cuts off the thread of life.*

FAUNA

In Roman religion, a rural deity, *god of animals and products of the fields;* also of *prophecy,* and, more particularly the *chastity of women.* Known as Bona Dea, the *good goddess.*

FEATHER

In early Egyptian religion where a feather symbolized *truth* and *righteousness,* the heart of a deceased person in the hall of judgment of Osiris was balanced against a feather. Among different symbolisms are:

In general symbolism, a goose feather is an emblem of *writing, literature.*

A white feather, *cowardice.*

Ostrich feathers, *distinction.*

Three ostrich feathers, originally the emblem of the Black Prince of Wales, with the implications *good thought, good deed,* and *good word,* eventually became the emblematic symbol of Wales.

FEET

Human feet in picture language signify *wanton desire.* In church symbolism, *ministry.* Ephesians 6:15.

FERN LEAVES

Humbleness, sincerity, from the natural haunt of the plant in the darkness of thick forests. In northern lands where palms cannot thrive, fern leaves have the same symbolism that palms have in more southern climes, *victory.* In Christian symbolism, the denotation is, *victory over death.* In Japan, from the profuse growth of ferns, the symbolism is *prosperity.*

The fern tree is the emblematic tree of New Zealand.

FETTERS

Symbol of *punishment, slavery, hopeless misfortune, power of Satan.*

SAINT FIACRE OF BREUIL

Patron saint of *gardeners, florists, trellis-makers, boxmakers, brass beaters, coppersmiths, lead founders, needle-makers, hosiers, tile-makers,* and *potters.* Protector of field and garden fruits. Pictured as a monk preaching to the birds or digging in the garden with spade, and with a book beside him. Special day, August 30.

FIG

The fruit is symbol of *fertility, fruitfulness,* from its abundance of seeds.

The tree symbolizes *fidelity, prosperity,* sometimes spoken of as the

103

tree of knowledge instead of the apple tree in the Garden of Eden narrative.

The leaf, from an allusion in Genesis 3:7 has become the symbol of *lust*.

The tree laden with fruit, in Biblical symbolism, denotes a *holy life rich with the fruits of the spirit*.

FIGURE

In symbolic picture language of a human figure:

Kneeling, *reverence*.

In cap and gown, *scholarship*.

A man or woman at desk writing, *prose*.

A classical figure examining a skull, *philosophy*.

A woman with cask in hand measuring a sphere with a compass, *science*.

Upright figure holding a small cross on high with the gesture of an orator, *rhetoric*.

FINCH

The purple finch is the emblematic bird of New Hampshire; the willow gold finch, bird of Washington State.

FINGERS

Rare representation in Biblical symbolism:

First or index finger, *Holy Spirit*.

Second, or middle finger, *Christ*.

Last two folded upon the palm, *dual nature of Christ*.

Thumb, *chief person of the Godhead*.

In recent times the shaping of the first two fingers of the right hand to form the letter "v," *victory*. Often referred to as the Churchillian "v" from the great English statesman who popularized the sign.

FIR

Tree of *fervor, power*, from habits of growth. In Japan, *longevity*. In Christian symbolism *patience, fire of the spirit, strength to abhor earthly wants*.

Legend relates that the fir was the tree of life, believed to have bloomed until Eve plucked its fruit, and then its leaves became smaller, and its fruit became inedible. However, according to legend, it bloomed again the night Christ was born.

FIRE

An open fire, the same as for a hearth, signifies *fervor*, which in church symbolic terms means *religious fervor*. A circle of fire is to be interpreted as *chastity, inviolability*. *Fire and flames*, stand for *martyrdom, punishment, retribution*. Also in religious symbolism, because of its illuminating characteristics, signifies the *Holy Spirit*. In decorative art of the Pentecostal season, flames on the heads of the Apostles, indicate the *presence of the Holy Spirit*.

FIREFLIES

In Japanese art represent *ghosts of slain warriors*. As glowworms, in general symbolism, fireflies denote *extended enlightenment*.

FIRESTONES

An outgrowth of the ability of the stones to endure excessive heat, *carnal passions*.

FISH

The use of a figure of a fish as a Christian religious symbol gained fast prevalence following its appearance on the walls of the catacombs of Rome. However, the fish served as a symbolic object in Apostolic days, and even in pagan times in early Greece. Among these employments, in both earlier and later times are:

By the cult of Adonis as an offering to the dead, *love's grievous separations*.

In ancient Syria and Mesopotamia, *luck and life*.

As found on engravings on rings in early Greece, *good fortune*, and *happiness*. Illustration p. 11:4.

As an *attribute of Saint Peter*, in reference to an allusion of his being a fisherman.

In the catacombs, besides serving as a pointer directing persons to special points where they might worship, the fish symbol denoted *Christ*. Here it also became a symbol of *baptism*, and was used as a marker on the tombs of those persons who had been baptized. (Water being the only element in which fish can exist.)

In Chinese art, a fish may signify *virility*, a *fruitful marriage*.

From Japan comes the popular acceptance that two fishes facing one another imply *good luck* and *happiness*, and even in modern marriage rites, two fishes are presented to the bride as a sacred offering. Illustration p. 17:10.

In Christian religion, a fish with the letters ICHTHUS stands for Christ, from the initial Greek letters of Jesus Christ, Son of God, Saviour.

A triangle of fishes represents the Holy Trinity, and when engraved on a baptismal font, *baptized in the name of the Father, Son, and Holy Spirit.*

FISHERMAN

Symbol of *baptism,* the fisherman being *Christ,* and the fish, representations of *faithful men.* In the catacombs Christ sometimes shown as fishing in the water from Peter's rock.

FISHHOOK

Symbol of *perfidy, faithlessness.*

FIST (see, also, hand)

Symbol of *deterrent capability.*

FIVE

This number generally in Christian symbolism denotes *sacrifice,* from the five wounds of the Crucifixion. Five also numbers the lesser sacraments — confirmation, penance, Holy Orders, matrimony, and the visitation of the sick.

A number sacred to Apollo. Plutarch, enumerated the attributes of the deity in the old school of philosophy as — *being, sameness, diversity, motion,* and *rest.*

FLAG

The flag of a nation generally symbolizes *patriotism, victory,* and more usually, *freedom.* As to the symbolism of the U.S.A. flag, we have the explanation of George Washington, the country's first president:

"We take the stars from heaven, the red from our mother country, separating it by white stripes, thus showing that we have separated from her, and the white stripes shall go down to posterity representing liberty." Illustration p. 22:8.

In the Christian flag, the cross symbolizes *God's love for man;* the blue background, *faithfulness of the Savior;* the white portion, *purity, innocence, peace.*

A flag at half mast, signifies *mourning.* A red flag, *danger, caution,* and in certain circumstances, *anarchy.*

FLAGON

In modern picture language, *wine-drinking*.

FLAMES

When thought of as fire as a benefactor, *zeal, fervor, purification;* when thought of as a destructive element, *condemnation, punishment.*

In Christian symbolism, when pictured in connection with Pentecost in the form of a cloven or seven-tongued flame signifies the *Holy Spirit.* Seven tongues of flame denote, the sevenfold gifts of the Holy Spirit — *wisdom, understanding, counsel, might, knowledge, fear, delight.*

From Japan, comes the signification, *wisdom.*

A never-ceasing flame in the U.S.A., burning as memorial for heroes, reflects a *remembrance of the principles for which our military men gave their lives.*

FLASK

As for flagon, in modern picture language, *intemperance, wine-drinking.*

FLAX

Symbol of *Northern Ireland* where linen-weaving is an important industry.

FLEECE

In the Greek story of the Argosy of Jason, the Golden Fleece signifies *wisdom.* In general symbolism, *alluring desire, closely guarded wealth.* In industrial picture language, a fleece is the emblem of a *wool* merchant.

FLEUR-DE-LIS

According to interpretations of the Gothics, the three division of the petals of this popular flower signify *faith, wisdom, valor.* In Christian symbolism, they stand for the three members of the *Holy Trinity.* As one of the flowers of the Virgin Mary, the denotation is *purity, spiritual light,* and *Annunciation.*

As an attribute of *royalty,* the fleur-de-lis appears on crowns and scepters of kingly saints. It is the emblem flower of the city of Florence. Illustration p. 10:6.

FLICKERTAIL

Emblematic bird for the state of Alabama; also of North Dakota.

FLORA

In the early Roman religion, fairest among the lesser deities, Flora is *goddess of flowers and trees.* When pictured scattering flowers, she is a representative of *spring.*

FLOUR

As an ingredient of the pancake, Shrove Tuesday food specialty among early Middle-European churchmen, flour signifies, *abundant life.*

FLOWERS

Flowers, generally speaking, are symbolic of *beauty, loveliness, divine approval.* Exhibited under different conditions, these symbolic interpretations are indicated:

Blossoms of any flower growing at the end of a long stalk, *grace.*

When fastened as an ornament to the end of a rod, *divine approval.*

A blossoming branch having foliage that does not change in color with change of season — *peace,* and *continuing vitality.*

Blossoms from a long-blooming plant, *long, active life.*

Flowers that bloom a second time in a season, *Au Revoir,* a safe *return.*

When flowers, as a part of liturgical rite are placed on the altar, the general meaning is *joy in the risen* Christ. However, the particular kinds of flowers used have special significations, as have colors for special occasions.

FLUTE

Musical instrument stemming from the pipes of Pan, symbol of *pastoral music,* the *dance,* and *love.* In Greek mythology, flute music was presided over by Euterpre, patron of *delight.*

FLY

Insect of *annoyance, trouble, bearer of evil* and *pestilence.* In Christian symbolism, *sin* or *minor troubles.*

FLYCATCHER

The scissor-tailed flycatcher since 1951 has been the emblematic bird of Oklahoma. Now becoming rare in U.S.A.

FLY WHISK

A brush-like device carried by Buddhist or Taoist priests, is a symbol of *leadership*. The whisk was designed as a protective instrument for those who are forbidden to kill even the smallest of insects.

FONT

As a receptacle for holding the sacramental baptism water, symbol of *regeneration, purification, new creation*. When eight-sided, there is implication of the eight Beatitudes, Matthew 5:3-12. Another far-fetched interpretation is that eight sides stand for the number of souls saved in Noah's Ark.

FOOD

A dish of smoking food in modern picture language represents *good cheer*.

FOOT

Because a foot touches the soil, it is an apt symbol of *humility, willing servitude*. A winged foot is symbolic of *speed*. One crushing a butterfly or other insect, *death*.

FOREHEAD

In Buddhism, *spiritual insight*, indicated through special markings on the forehead. Among certain groups of Christian believers, markings of ashes on the forehead, as a part of Ash Wednesday observances, signify *humility, penitence*.

FORGE

In industrial picture language, the insignia of *mechanics*.

FORGET-ME-NOT

Flower of *love, hope, friendship, remembrance, fidelity*. Emblematic flower of the State of Alaska.

FORK

The barbed fork, torture instrument of demons, symbolizes *spitefulness*. A three-tined fork denotes *good luck*. As an implement of Neptune, a fork signifies *sea power*.

FORSETI

Norse deity worshipped as god of *justice*.

FORTUNA

In Roman mythology, attendant of Jupiter, goddess of *fortune* and *plenty*. Pictured as a young woman with revolving wheel, sometimes winged, generous in her predictions for a bright future for those who sought fortunes. Fortuna has become a favorite character in literary writings.

FORTY

Known as a *generous* number, but not always to be interpreted as an exact number, especially in Biblical references. Leading Bible scholars agree that the forty days of Moses on Mount Sinai, or Christ's forty days of temptation are to be interpreted as meaning a *great length of time*.

FOUNTAIN

In Biblical symbolism, *water of life, miraculous refreshment*. Numbers 20:1-11.

Historically, from the story of Ponce de Leon's visit to the Americas, the fountain is a symbol of *eternal youth*.

An attribute of Saint Clement who miraculously found water in the desert for his thirsty followers.

FOUR

Number of *stability, totality, completeness*. The four cardinal virtues are: *justice, prudence, temperance, fortitude*. Four horsemen of the Apocalypse: *conquest, war, pestilence, death*. Four evangelists: *Matthew, Mark, Luke, John*.

FOX

From its natural characteristic traits, the fox is symbol of *cunning, subtlety, craftiness, fraudulence*. In Japan, the animal serves as messenger of Inari, goddess of rice. Illustration p. 17:2.

FOXGLOVE

Flower called the "glove of Mary" which name gives us the basis for its symbolical meaning, *adulation, sincerity*.

SAINT FRANCIS OF ASSISI

Patron saint of *animals* and *animal welfare societies*, also of *tapestry weavers*. Small, bearded Franciscan with stigmata on hands and feet, he had gifted power over wild beasts and lesser creatures, culminating in his beautiful sermon to the birds, a prized document for every age. His festival day, October 4.

FRANKENSTEIN

From the monster created by Mrs. Mary Shelley, poetess, this character has become a symbol for *one who is destroyed by his own shortcomings.*

FRANKINCENSE

In association with the gifts of the Magi at Christ's birth the signification is *adoration, holiness, nobility, consecrated power.*

FREY

Norse religious sun-god of *fertility, rain, sunshine,* and *summer showers.* Patron of *seafarers.* Like Adonis, fabled as having been killed by a boar, Frey is seen in art as riding a golden-bristled boar across the sky, scattering flowers along the way.

FREYA

In Norse mythology, sister of Frey, and goddess of *beauty, flowers, music,* and *awakening of spring.* She rides a chariot driven by cats.

FRIGG or FRIGGA

In Norse mythology, wife of Odin and goddess of *love, marriage,* and the *home,* and with Odin shares dominion in heaven and knowledge of the world's fate.

FROG

From the Biblical allusion to the rain of frogs as one of the plagues of Egypt, comes the symbolism of *sin, destroyer of life's pleasures.* The tree frog signifies *perseverance.* In church symbolism there is rare use of the frog denoting *resurrection,* associated with its reappearance after winter hibernation.

The decorative frogs or fasteners on Chinese garments suggest *longlife, happiness.*

FROST

A symbol of Christmas festivities, meaning *friendliness,* in contrast with the temperature of its crystal flakes. This implication may, also, have come from an association with the friendly Jack Frost, wood-sprite, or elf in his flitting about in garments sparking with hoar.

FRUIT

In general symbolism, *achievement*. Often bears implications of the twelve fruits of the spirit: love, joy, peace, long-suffering, gentleness, goodness, faith, meekness, patience, modesty, temperance, and chastity.

Fruit in a basket, or pouring from a cornucopia, or in a festoon with flowers signifies *plenty, harvest, good works of the righteous.*

FUCHSIA

From characteristics of the growth of the flower, *romantic melancholy, wistful tenderness.*

FUGIYAMA

Sacred mountain in Japan, emblem of *good luck.*

FUKUROKUJIN

For the Japanese, one of the seven gods of *luck* with special gift of prophecy, and working of miracles.

FUNGUS

Chinese plant of *long life*, a special attribute of Shun Lao, god of longevity.

FURIES

In early Greek religion, any one of three snaky-haired women who pursued evil doers and inflicted madness, symbols of *anarchy.*

FYLFOT

A cross, in shape identical with a swastika, but when used with religious symbolic implications, the term *fylfot* has gained in popularity, with denotations of *Christ the sun of righteousness.* There is speculation as to the origin of this design, and it appears to have a significant meaning in pagan times. Earliest Christian use was in the catacombs. P. 12:12.

G.

SAINT GABRIEL, THE ARCHANGEL

Guardian of *purity*. His special day is March 24. His chief attribute a *lily*, and in some pictures, he carries an olive branch to the Virgin Mary.

GAEA

In Greek mythology, the *earth goddess*, and *female principle in nature*. She was mother of the Titans, the Cyclops, and the giants, and known as the *nourisher of youths*.

GALLOWS

In modern picture language, symbol of *execution, disgraceful death*.

GANESHA

Hindu elephant god of *wisdom, good fortune, remover of obstacles*, having supremacy over all other gods except Shiva, god of the universe. His image, a many handed figure with head of an elephant, is placed at the gate of all temples. When the statues show sixteen arms, the signification is *overwhelming power of God*. Illustration p 9:4.

GANYMEDES

In Roman mythology, son of Tros of Ilion, a beautiful boy, who while still young was carried up Mount Olympus by the eagle of Zeus to become supbearer of the gods. His attributes a *Phrygian cap and ewer* and *two-handled drinking vessel*.

GARDEN

In early Christian symbolism an enclosed garden suggested the *Immaculate Conception of the Virgin*, an allusion taken from the Song of Solomon 4:12. Later, the implication became *any bride*. A garden with gates closed is symbolic of *paradise, heaven*.

GARDENIA

Lovely flower of the madder family with showy, fragrant white or yellow blooms. From the color, has arisen the symbol, *chastity;* and from the fragrance, *feminine charm*.

GARGOYLE

In early Gothic architecture, gargoyles, besides serving a useful purpose as waterspouts, provided a grotesque form of decoration in Gothic architecture. Some were humorous, but most were serious and strikingly hideous, depicting *evil*, or *evil forced to serve the good*.

GARLANDS

In Christian symbolism, a garland of flowers, leaves or branches signifies *good works of the righteous*. In classical times, they were given as an award of honor to a victor, or to one who had shown outstanding skill and accomplishment. Pictures from this period show flutes, pipes, or winecups garlanded with flowers, or the skull of a horned animal festooned with a garland.

GARMENT

The seamless garment, one of the thirteen symbols of the Crucifixion, signified the *Passion of Christ*. A spotted garment in church symbolism denotes *iniquity*. The robe of the High Priest is symbolic of *Christ's ministry of Intercession*.

GARNET

This gem of beautiful red hue symbolizes *friendship, constancy*. It has been chosen as birthstone for January.

GARUDA

In Hinduism, a supernatural being, half man and half bird with golden body and red wings. It serves as a means of transportation for Vishnu in his trips through the skies. Strong enemy of the nagas (serpents) maintained to be half brothers of the garuda. Seen on the roofs of Hindu temples usually with a serpent in its beak. Believed by the common people to ward off evil. Illustration p. 8:10.

GATE

In Biblical symbolism, *power, security, imminency*, stemming from Psalms 9:13 and 147:13. An open gate signifies *an invitation;* one closed, *forbidden protection*. A gate pictured in the bronze door of the Baptistry of Florence is the symbol of the *tribe of Simeon*.

A gateway, in church symbolism, denotes *heavenly authority*.

GAUTAMA (see Buddha).

GAVEL

In modern picture language, *order, discipline*.

GAZELLE

From natural characteristics, *gentleness, gracefulness*.

GEESE

From Japanese art, comes the symbolism of a flock of wild geese, as a depiction of *autumn*.

GEHELIA

In Zoroaster's *Oracle*, represents *birth and growth*, as one of the nine spirits of intelligence.

GEMINI

The heavenly twins, Castor and Pollux in the sign of the zodiac for May. Always, they stand for opposites: *morning and evening; light and darkness; summer and winter; male and female.*

SAINT GEMINIANUS

Presides over the powers of *healing*. In art, pictured as holding in his hand a mirror reflecting an image of the Virgin Mary.

GEMS

Gems, as precious stones, are symbols of *elegance, refinement*. In many countries of the world, though there has been no official adoption, the following emblematic gems have been assigned as birthstones for persons born in one of these months of the year:

> January – Garnet
> February – Amethyst
> March – Aquamarine, or bloodstone
> April – Diamond
> May – Emerald
> June – Pearl
> July – Ruby
> August – Peridot, sardonyx
> September – Sapphire
> October – Opal
> November – Topaz
> December – Turquoise

SAINT GENEVIEVE OF PARIS

Patroness of Paris. Her special festival day, January 3. Her chief attributes, *book, candle,* and *torch*. Pictured restoring sight to her mother.

GENTIAN

Flower of *hope* and *longing*, in that it blooms late in the season. Emblematic flower for October.

GENUFLEXION

In religious rites, this act of bending the knees, denotes *reverence, humility*.

SAINT GEORGE OF CAPPADOCIA

Patron saint of *armorers, artillerymen, horsemen, all soldiers,* and *knights*. Also in England, Venice, and Ferrara, Italy. His special day, April 23. Declared a hero for having slain a terrible dragon that was at the point of devouring the daughter of the king. Vividly pictured as a young knight on horseback, in richly emblazoned armor, bearing a shield with lance and red cross.

GERANIUM

Typifies *family closeness, congeniality,* from the arrangement of the long, slender carpels of the flower.

GERAS

In Greek religion, divinity of *time,* and symbol for *the aging*.

GERYON

In Greek mythology, a monster having three bodies and powerful wings. Son of Chrysaor and Callirrhoe. The demon slain by Hercules.

GHOST

A disembodied, shadowy human being, most usually a female, unharmful, and having the gift of prophecy. A figure invaluable as a device in stories of mystery and magic. Of recent times, the ghost in the form of a witch presides over Halloween festivities.

GIANT

A mythical, man-like monstrous being denoting *superhuman strength, despotism, impending evil*. Said to have more than mortal, but less than godlike power and endowment.

GIBBET

A kind of gallows on which in early times violators of the law were hanged in chains, and left in that position as a warning to other offenders. Symbol of *execution, disgraceful death*.

GIBRALTAR

Pictorial figure of a triple-towered castle on a rock, symbol of *firmness, strength.*

GILLY-FLOWER

Known in Mediaeval days as the clove pink, and in later times as wall-flower or stock. Symbol of the *Passion* in church representations, from the crosslike four-petal corolla of the blossom. Also one of the Virgin's flowers in scenes of the Annunciation.

GIRAFFE

Bears the symbolism of *ambition,* from the capability of the animal to reach high for its food.

GIRDLE

The girdle of Venus signifies *grace, charm, amiability.* In liturgical vestment the significance is *self-restraint, continence, power, activity,* the meanings stemming from Job 12:18.

GIRL

Figure of a young girl dancing, *fascination, grace.*

GLADIOLUS

Flower of *stately beauty,* in that it bears large showy flowers without restraint. Further implications are, *brotherly love, generosity,* and *abundance;* also, in church symbolism, *incarnation* and the *word made flesh.* Illustration, p. 21:8.

GLASS

In Biblical symbolism, *purity* and *peace,* from the allusion of "sea of glass like unto crystal" in Revelation 4:6.

The ritual of breaking a glass at the close of a wedding ceremony, an ancient Jewish custom, signified the *destruction of Jerusalem.*

GLAUCUS

In Greek mythology, a sea god who became immortal by eating magic grass. Said to have been helmsman of the Argo, ship in which Jason with a band of followers sailed to Colchis. Lover of Scylla, horrible sea monster who made life hazardous for seamen. She tormented Glaucus until he begged Circe to give him a drink which would compel her love rather than her wrath. Instead, Circe caused her to become a loathsome monster.

GLOBE

When surmounted by a cross, *Christ's sovereignty, His victory over the sins of the world, salvation, enlightenment, unity of spirit.* When the globe is encircled by a serpent, the interpretation is, *the fall of man through the temptation of a serpent.*

In commercial art, a globe, sometimes in the hands of a boy or man, denotes *enterprise, world interests.*

GLOVE

White gloves traditionally stand for *pure heart and clean hands.* In the realm of fashions, they signify *elegance, good taste.* Earlier, white gloves worn by participants in funeral occasions, were a sign that the deceased was unmarried. More recently, in general symbolism, they denote *mourning, sorrow, grief, reverent respect.*

GOAD

Symbol of *action, labor.*

SAINT GOAR OF TRIERS

Patron saint of *potters;* his attributes, an earthenware jug or vessel, with three stags near at hand. His special day, July 6.

GOAT

Animal of *agility, selfish pleasures.* When resting, and seemingly chewing a cud, *meditation.* In art, when a goat is seen climbing a mountain, the signification is, *a soul seeking heavenly things.* Also, in scriptural depiction, *wicked persons,* stemming from Matthew 25:33. Illustration, p. 17:1.

In the zodiacal figure for December, the goat is the *generator.*

GOBLIN

Grotesque sprite, symbol of *malice, terror,* and, as a creature presiding over Halloween festivities, *mischief.*

GOLD

As a color in liturgical symbolism, signifies *celestial light, fineness, joy, majesty, honor.* Tassels or fringes of gold used on church vestments or other objects of decoration, denote *glory of God, virtue, Christian might or worth.* When used as background color in early paintings, the implication is *heaven,* in that the color reflects much light.

118

Gold as a metal, symbolizes *life, light truth, majesty, riches, honor, the triumph of faith in time of adversity.*

In Biblical literature, the denotations, *worldly wealth, idolatry,* stem from the story of Aaron (in Exodus Chapter XXXII) who, in the absence of Moses, fashioned a golden calf to be worshipped instead of the true God.

Gold thread as a symbol of *long life* has come to us from Japan.

The term "golden age" has become a personification of *opportunities for many.*

GOLDENROD

Flower of *encouragement,* in that it brightens the autumn months with its enlivening showy flowers.

In 1895 it was made the emblematic flower of Nebraska; in 1926, Kentucky, and in 1927, Alabama.

GOLDFINCH

In church symbolism, *Christ's Passion, Christ's crown of thorns,* in that the bird is fond of thistles and thorns as part of its diet. It has been adopted as a state emblematic bird for Iowa, Minnesota, and Washington.

GOMORRHA

(see Sodom, and Genesis Chapters XVIII and XIX.)

GOOSE

Since the Roman era, the goose has become the symbol of *watchfulness, warning, providential guardianship,* from the story that geese saved Rome from the invasion of the Gauls. The goose was sacred to Juno.

From Japan, we get the symbol *matrimony.* For marines, the fowl is an omen of *good luck,* in that it "swims on top of the waters and sinks not."

A goose quill is the emblematic figure for *authors.*

GORGON (MEDUSA)

In Greek mythology, with her two sisters, Athene and Euryal, featured in myths of the underworld. Symbol of *frightfulness* and *hideousness,* her repulsiveness is said to have turned to stone any one who looked upon her face, and her hair of snakes.

Legends reveal that eventually she was killed by Perseus who succeeded in cutting off her head while looking at its reflection in his

119

shield. He gave the head to Medusa's rival, Athene, who had earlier brought about the transformation of hair into serpents. Athena placed on her own shield a setting of the Medusa head pictured page 7:10.

A Gorgon head, without the snaky hair takes on the denotation of a full moon, and the symbolic meaning becomes *protection, defense of both the living and the dead.*

GOURD

A vining plant, symbol of *longevity,* from the length of the vine and the hardness of the shell of the gourd.

From the Biblical story of Jonah, the implication is *resurrection,* Jonah Chapter IV.

In China, the gourd is popular as a New Year's symbol of *progeny* because of its many seeds.

GRACES

The Three Graces, daughters of Jupiter and Eurynome, are goddesses of everything which lends charm and beauty to nature and human life. Patronesses of *tasteful dress, domestic arts, personal* and *household ornament.*

Agalaia stands for *splendor.*

Thalia, *luxuriant beauty.*

Euphrosyne, *good cheer.*

GRAEAE (GRAIAE)

In Greek mythology, the three daughters of Phorcus — Deino, Enyo, and Pephedro, who in myths, serve as sentinels for the Gorgons.

GRAIL

The Holy Grail, in literature often, *Sangreal,* refers to the cup used by Christ at His Last Supper with the Apostles. Symbol of *mystery,* in that it has always disappeared mysteriously when approached by an impure knight in search of the vessel.

GRAIN

General term for wheat in John 12:24, a well-known Eucharistic symbol suggesting the *human value of Christ.*

GRAMPUS (see DOLPHIN)

GRAPE

As suggestive of the bacchanal feast, the fruit of the grape from which wine is made denotes *pleasure, good cheer, youth, fruitfulness.* Illustration, p. 20:3.

In Christian symbolism, with wheat heads, the bread and wine of the *Eucharist,* or the *Blood of Christ.* Twelve bunches of grapes in art ornamentation suggest the twelve apostles. Grapes with leaves signify *God-given earthly abundance.* The grape vine with many leaves, *fruitfulness.*

The flower of the holly-grape, now called the Oregon grape, since 1899 has been the chosen state emblematic flower of Oregon.

GRASS

In ancient times grass was a symbol of *victory.* In Japan it signifies *humility,* being close to the ground.

In church symbolism, *temporary prosperity, frail beings,* from allusions in James 1:10; Isaiah 40:6,7.

GRASSHOPPER (See locust).

GRATE

The same symbol as for hearth or fireplace, *good cheer.*

GRAVESTONE

Symbol for *mortality.*

GREEN

The predominant color in nature is regarded as the universal color; in Christian symbolism it expresses *hope, regeneration, resurrection,* and *growth of the spiritual life of a believer.*

In floristry, green used alone or in combination with other colors, signifies *freshness, youth, hope, life, vigor, bountifulness, merit, prosperity.*

From an early Chinese symbolism, *disgrace,* there has spread the idea of *envy, jealousy.* As a signal, green denotes *safety.* As a liturgical symbol, green is the color for Epiphany and the Trinity Season. (See liturgical colors.)

SAINT GREGORY THE GREAT

Patron of *choirmasters, scholars, singers, fringemakers, students* and *teachers.* His special day, February 13. In art, he wears the tiara of a

Pope and carries the crosier with double cross. His special attribute, a dove whispering into his ear. It was believed that the Holy Spirit in the form of a dove gave him the information for his writings.

GREY

Springing from monastic life, the color symbolizes *discretion, penitence, humility, barrenness, retrospection, renunciation, grief, unfruitfulness.*

In the fashion world, the color is suggestive of *calmness, serenity, dignity,* and in some countries, *mourning.*

GREYHOUND

Sarama's dog, animal of the dawn, gives us the symbols *speed, keen-sightedness.*

GRIDIRON

Symbol of *martyrdom,* attribute of Saint Lawrence who in A.D. 258 suffered death by being roasted alive.

GRIFFIN

In Greek mythology a fabulous chimera with body and legs of a lion, and with beak and wings of an eagle, symbolic of *superiority, enlightenment.* Illustration, p. 8:1.

A pair of griffins denotes *wisdom and enlightenment,* which meanings, in Christian symbolism stand for a combination of the *divine* and *human nature* of the Lord.

GROUSE

Symbolic bird of Pennsylvania since 1931.

GUILLOTINE

Instrument of *martyrdom,* symbol of *execution.*

GULES

A succession of red parallel lines forming a field of gules on engraved escutcheons, early in heraldry took on the significance of *royalty.*

GULL

Same symbol as for terns, *usefulness,* suggesting their help to man as scavengers; *versatility,* from their habits of frequenting both land and waters.

Symbolic bird of Utah.

H.

HAG

Female demon pictured with bat's wings, fangs, claws, and streaming hair. Symbol of *famine.*

HAIR

The custom of hermits allowing their hair to grow long stems from Luke 7:37-38 and symbolizes *penitence.*

Lock of hair on forehead of Father Time, *opportunity.*

Lock of hair in general symbolism, *remembrance.*

Long hair for men may symbolize *strength,* as in story of Samson. Judges, 16:17.

HALBERD or HALBERT

Implement of *martyrdom* stemming from the attribute of Saint Jude who was killed with a halbert as a Christian martyr.

HALO

(See nimbus.)

HAMADRYAD

A nymph who has taken on the semblance of some divinity of Greek mythology, and inhabits as a spirit some individual tree. A good example is that of Daphne who inhabited a laurel tree.

HAMMER

In commercial art, symbol of *work, mechanics, geologists.* In church symbolism, one of the thirteen objects used as symbolisms of the Crucifixion; pictured with pincers, denotes *Christ's Passion.* Hammer of Thor in Norse mythology, signifies *force.* Illustration p. 13:13.

Hammer pictured with a sickle, emblem of *Soviets* and *Sovietism.*

In Japan, a hammer is signification for *diligence.*

HAND

The position in which the hand is held, or the objects with which it is pictured determines its symbolic meanings:

A hand emerging from the clouds, *Jehovah,* or *God the Father.*

Attached to the end of a scepter, *sovereignty.*

Right hand open, *plenty.*

Left hand closed, *protection.*

Right hand extended with a gift, *benevolence.*

A black hand, *warning of death.*

Lifting up right hand, *promise,* or *oath, benediction.*

Folded hands, *prayer,* or *resignation.*

Palms together, fingers pointed upward, *prayer, supplication, worship* and *adoration.*

Clasped hands, *brotherhood, fraternity, friendship, concord.*

Clasped hands of two persons under the clasp of another, *oneness of union, conjugal love,* (with some peoples, part of a marriage service).

Handshaking, symbol of *friendship, warm greeting.*

First and second fingers extended in an upright "V" shape, *V-for-victory,* a symbol given universality through the use of Sir Winston Churchill.

In Christian symbolism, hands over a basin signify *waiving of responsibility,* in reference to Pilate's washing his hands from the conviction of Christ.

HAND PRESS

In commercial art, emblem of *the printing trade.*

HAN HSIANG-TZU

As one of the seven immortals of Taoism signifies the *power of growing.*

HANUMAN

Monkey god of Hindus, helper of Rama, symbol of *loyalty.* The monkey is still held sacred to loyal Hindus, and it is given full freedom, even to the extent of eating of the food presented in the temples.

HARBOR

A pictured harbor represents *security, comfort,* and, in church symbolism, *eternal life.* Ships sailing toward the harbor denote *souls in search of heaven;* or *souls on a journey.*

HARE

From accustomed habits of the hare, *swiftness, resourcefulness,* yet, also *lust* and *fecundity.* One of the favorite symbolic objects of Easter festivities, from the active movements of the little animal among the new-growing plants of this early season. Three hares forming a triangle within a circle, in Christian art, is representative of the *unity of the*

Trinity. A white hare pictured at the feet of the Virgin Mary signifies her *triumph over lust.* Illustration of a hare, p. 17:4.

HARE-BELL

The wood hyacinth, one of the flowers of the Virgin, signifying *peace of mind.*

HARLEQUIN

A buffoon depicting a *carnival spirit.* Often characterized in comedies and pantomime by his shaven head, marked face, garish tights, and crude imitation of a sword.

HAROSET

A pasty combination of apples and nuts, symbolizing the *mortar* used by the Jewish people as they labored under Pharaoh.

HARP

When used as a decorative design, *joy, praise.* Symbol of *poetry, music.* Emblem of national Ireland.

HARPOCRATES

Roman god of *silence* identified with Egyptian Horus, hawk-headed deity of the rising sun. Pictured as a child-god seated on a lotus flower, his finger on his lips.

HARPY

In classical mythology, one of a group of foul creatures, half woman, half bird, who snatched away the souls of the dead, or poisoned the food of those whom they seized. Thought of in literature as personifications of the *disturbing elements of nature — storms on land or sea.* Illustration, p. 9:9.

HARROW

One of the implements of martyrdom, signifying *tribulation.*

HART (also HIND)

Stemming from the habits and physical features of the animal, *solitude, purity, piety, religious aspirations.* Psalm 43:1.

HAT

In religious symbolism signifies *missionary, pilgrim,* arising from the hat and staff which were emblems of James, major missionary of New Testament history.

HATCHET (see, also axe)

Symbol of *execution*. In the U.S.A., thought of as symbolical of *truth*, in allusion to the confession of George Washington "I cannot tell a lie," in connection with his having cut down a cherry tree in his early youth.

HATHOR

In early Egyptian religion, goddess of *love, mirth, pleasure,* and of *war*. Represented with a cow's head or ears. Had the power to foretell the future of a child when she was an attendant at its birth. In Greek mythology, identified with Aphrodite.

HAWK

From its strength, rapid flight and quick swoop, symbolism of *speed, ferocity*.

Sacred bird of the Egyptian sun god, Horus, with the signification of *power*. Still thought of in Egypt as the bird of *fire*, it being the only bird which can focus its eyes upon direct, bright sun rays.

HAWTHORNE

Symbol of *spring, constancy*. Among early Greeks held as symbol of *family, unity,* and the flowers were used traditionally as a part of the wedding festivities.

HEAD

The use of a head with symbolic implications is dependent upon the person or animal with which there is an association. Among the denotations are:

Head of Apollo — *music and the arts.*

An ass — *ignorance.*

Athene — *wisdom, knowledge.*

A bull — *Astarte.*

A cat — *Bast, Pasht.*

A cock — *Abraxas.*

A cow — *Astarte, Hathor, Isis.*

An elephant — *Ganesha.*

A dog — *Anubis,* also *contention, litigation.*

A goat — *India,* also *diligent workman.*

Head of Hermes — *industry, commerce, medicine.*

Head of Zeus — *classics, religions.*

Head of maiden wearing crown of flowers — *caprice.*

Head on a platter – *Saint John the Baptist.*

Shaven head, in Buddhism – *giving up pleasures of the world.*

Hydra-headed monster – *evil having many sources.*

HEART

General symbolism, *love, religion, compassion, will-power, charity.* Special significations:

Flaming heart, *intense zeal* or *devotion, fervent love and devotion.*

Flaming heart encircled by thorns, *Sacred Heart of Jesus.*

Flaming heart pierced by seven knives, *Sorrows of the Blessed Virgin.*

Heart pierced by an arrow (Cupid's dart), *love.*

Heart combined with a cross and anchor, *love, faith, hope.*

HEARTH

Symbol of *home, domestic felicity, hospitality.* When there is a fire burning, *good cheer, benevolence,* a *burning welcome.*

HEATHER

Humility, from the natural habitat of the shrub, frequenting heaths and waste-lands.

From early days, a customary nuptial flower in Great Britain, signifying *good luck, happiness.*

National flower of Norway.

HEBE

In Greek mythology, goddess of *youth,* daughter of Zeus and Hera, and cupbearer of the gods before Ganymede was chosen for that honor.

HECATE

In Greek mythology, goddess of the *underworld, night,* the *moon,* and later of *ghosts* and *magic.* Daughter of Zeus and Asteria, she was *protectress of crossroads.* Pictured as having three bodies placed back to back, holding a pitcher and sacrificial saucer.

HEDGEHOG

In U.S.A., the porcupine, symbol of *strong defense.*

HEEL

From the reference in Homer's *Iliad* to Achilles, whose heel was wounded by the arrow of Paris, the symbolism is *susceptibility, vulnerableness.*

HEIMDALL

In Norse mythology the *watchman* of Asgard, meeting place of the gods.

HEL

In Norse mythology, half black and half blue, goddess of the *underworld*, living daintily on the brains and marrow of the deceased. Daughter of Loki, contriver of discord and mischief.

HELEN OF TROY

In literary allusion, stands for a *beautiful dawn* or *twilight*. Born of Jupiter (the sky) and Leda (night), carried away by Paris, admirer of her beauty.

SAINT HELENA

Patroness of *dyers, nailsmiths, needlemakers,* mother of Constantine the Great, and discoverer of the true cross. Her special festival day, August 18. Usually represented wearing a royal crown, and bearing a large cross; also hammer and nails.

HELIOS

In Greek mythology, god of the *sun,* as one of the personages of Apollo. His special symbols were *horses'-heads,* a *cornucopia* with *ripened fruit,* and a *crown with seven bright rays.* Represented as driving a four-horse chariot through the heavens.

HELIOTROPE

As a flower, signifies *eternal love* from the natural tendency of the flower to turn its head with the sun's changed position. As a color, the significance is, *truth and loyalty,* from the common mixture of blue and red.

As a gem, see *bloodstone.* The emblematic stone for March.

HELLE

In Greek cloud-myth story, emblem of *condensation of vapor.* To free her and her brother Phrixos from the cruel treatment of their stepmother, Ino, Neptune sent them a winged, golden-fleeced ram to transport them to Colchis. The ram flew over land and sea, but Helle, frightened at the loud-roaring waves beneath her, lost her hold and fell into a body of water which later became the *Hellespont,* from her name.

HELMET

Symbol of *prowess, knighthood.*

In church symbolism, *salvation, ability to resist.* Ephesians 6:17; Thessalonians 5:8.

HEMLOCK

Death potion of Socrates, symbol of *evil, poison.*

In its evergreen leaves, lies the symbol of *faith in immortality.*

Since 1931, the emblematic tree of Pennsylvania.

HEN

In symbolic picture language, *providence, maternity.*

HEPHESTUS

In Greek mythology, son of Zeus and Hera, god of *blacksmiths* and *craftsmen* in general. He was instructor of the Cyclops, race of giants having only one eye. He manifested his power in volcanoes, hot springs, and burning gases. Pictured as a lame smith, holding a hammer, and wearing a leather apron and cap.

HERA (Same as Roman Juno)

In Greek mythology goddess of *women, marriage, fertility,* and *the weather.* Daughter of Kronos and Rhea; sister and also wife of Zeus. In literature often depicted as being capricious, jealous, vengeful. Pictured page 7:9, with her chief attribute, a *peacock.*

HERBS

Symbol of *healing.*

HERCULES

In Greek mythology, son of Zeus and Alcmene, noted for his strength; god of athletic games, and symbol of an *unconquerable spirit.* His chief attribute a *club* and a *lion-skin.* As a child, he strangles a serpent in his cradle, and continues through life attacking dangerous enemies. His crown is of poplar leaves. Pictured with club, p. 7:5.

HERMAPHRODITUS

Fabled son of Hermes and Aphroditus, who, while bathing in the sea became enjoined with a nymph, an involvement which brought about the coupling of both sexes within one body. He has become a symbol of *indissolute marriage,* and the *twofold aspect of nature.*

HERMES (Same as Roman Mercury)

In Greek mythology, son of Zeus and Maia, (sky and the plains). He was the *herald and messenger of the gods,* guardian of travelers, marshall of departed souls, patron of commerce; also of thieves and liars. He is more popularly referred to as patron of the *gymnasium and protector of youths.* He is symbol of *inventiveness, versatility,* and *communication.*

HERON

Bird of early morning. In Egypt symbol of *regeneration.*

HESPERIDES

In Greek mythology, the nymphs, who, with the aid of a dragon, watched over the garden in which grew the Golden Apples which Gaea gave to Hera as a wedding present. Symbol of the *western sky, clouds at sunset,* and of *wisdom.*

HESTIA (Same as Roman Vesta)

In Greek mythology, daughter of Kronos and Rhea. Virgin goddess of the *hearth, home fires, family life,* and of *modesty.*

In literature and art, represented by a middle-aged, sedate woman without distinguishing attributes, but whose gown is richly decorated with fruit and flowers.

HEXOGRAM

Known among the Jewish people as David's shield, with implication of *divine protection.*

HIBACHI

A Japanese firebox, symbolizing, as for hearth, *domestic felicity.*

HIBISCUS

Symbol of *short-lived glory* from the characteristic of the flower blossoms which open in the morning and droop at night. With the ilima, is celebrated as Hawaii state flower.

SAINT HILDA OF WHITBY

Learned nun of the seventh century. Her special day, November 17. In pictures she is throned, attended by scholars, with Caedmon, the Anglo Saxon poet, appearing before her.

HILL

In art, a pictured hill represents *constancy, stability, long-lasting attributes.*

HIND

Adult female of the red deer, symbolizes *solitude, purity of life, piety,* and *religious aspiration.* In Biblical symbolism, *agility, affection,* Psalms 18:33; Proverbs 5:19.

HIMEROS

In Roman mythology, follower of Venus, divinity of the great desire for love, and symbol of *longing.*

HIPPOCRENE

In Greek mythology, fabled fountain on Mt. Helicon in Boeotia said to have burst forth where the hoofs of Pegasus touched the earth. Its waters promote *poetic inspiration.*

HITSUJI

In Japanese zodiac, the goat, symbol of *procreation.*

HO-BIRD

In Japan, the phoenix, symbol of *fire, immortality.*

HOE

In modern picture language, *diligence.*

HOG

Symbol of *greed, self-indulgence, selfishness, sloth, sensuality,* and *gluttony.*

HO HSIEN

One of the seven Taoist immortals, patron of the *house.*

HOLLY (See also ilex)

Symbol of *hospitality, aspiration, rejoicing, good will, eternal life.*

Used by the pagans at the Saturnalia festival in Rome as a symbol of *health, and well-being.*

Among Christians, used in Christmas decor as a token of good *will,* and *Christmas joy.* A branch with thorns signifies *suffering, Christ's Passion.* Without thorns, but with red berries, emblem of *endless love.*

Since 1939 the state tree of Delaware.

HOLLYHOCK

Ambition, from habits of growth of this sturdy plant.

HONEY

Besides *sweetness,* honey symbolizes *knowledge, wisdom,* particularly that which is gained through experience.

In Christian symbolism, the *work of God,* and *ministry of Christ,* and the precious results of *spiritual experience.*

SAINT HONORIUS

Patron of *bakers,* with special day, September 30. Attributes, a baker's shovel with three loaves of bread upon it.

HOPE

In Greek mythology, the beneficent spirit in Pandora's box containing all human ills, the only one spirit not escaping when Pandora, through curiosity, opened the box. Remaining to alleviate human suffering, Hope has become the symbol of *aid to struggling humanity,* and *bright prospects for the future.*

HORAE

In Greek religion, a collective name for three goddesses of the seasons, daughters of Zeus and Themis: Eunomia who presided over *good order;* Dike, over *justice;* and Eirene, over *peace.* Jointly they are credited with providing *stimulation for plant life,* and later regarded as the *Hours of the Day.*

HORN

As a musical instrument, *call of the spirit.* In Biblical symbolism, *power, glory.* Psalm 75:10; Daniel 7:8.

Horn of an animal, *strength, dignity, authority, protection against the evil eye.* When placed on walls of tombs in guardianship of the dead, *protection.*

When placed on the head of the Lamb of God, *power against evil.*

When placed on the head of a man, a *cuckold.*

Horn in the form of a cornucopia, *horn of plenty,* a symbol derived from the horn of Amalthea in classical mythology wherein a goat's horn was endowed with the virtue of becoming filled with whatever its possessor wished.

HORSE

In general, is symbol of *intellect, speed,* but with various surroundings has different implications as:

Wild horse — *untamed power.*

Balking horse — *obstinacy.*

Galloping horse — *zealous Christian.*

Winged horse (Pegasus) — *poetry.*

A saddled horse before a milestone — a *Christian who has reached his goal and ready to receive his reward.*

A riderless horse in funerals of men of state — *mourning.*

A grey horse in Wales — *the Devil.*

Horse in Russia — *domestic happiness, marriage.*

In heathen days — a horse with palm in his mouth — *victory, reward for labor.*

Pictured with a Chi Rho on his buttock — *a Christian.*

Skull of a horse — *mortality, death.*

White horse in ancient times — the *sun.*

HORSESHOE

Symbol of *protection and luck.* The origin of this implication is speculative, possibly from its shape of a crescent, or, that iron, of which the shoe was made, was habitually regarded as giving protection from harm. Still to be seen above entrances to mosques as a protection against evil.

One of the bridal "good luck" symbols.

The emblem of *blacksmiths and farriers.* Illustration, p. 15:7.

HORUS

In early Egyptian religion, the hawk-headed *god of dawn of day,* son of Osiris and Isis. Represented as a child with side locks, sitting on a lotus flower, with finger on his lips, indicating *silence.*

HOST

In rites of some of the Christian churches, the Eucharist wafer (usually round) or bread, symbol of *sacrifice*, or of *Christ's body* at the sacrament of the Holy Communion.

HOTEI

In Japan one of the seven gods of *luck* and *wisdom*.

HOUND

(See dog)

HOURGLASS

Symbol of *time, shortness of life*. With sand run out, symbolizes *death as the end of life*. Frequently seen on gravestones of the eighteenth century. Illustration p. 15:6.

HUA HSIEN

In Taoism, a *flower deity*.

SAINT HUBERT

Patron of *huntsmen, mathematicians*, and *metal workers*. His special day, November 3. Pictured as a huntsman adoring a stag with a crucifix between its horns, and an angel presenting him a stole.

HUGIN

In Scandinavian myth, the raven of Odin symbolic of *thought* and *memory*.

ONE HUNDRED

As a number, emphasizes *completeness*.

HYACINTH

This gem, also called zircon is a symbol of *constancy, deep love*, in association with the symbolism of red in its coloring. It has become the birthstone for January.

The symbol *grief, deep sorrow*, of hyacinth, the flower has come to us from ancient Greeks who maintained that petal markings formed the letters *Ai! Ai!*, or *woe, woe* which for them spelled *grief*.

The flower, in Christian symbolism stands for *peace of mind, desire for Heaven*. Illustration, p. 20:9.

134

HYDRA

Symbol of *multifarious evil*, stemming from the Greek legendary account of Hydra, a serpent monster, slain by Hercules. It had nine heads, any one of which when severed from the body was supplanted by two others unless the wound had been cauterized.

HYENA

Animal large and strong, but cowardly; hence the symbolic *cowardice, evil, Satan.*

In India and the Orient, symbol of *witchcraft, sorcery.*

HYGEIA

In Greek mythology, goddess of *health.* She was a daughter of AEsculapus, the noted physician who watched over the health of men.

Hygeia seen in art as a maiden holding a kantharos from which the serpent, attribute of her father, is drinking.

HYMEN

In Greek mythology, god of *marriage,* an attendant of Venus on her way to Mount Olympus after she flung her garments to the waves of the sea. Pictured as a mature cupid with bridal veil and necklace.

HYPERION

In Greek mythology, a Titan, father of the sun, moon, and the dawn. He was the incarnation of *light and beauty,* having charge of the sun chariot which ancients believed was driven daily across the sky.

HYPNOS

In Greek mythology, god of *sleep,* son of Nix (night) and Erebus (darkness). He spent his life between earth and the land of dreams. Represented in art as a winged god in company with his twin brother Thanatos (death) who emerged from the underworld to cut a lock of hair from the head of the dying, and to hasten the last breath.

HYSSOP

Symbol of *penitence, humility,* in association with the natural habits of its growth among stones in secluded places.

In Jewish ceremonial a bunch of hyssop on the end of a reed signifies *cleansing, purification,* stemming from the purgative qualities of the plant.

In Christian symbolism, *innocence regained through the rite of baptism.* Psalm 51:7.

I

In Christian symbolism, the letter *I*, from the first letter of *Iseu* stands for *Jesus Holy One*.

In Japanese zodiac, the letter indicates the *boar*, symbol of *courage*.

IBIS

The sacred ibis of ancient Egyptian religion symbolized *protector, defender,* from its usefulness in destroying venomous reptiles.

ICARUS

As for his father, Daedalus, *cunning worker,* because of their initiative and ingenuity in the art of flying.

ICTHYS

An anagram made up of the first letters of the Greek word for fish, used for secrecy by the Christians in the catacombs for *Jesus Christ, Son of God and Savior,* when their religion was unpopular. Pictures of a fish, likewise, implied the same meaning.

IDOL

An image, whether of man or of other representations of natural objects, when holding an especially important place in religious rites implies *idolatry, paganism, devout reverence.*

IDUNA

In Scandinavian myth, wife of Bragi, and goddess of *youth, dawn.* She makes the world young again each morning. Her attribute is an *apple* and she is usually shown with a box or basket of this fruit, signifying the golden apples which the gods ate, and so making themselves young again.

SAINT IGNATIUS LOYOLA

Founder of the Society of Jesuits. Special day, July 31.

IHS

A sacred Christian monogram, abbreviation for the Greek word *Jesus.* A frequently-used church ornamentation in carvings, needlework, paintings, and on publications.

ILEX (see holly).

With early Britons, *aspiration*, the *Great Spirit*.

ILIMA

With the hibiscus, serves as the state flower of Hawaii. When woven into leis, the signification is *royalty, high estate*.

INCENSE

Symbol of *adoration, thanksgiving, prayers rising to the throne of God.*

A pot of incense, reflects a *grateful and pious heart*. With a perpetual fire burning, typifies the *perpetual intercession of Christ*, or the *Virgin Mary*.

In China, incense signifies *scholarship*.

INDIAN

An American Indian in picture language in U.S.A. generally means a *pathfinder, sagacity, cunning*, or *the art of woodcraft*. A young Indian or a warrior, armed with bow and arrows, often couching, is a popular personification of *America*.

INDIAN PAINTBRUSH

By legislative action in 1917 this colorful wild flower became the state emblematic flower of Wyoming.

INDRA

In ancient Hinduism, god of thunder, rain, *storm winds*, identical with Scandinavian Thor, Greek Zeus, or Roman Jupiter. Pictured in splendor, riding his elephant, Airavata, or in a golden chariot drawn by from two to eleven hundred horses.

INK BALLS

In commercial art, one of the emblems of *printing*.

INO

In Greek mythology, a sea *goddess*, Daughter of Cadmus, symbol of *broad daylight*. Persecuted by her husband until, with exasperation she threw herself into the sea.

INRS

Initial letters for the Latin superscription on the cross at the Crucifixion of Christ — *Jesus of Nazareth, King of the Jews.*

In Hebrew the initial letters for the four elements:

Iaminim — *water.*

Nour — *fire.*

Ruach — *air.*

Iebschah — *earth.*

INTERLACINGS

In architectural designs (see illustration, p. 19:8) stand for *co-operation.* In church architecture or art, the *mystery of life and death.*

INU

In the Japanese zodiac, represented by the *dog.*

IO

In Greek mythology, a beautiful nymph, personification of the *moon.* Juno, jealous, through Jupiter's affinity with Io, had the maiden changed into a heifer, setting one-hundred-eyed Argus to keep watch over her.

IOLE

In Greek mythology, a beautiful maiden taken captive by Hercules, when she failed to fulfill her agreement that she would give her hand to the suitor most successful in a contest of archery. The winner was Hercules.

IPHIGENIA

In Greek mythology, daughter of Agamemnon and Clytemnestra, offered by her father to Artemis for an object of sacrifice that the gods might be appeased. Instead of allowing the maiden to be burned, Artemis snatched her into the clouds, leaving in her stead a young deer to be sacrificed. Iphigenia's story serves as a basis of many dramatic plots.

IRIS

Greek goddess of the *rainbow,* and the swift messenger of Zeus and

Hera who carried good news, only, along the bridge from gods to men. She, also loosened the hair of dying persons, that their spirits might depart more readily. Appears in pictures clothed in bright colors, with wings of butterfly or moth, bearing a heraldic wand.

IRIS

The flower, from its multi-colored blooms, took its name from the Greek goddess, Iris, who presided over the rainbow. In Christian symbolism, from the three distinct divisions in a conventionalized form of the flower, the significance is the *Holy Trinity*, and when the letters IHC appear on these divisions, the meaning is *Christ*. As one of the flowers of the Virgin, the significance is *Passion of Christ*, or the sorrows of the *Virgin*, in association with the sword-like end of the sturdy leaves. See, also fleur-de-lis and illustration p. 10:6.

IRON

When reference is to rods or bars of the metal, the denotation is *strength, irresistible power, obduracy.*

SAINT ISABELLA OF FRANCE

Sister of Saint Louis, with special day, August 31. Pictured in lavish gown with the diadem of a princess, holding a lily, or a conventional building in her hand.

SAINT ISADORE

Patron saint of *laborers;* also of Spain and of Spanish agriculture. His special day, May 10. Pictured holding a spade or rake; or praying before a cross; or near him, an angel plowing with white oxen.

ISIS

Egyptian *moon* goddess, sister and wife of Osiris, god of the underworld. She was also goddess of *motherhood* and *fertility*, and usually represented with the head of a cow, or by a crowned woman seated on a throne placed between two horns.

SAINT IVES, or YVES

Patron of *lawyers, judges,* and *notaries*. His special day, May 19. Pictured wearing fur robe and bonnet of a judge or doctor, enthroned between rich and poor litigants, inclining a bit toward the poor.

IVORY

Symbol of *purity* and *moral fortitude,* from the color and the firmness of texture.

It is said that the practice of carving crucifixes of ivory, springs from ivory as a symbol of *Christ* with reference to the *incorruptibility of His body* in the tomb.

IVY

For this vine there are many symbolic meanings:

In ancient Greece it was sacred to Dionysius, and, together with other evergreens it signified *immortality.* In its dedication to Dionysius (Bacchus) it also stood for *conviviality.*

From its natural clinging tendencies, it signifies *friendship, fidelity, dependency, undying affections,* and *family closeness.*

For its lasting green, it is the symbol of *eternal life, remembrance.* Added to a bridal bouquet, *faithfulness, good luck.*

Ivy-covered walls depict, *dignity, stability, maturity, excellence.*

IXIOM

In Greek mythology, king of the Thessalian people, bound to an endlessly revolving wheel by Zeus for aspiring to the love of Hera. From this legendary reference has grown the symbol, *unending emotional stress.*

JACINTH

Gem of *strength, endurance,* from the hardness of its texture, and the strength of its pure orange color.

JACKAL-HEADED MAN

Figure of the *crucified Christ in derision.*

JADE

A charm of happy omen, signifies *virtue.* In ancient China, jade stood for *esteemed possessions,* something too precious to be given up readily.

SAINT JAMES THE ELDER

Patron saint of *millers;* also of Spain. As one of the Apostles, in art, he is pictured as bearing a scroll in one hand with Biblical passages written upon it. His special day is July 25.

SAINT JAMES, THE LESS APOSTLE

Patron saint of *hatters.* His special day May 1. Meeting his death from an enraged mob, his attribute is a *club.*

JANUS

In Roman mythology, two-headed porter of heaven, god of *arches and doorways,* of *gates,* and of *all beginnings* — first hour of the day, first day of the month, and first day of the year (his name gives us January). He is represented with two faces looking in opposite directions, whereby he is able to see the past and the future at the same time.

JAROJIN

One of the seven gods of luck of Japan, symbolizing *longevity.*

JASMINE

Symbol of *divine hope, heavenly felicity, grace, elegance, amiability, feminine loveliness,* implications stemming from the white color and fragrance of the flower.

JASON

In Greek mythology, nephew of Pelias, King of Ioleus, who kept him from the throne by sending him in quest of the Golden Fleece. After slaying the dragon (demon of drought) with the aid of Medea (the dawn), he succeeded in capturing the Golden Fleece (rays of the sun).

JASPER

The red variety symbolizes *strength, courage, fortitude, happiness.* The light-colored variety with red stains symbolizes the *spiritual grace* which preserves men from vain terrors.

Ancients believed jasper to have wonderful magic power of protection against death from wounds or from hemorrhage.

JAVELIN (See, also spear)

Symbol of *valor, supreme honor, war,* or *intimation of war.*

SAINT JEROME THE GREAT

One of the four great Latin Fathers of the Church, known principally for his translation of the Old Testament into Latin, the Vulgate. Patron saint of *scholars, students.* His special day, September 30. In art usually accompanied by a lion, in association with the legend relating the saint's having removed a thorn from a lion, which animal became his constant companion. More familiar in art is the picture showing him as a hermit in the desert beating his breast with a stone and praying or writing. Near him, his attributes, a *skull* and an *owl.*

JERUSALEM

Often personified as *utopia, heaven.*

JESSAMINE

The yellow jessamine by vote of the General Assembly of South Carolina in 1924 became the emblematic flower of the state.

JESSE TREE

A popular design of candlesticks made in the shape of a tree, in the Middle Ages in religious symbolism represented *Jesus' royal genealogy.*

JET

Symbol of *grief, mourning* when made up in dull finish.

JEWELS

In general symbolism, *pride* and *ostentation, wealth, wisdom.*

SAINT JOACHIM

Father of the Virgin Mary, with special day, March 20. His attributes are, the *lamb,* and *lilies.*

SAINT JOAN OF ARC

Patroness of *France,* cannonized in 1920. Her festival day, May 30. Represented in art, in armor with hair flowing down her back to show she is a maiden. She holds lilies of France.

JOB

Symbol of *patience.* Old Testament patriarch who experienced one affliction after another. Job 2:7-13.

SAINT JOHN, APOSTLE AND EVANGELIST

Patron of *art dealers, bookbinders, book-sellers, compositors, engravers, lithographers, painters, printers, publishers, papermakers, sculptors, writers.* Often referred to as "the disciple whom Jesus loved." His special day, December 27. His emblem pictured p. 10:11.

SAINT JOHN, THE BAPTIST

Patron of *cutlers, farriers, tailors.* His attribute is the *lamb.* A dish or platter bearing his head, refers to his execution. Sometimes in art he holds a reed cross or carries a banner with reed cross. His special day, June 24.

JONAH

Symbol of *resurrection.* Images of Jonah appear at different points in the catacombs, as a sign of the *risen Christ.* In art, represented seated under a gourd vine, with whale and ship, his attributes, in the distance.

JONQUIL

Symbolism the same as for the crocus, *cheerfulness, mirth, spring greeting, charity.* The flower for the month of March. Illustration p. 21:3.

SAINT JOSEPH, HUSBAND OF THE VIRGIN MARY

Patron of *carpenters, confectioners, engineers, househunters, pioneers, travelers, married couples,* the *dying.* His attributes are a carpenter's plane, saw, and hatchet. Often in scenes of the Presentation he carries a lily and two doves in a basket. At other times pictured with a budded staff in hand, from the legend that his staff, left in the temple was the one that budded into leaf and from it flew a dove into heaven. His special day, March 19.

SAINT JOSEPH OF ARIMATHEA

Patron of *gravediggers* and *undertakers.* In art seen taking the crown of thorns from the dead Christ. His special day, March 17.

JOTMA

Among the ancient Hindu gods, he stands for *might.*

JOTUN

In Norse mythology, Jotun represents a *giant.*

JOVE

In early Roman religion, god of the *sky.*

SAINT JUDE, THE APOSTLE

Patron of the helpless. His special day, October 28. His attribute is a *lance* or *halberd,* weapon with which he was beheaded. In art, bearded, holding in his hands a long cross, a knotted club, a halberd, boat, oars, carpenter's square, and a ship with sails and an inverted cross. He is reputedly the author of the book *Revelations.*

JUG

In modern picture language symbol of *intemperance,* or the *water of life.*

SAINT JULIAN, THE HOSPITATOR

There are many references to Saint Julian in literature, particularly in prose works, as the patron of *travelers, minstrels, innkeepers, musicians, ferrymen,* and of *hospitality.* His special day, January 9. Generally in art, pictured as a huntsman with stag by his side, and river and boat as background.

JUNIPER

Its branches signify *resilience* because of their power to withstand wind and storm without breaking.

JUNO

(See Hera.)

JUPITER

In early Roman religion ruler of the gods, father of gods and demigods, *protector of man.* The *thunderbolt* was his chief attribute, and the *eagle* his emblematic bird. A Jupiter allusion is not uncommon in literary writings. Same as Greek Zeus, pictured p. 7:11.

JUSTICE

In Roman mythology an abstract representation of Greek Themis, mother of the seasons. Pictured in art as a blindfolded or headless woman, holding aloft a balanced scale in her right hand and a sword in the other, as a symbol of *justice.*

K.

KAKIA

In Roman mythology, goddess of *vice*. She tried to mislead young Hercules by asking him to choose between Arete (virtue) and herself (vice). Though she promised riches, ease, and love, she could not dissuade him.

KALLIOPE (Also Calliope)

In Greek mythology, chief of the nine muses, the sweet-voiced one who presided over *eloquence,* and *heroic* epic. Mother of Orpheus, with attributes, a *crown of laurel* and a *writing tablet.*

KAMADEVA

In early Brahman religion, god of *love,* represented as riding on a dove, armed with an arrow of flowers and a bow whose strings are formed of bees.

KANGAROO

The animal, kangaroo, in 1912 was designated as the symbol of *Australia.*

The flower, kangaroo paw, accordingly, is regarded as the emblematic flower of Western Australia.

KANNON

In Japan, honored as the goddess of *mercy.* A huge statue of her has been erected atop Otsuboyama Hill southeast of Tokyo.

KAPOK (Also ceiba)

Known as a silk-cotton tree in Argentine. Made emblematic tree of that country by presidential decree in 1942.

KARPO

In Greek mythology, known as goddess of *fruitage* and *stimulation of plant life.* One of the beautiful daughters of Zeus and Themis.

KEB

In ancient Egyptian religion god of the *earth.*

KEY

Symbol of *knowledge, authority, circumspection, high office.*

Among prominent Christian churchmen, the key denotes *spiritual or temporal power.*

Two crossed keys are an attribute of Saint Peter, the Apostle. Illustration, p. 10:7.

A key when held by Cupid signifies the *power of love.*

KEYSTONE

In architecture, symbol of *stability, firmness.*

KHEM

In early Egyptian religion god of *generation* and *reproduction,* the same as the garden-god Ranno who was represented by an asp, a figure of which is to be seen still on winepresses, garden and agricultural implements. Identified as Pan by the Greeks.

KITE

Symbol of *venture, theory, experiment.*

KIWI

Emblematic bird of New Zealand. Unknown in other countries.

KLEIO

(See Clio.)

KNEE

In genuflexion implies *reverence, subjection,* stemming from Ephesians 3:14 and Philippians 2:10.

KNIFE

As one of the implements of martyrdom signifies *sacrifice.* A flaying knife on a Bible is the emblem of Bartholemew, with reference to his martyrdom.

148

KNOT

One of the eight Buddhist symbols, standing for *longevity*. Ribbon ends knotted when accompanying flowers or wrapped gifts express *many good wishes*.

KONOHAMA SAKUYAHINE

Japanese goddess of *living flowers*. Her sister Chiruhime is goddess of *cut flowers*.

KOTO-BUKI

A variation of *lowtow* which in China and Japan is the prostration made by kneeling and touching the forehead to the floor or ground. The act signifies *welcome, happiness, long life*.

KRISHNA

Hindu god of *love*, the eighth incarnation of Vishnu. Represented as a beautiful youth. In the literature of many countries, popular hero of spectacular exploits, sometimes referred to as a type of Christ.

KRONOS (Cronus)

In Greek religion, god of the *harvests;* identified with Roman *Saturn*. The son of Uranus, Kronos killed his father, seized the throne and for years ruled in satisfaction. Eventually was dethroned by his son, Zeus.

KUANYIN

Among the Buddhist goddesses stands for *mercy*, and *protection* of children.

KUVERA

In early Brahman religion, god of *riches*.

L.

LACHESIS

In Classical mythology, the second of the three fates, whose function is to determine the course and length of life. She is the *measurer, bearer of the rod and staff, disposer of lots.*

Her sisters are Clitho, the spinner, who spins the thread of life; and Atropos, the inflexible one, who cuts off the thread.

LADDER

In church symbolism, one of the thirteen symbols of the Crucifixion, suggestive of the implement used by the mockers to reach Christ. Illustration, p. 13:6.

In general symbolism, a ladder reflects the *way to perfection, to spiritual beauty.*

LADYBIRD

A beetle, symbol of *good luck.* An outgrowth of its value in destroying other insects.

LADY'S SLIPPER

Commonly called the wild orchid. Adopted as symbolic flower of Minnesota by act of legislature in 1902.

LAIUS

King of Thebes, father of OEdipus. Learning from the oracles that he was to be killed by his own son, he left him in an exposed place to die. He was rescued by the King of Corinth, and later, unwittingly he slew Laius.

LAKSHMI

Among the Brahmas, goddess of *wealth,* wife of Vishnu. Her attributes are a lotus blossom, jewels, and sumptuous fabrics.

LAMB

In general symbolism, *meek submissiveness, innocence, sacrifice.* A favorite Christian symbol, clearly pictured on the walls of the catacombs of Rome where it was usually surrounded by a nimbus with three rays. The symbolic meanings are determined by the pose:

Reclining, holding a banner — implies *suffering*.

Lying down with a lion — *concord*.

Having human hands and arms — *power of the Father*.

Reclining, haloed, holding a Latin cross — *atonement*.

Lamb standing — the *triumphant, risen Lord*.

As cemetery marker for a child's grave, if reclining on a Bible — *innocence;* displaying a banner — the *resurrection*.

One of the principal attributes of Saint Francis of Assisi. In Mediaeval *Bestiaries*, symbol of the *soul*, or a *believer*.

SAINT LAMBERT OF MAESTRICHT
Patron of *children's nurses, dentists, surgeons, trussmakers*. His special day, September 17. Pictured as a bishop with two armed men under his feet. He holds a sword and open book.

LAMP
In general, signifies *wisdom, knowledge, guidance, enlightenment*. A popular key emblem for honors in the educational field, especially as a lighted Roman lamp. In Christian symbolism, *truth, reverence, righteousness, piety, immortality*, the *word of God*.

LAMPREY
When entwined with a viper, *adultery*.

LANCE
One of the thirteen symbols of the Crucifixion, with reference to the piercing of Christ's sides in Saint John 19:34. Illustration, p. 13:2.

In general symbolism, a lance denotes *knighthood, chivalry, truth*.

LANTERN
Symbol of *light in darkness*, a *search for truth*, a *signal*. In church symbolism, *Christ's Passions* or *the betrayal*, in reference to John 18:3, pertaining to the entrance of Judas and his companions into the Garden of Gethsemane, with lanterns.

LAN TR'AI-HO

In Taoism one of the seven immortals, patron of the *flowers*.

LAOCOON

In classical mythology, a Trojan priest who distrusted the wooden horse, and with his two sons was crushed and killed by two mammoth serpents which Athera caused to come up out of the sea. This episode is a favorite story among poets and artists. The statue of Laocoon in the Vatican is one of the finest works of art in the world.

LAPAGERIA

Also called bell flower in Chile has been adopted as the national emblematic flower of that country.

LAPIS LAZULI

This stone, the sapphire of the ancients, is a symbol of *heaven*, reflecting the blue of the sky as a background and a sprinkling of golden spots, as stars. In more modern implications, lapis lazuli denotes *success, prosperity, fruition, cheerfulness*. With the turquoise, it is birthstone for December.

LARK

Is symbolic of *joy, gaiety*, in that the bird flies high, and sings best when in flight.

In church symbolism, the lark signifies the *humility of the priesthood or ministry*.

The lark bunting since 1931 has become the state bird of Colorado. Six states claim the meadow lark as symbolic bird: Oregon and Wyoming since 1927; Nebraska, 1929; Montana, 1931; North Dakota, 1947. Kansas school children in 1925 proclaimed the bird as their favorite, with legislative adoption coming later.

LARKSPUR

Flower of *good welfare, well-being*, stemming from the fact that the leaves do not drop off until new ones have become fully grown. Illustration, p. 21:7.

LASSO

(See noose.)

LATONA

Same as Leto, mother of Apollo and Artemis, a personification of *night*.

LAUREL

Ancient Greeks crowned their victors with laurel as a symbol of *achievement, victory.* Additional implications are: *fame, valor, distinction, reward of merit, academic honors.* Illustration, p. 22:6.

Laurel is said to be the first plant to be used as a Christian Nativity decoration.

Mountain laurel, since 1907 has been the adopted emblematic plant of Connecticut; and since 1933 is Pennsylvania.

SAINT LAURENCE

Patron of *brewers, confectioners, cooks, cutlers, school boys and other students, washerwomen, glaziers* and *armorers.* His chief attribute, a gridiron with reference to his execution by slow roasting. Also he is represented with a dish of coins, alluding to his distribution of the church treasures to the poor around him. His special day, August 19.

LAVENDER

As a color, in some countries is emblematic of *mourning.* In fashion design, *gentility.*

As the flower of a fragrant mint plant, *voluptuousness.*

LAVER

Vessel of brass for holding water for the use of priests of the Temple of Solomon, *consecration.*

LEAVES

In floristry, when used as background greenery, *hope.*

LEEK

Plant emblem of *Wales.*

LEI

Necklace garland of leaves or flowers, popular in Hawaii as an offering of *friendship, hospitality*. The special symbolism which each lei holds is dependent upon the type of flower woven into the garland.

LEMON

Symbol of *fidelity*, and with the meaning of *fealty* often associated with the Virgin Mary. Often, also, depicted as the fruit of the tree of knowledge of good and evil in the Garden of Eden narrative.

SAINT LEONARD OF LIMOGES

Throughout Europe held to be patron saint of *fruiterers, greengrocers*, and of *prisoners* and *captive slaves*. His special day, November 6. Represented as a church deacon bearing broken fetters in his hand, or with prisoners kneeling at his feet.

LEOPARD

In general symbolism, *stealth*. When couching, *jealousy*. In church symbolism, *dominion*, in reference to Daniel 7:6.

One of the beasts of the chariot of Bacchus. Illustration, p. 17:7.

LETHE

In Greek mythology, denotes *forgetfulness of the past, oblivion*, from a river in Hades which separated Elysian fields from the world of darkness. Its waters were said to create forgetfulness.

LETO

(See Latona).

LETOPHORO

In Zoroaster's *Oracle* stands for *dangerous maladies, death*, as one of the nine spirits of intelligence.

LETTER

In modern symbolism, an envelope sealed is a symbol of *special message*.

LETTUCE

Both the wild or garden variety, symbol of *temperance*. Stemming from the fact that the milky juice is only mildly stimulating.

LEUCOTHEA

(See Ino.)

LEVEL

A carpenter's tool for establishing a horizontal line, symbol of *equality*.

LIBATION

Ancient rite of pouring wine on the earth or individual, as an honor to a *deity;* if blood is used, the act stands for *purification of the soul,* or *pledge of faith.*

LIGHT

Radiating from any object which emits rays, such as a lamp, signifies *joy, truth, glory, faith, purity, increasing knowledge.* Other meaningful reflections are:

Altar lights — Christ the Light of the World, John 8:12.

Very distinct radiating light — *force.*

Zig-zag flashes or rays — *electricity,* or *power held in reserve.*

Green or white light — *safety.*

Red light — *warning* or *danger.*

LIGHTHOUSE

Symbol of *safety, vigilance, watchfulness.* In early Christian cemeteries as a gravemarker, the *final port.* Illustration, p. 19:6.

LIGHTNING

A flash of lightning in symbolic picture language denotes *divine power, expedition, vengeance, wrath.*

LILAC

The color is symbol of *fidelity in love,* stemming from the red-blue tones of the color.

In 1919, by legislative act, the lilac became the state flower of New Hampshire.

LILY

From the natural characteristics of the lily, the symbolism is *loveliness, regal beauty.*

As one of the widely pictured flowers of the Virgin Mary, most often in Annunciation scenes, *purity, chastity, innocence, righteousness, heavenly bliss.*

As an Easter flower, the lily stands for the *resurrection, immortality.* With these implications goes the story of the growth and development of the stalk of flowers. The bulb decaying in the soil produces a new bulb, stem, leaves and flowers, all rising in glory above the dark earth in which the process of death and the release of new life are inseparable; thus exemplifying the experiences of the human life from birth to death, and the new life. Illustration, p. 16:8.

The lily is the emblem of Florence, and, together with the violet and daisy, a national flower of Italy.

The orange lily, from its color, in Christian symbolism denotes *Christ's blood.*

LILY OF THE VALLEY

As one of the earliest blossoms of spring, *delight, happiness.* As a flower of the Virgin Mary, *humility, purity.*

A favorite flower of brides with the denotation of *happiness, perfect bliss.* Illustration, p. 21:5.

LINES

The direction in which lines are drawn carries great meaning in architecture, in nature paintings, and in flower arrangement:

> Straight lines — in general, signify *nobility, grandeur, firmness, infinity, aspiration, uprightness, strength.*
>
> Curved lines — *grace, elegance, suavity, movement, beauty.*
>
> Horizontal lines — represent *repose;* parallel lines, *harmony.*

In flower arrangement, branches with sharp bends denote *caprice, indecision;* drooping or wilting, *sorrow* or *discouragement;* extending branches *repose, benediction;* a group of many crossing lines of branches, *anxiety, conflict.*

LINGAM

In Buddhism, symbol of *life.*

LION

In general symbolism, *courage, ferocity, power, guardianship, vigilance, kingship,* meanings dependent upon the circumstances surrounding the beast or whether his position is reclining, couchant or pictured with other animals. Illustration, p. 9:5.

When appearing in sculpture at entrances to temples, museums, and gates of walls, the symbolism is *protection, guardianship.*

With head bowed and neck pierced by a caduceus, *force.*

When lying down with a lamb, *concord.*

For early Romans, the male lion represented *majesty, kingship.*

Lion as emblem of Saint Mark, the Evangelist, in that in his gospel he emphasizes Christ's kingly character like a lion crying in the wilderness. Lion is the symbol of Judah in the bronze door of the Baptistry in Florence.

LIONESS

The symbolism, *resurrection,* stems from the fable that all lions are born dead, and are not brought to life until the third day by the loud roaring of the father. Often found with this symbolism in the literature of late Middle Age. In *Bestiaries,* also denotes *Satan.*

LITERATURE

Popular emblem of literature, book and lighted candle. Illustration, p. 19:7.

LI T'IEK-(KUAI)

In Taoism, patron of the *beggars.*

LITURGICAL COLORS

White, red, green, violet, and black, as emblematic colors are more or less in strict usage among Christian churches of high rituals. Their chief purpose is to create a worshipful atmosphere, and add beauty to the visible part of the services. Each color has a special symbolism, and, where the church observes the proper division of a fixed calendar year, there is a special color for each occasion, displayed in the hangings, or paraments which adorn the altar, pulpit, lectern, and Bible marker. The symbolic meaning and proper time for use of each color follows:

White, symbol of *light, faith, purity, innocence, virginity, divinity,* and of *angels* has special use at these times:

From and with vespers of the Eve of the Nativity, through the Epiphany season (except Saint Stephen's day, on which day it is red.) (For explanation of the seasons mentioned see year, symbolic church year.)

From Easter day to the vespers of the Saturday before Whitsunday.

On the festival of the Transfiguration.

On the Presentation.

On the festival of the Holy Trinity and its octave.

On days of the Annunciation and of the Visitation.

On the day of Saint Michael and all angels.

Red, the symbol of *fire, blood, zeal, love, youth, fervor,* and of *sin* and its *atonement:*

From and with vespers of the Saturday before Whitsunday to the vespers of the Saturday before the festival of the Holy Trinity.

On all Apostles' days, and on all Evangelist days (except that of Saint John).

On days of the martyrs.

On all church anniversaries.

For the festival of the Harvest.

For Thanksgiving day.

Green, symbol of *fidelity, hope, immortality, growth, life and nature:*

From and with vespers of the Saturday before Septuagesima to vespers of the day before Ash Wednesday.

Beginning with the second Sunday after the festival of the Holy Trinity and throughout the Trinity season to vespers of the Saturday before Advent Sunday.

Violet, the symbol of *penitence,* and *Christ's Passion* is the color for, from and with vespers of the Saturday before Advent Sunday to vespers of the Eve of the Nativity.

From the vespers of the day before Ash Wednesday throughout Lent (excepting Good Friday) to vespers of the Eve of Easter.

Black, the symbol of *death,* and *mourning* is used for Good Friday, and for a day of Humiliation.

LIZARD

Symbol of *piety, religion, spring, health, security*. When the lizard is thought of as a salamander, the idea is a *lover*.

LOADSTONE, or LODESTONE

The symbol is *love*, in that the stone possesses great polarity; hence for human beings the implication is having strong attractive power in amours.

LOBSTER

In Japan, *longevity;* in U.S.A. a *bigot*.

LOCOMOTIVE

In architectural ornamentation of public buildings, the emblem of *commerce*.

LOCUST

Destructiveness, and, from the migratory habits, *restlessness*.

LOGS

(See Yule logs.)

LOKI

In Norse mythology, god of *discord* and *evil*, called by some the mischief maker of the gods, and the first father of lies. He was slayer of Baldur the Beautiful, usually accompanied by Fenris, the Wolf, by Hela or Death, and by the Midgaard Serpent.

LOOM

A symbolism of the *mystery of life*, from the interweavings of yarns within a fabric. Also *feminine industry*.

A loom is the emblem of *textile manufacturing*.

LOTIS

In classical mythology, a nymph who was changed into a lotus flower to escape the pursuit of Priapus, god of the shade.

LOTOPHAGI (THE LOTUS-EATERS)

In the *Odyssey*, a people whose sole food consisted of the lotus fruit and blossoms; hence, in literature thought of as *inducers of sleep* or of *dreamy indolence*.

LOTUS FLOWER

Flowering water plant with a wide range of symbolic implications:

In early Greek legend of the Lotophagi, it is symbolic of *dreamy contentment*, but for the peoples of Greece it suggested *vigor, youthful bloom.*

In Egypt where the plant propagates in profusion, it became the symbol of *reproductive power of all nature*, and was widely used in religious rites and ceremonies. One variety has become one of the emblematic symbols of the country.

In India, a full blown red lotus flower, with eight inner and eight outer petals in a conventionalized pattern has become the emblem of the country.

The Hindu sees in the lotus the symbolism of *superhuman or divine birth*, the *flowering of the human spirit.*

To the Buddhist, it suggests *benignity, spirituality, perfection* and *immortality.*

In Japan, *purity of heart, spiritual realities.*

In Chinese art, *prosperity.*

In Christian religion symbolism the significance is *spiritual enlightenment, beauty, purity*, in reference to the natural growth habits of the plant which has its roots in the quagmires, its stems in the muddy waters, but emerges as a flower of exquisite beauty. In like manner Christians are to rise above all passions and selfish gains. Illustration, p. 20:2.

SAINT LOUIS OF TOULOUSE

Patron saint of *France*, and of *hairdressers.* Pictured in royal robes, and with a fleur-de-lis. His festival day, August 25.

LOVE-LIES-BLEEDING

Also known as bleeding heart, symbol of *immortality.*

LUCIFER

By early church fathers, and by Milton in Paradise Lost, called *Satan*, because of the belief that he was fallen from Heaven.

SAINT LUCY OF SYRACUSE

Patroness of *tailors, cutlers, glaziers, pedlars, servant girls, scribes, weavers, saddlers,* and *notaries.* Her special day, December 13.

Her lover, angered at Lucy's gift of her heritage to the poor, denounced her as being a Christian. The governor ordered her to be dragged to death, but because of some miraculous strength she had acquired, the soldiers could not move her; then she was to be burned, but flames would not touch her. Eventually she was stabbed to death in the neck.

Pictured with a lamb to suggest *divine light and wisdom.*

LUCINA
In Roman mythology, goddess of *childbirth.*

SAINT LUKE, THE EVANGELIST
Patron saint of *painters, bookbinders, sculptors, goldsmiths, notaries, doctors,* and *butchers.* His special day, October 18.

Legend has it that he was a painter of Christ and of the Virgin Mary. His most frequent attribute is the winged ox (see illustration, p. 10:10.) in that his gospel emphasizes the ministry and sacrifice of Christ. The ox, being the symbol of *sacrifice.*

LUNAE
(See Diana) She is the *moon-goddess,* and from her name we get *Monday.*

LU PAN
In China, god of the *carpenters.*

LUPINE
Also called blue bonnet and Buffalo clover, the state emblematic flower of Texas since 1901.

LUSTRATION
A religious ceremonial rite of ablution made upon entering a place of holiness. Its significance, *purification.*

LUTE
Prince of instruments, symbol of *lyric poetry, scholarliness, marital bliss.*

LU TUNG-PIN

In Taoism one of the seven immortals. He grants *supernatural power.*

LYNX

From the animal's natural tendencies, *cowardice.* Illustration, p. 17:6.

LYRE

In Greek mythology, symbol of *choral lyric* presided over by Terpsichore (delight in the dance).

Emblem of Apollo, god of poetry and song; and of Orpheus, sweet music charmer. The decorative character of the lyre makes it a pleasing design subject for distinction in music and song. In modern form, called the harp. Illustration, p. 16:6.

M

MA

In early Egyptian religion twin goddess of *truth* and *justice*, Daughter of Ra, great god of the *sun*.

MAAT

In early Egyptian religion, a goddess of *truth, justice,* or the *law.* In judgment scenes in which she appears, in one pan of the scales there is a feather, in the other a heart, whereby she weighs the souls of the dead to determine the region into which it is to be sent for its final home. She is daughter of Ra, great god of the *sun.*

MAB, QUEEN

Messenger of dreams, appearing in literary scenes as a fairy midwife who delivers dreams.

MACE

A heavy staff used in the Middle Ages as an implement for breaking strong armors. When borne by a dignity it signified *authority, distinction, power.*

MAENAD

In Greek mythology a nymph attendant upon Bacchus, god of wine; hence a *woman given to revelry and debauchery.*

SAINT MAGLORIOUS OF DOL

Patron of *glovemakers,* with special day, October 24. In art, pictured as administering the Holy Communion to an angel.

MAGNOLIA

The flower signifies *virtue, loveliness, feminine beauty, youthfulness,* in reference to the fact that the blossoms appear in early spring before the leaves.

The leaves, with the same significance as bay leaves, denote *victory.* In Japan, the tree symbolizes *power, affluence.*

Adopted in 1900 by both Louisiana and Mississippi as emblematic state flower.

SAINT MAGNUS OF ITALY

Patron of *fishmongers*. Pictured with crosier in hand, monsters and reptiles at his feet. His day, January 1.

MAHONIA

An evergreen shrub of the barberry family, called Oregon grape. The shrub is the emblematic foliage plant of the state of Oregon.

MAIA

In Greek mythology, goddess of the *plains*. The eldest of the Pleiades and mother of Hermes.

MAIDEN

Symbol of *grace, gentleness, promise*. Draped, and crowned with wheat heads, holding a sheaf, symbol of *abundance*.

MAJA

Of the ancient Hindu gods, the *allmother*.

MALLET

Symbol of *order*, and, coupled with a chisel forms the emblem of *sculptors*.

MAMAS

Patron of *shepherds and nurses*. His special day, August 17.

MAMMON

One of the fallen angels in Milton's Paradise Lost. From New Testament narrative, symbol of *demon of riches, greed, avarice*.

MAN

Dependent upon the circumstances, a man pictured, is symbol of:

Winged man — *humanity*. The attribute of Saint Matthew in reference to his having written much about Christ, the man. Illustration, p. 10:8.

Man armed — *guardianship*.

Spectacled and with a book — *scholarliness*.

With hand on head deep in thought — *meditation.*

Carrying a heavy weight — *strength.*

With ass's head, declaiming — *ignorance.*

With a muck rake — *avarice.*

Old man with scythe and hourglass — *Father Time,* or *Old Year.*

MAMA-BOZHO

With early American Indians, god of *dawn, air, fire.*

MANDRAKE

A plant of the nightshade family, symbolizing *delirium, witchcraft,* its forked roots subject of many superstitions. Symbol of the tribe of *Reuben* in the bronze door of the Baptistry of Florence.

MANGER

In Christian symbolism, an infant in a manger signifies the *Nativity of Christ.*

MANIPLE

In liturgical vestment, narrow strip of silk worn over the alb, carried suspended over the left arm of the celebrant of the mass, symbolic of *good works, vigilance, penitence.*

MANJUSAI

Among the Buddhist deities, god of *wisdom.*

MANNA

In church symbolism, denotes *spiritual provision* in reference to Exodus Chapter XVI and Revelation 2:17.

MANTELLETTA

In liturgical vestment, a knee-length, sleeveless outer garment open in front, sign of *limited jurisdiction, or authority.* Those worn by bishops are purple; those of the archbishops, red.

MANTIS

The praying mantis, because of its attack upon other insects, even those larger than itself, is the symbol of *courage.*

MAP

Symbol of *exploration, travel.*

MAPLE

The maple leaf since 1867 the official emblem of Canada, suggests *faithfulness to the end.*

MARDUC

Among ancient Babylonian gods, the *Creator.*

SAINT MARGARET OF CORTONA

Patroness of *spinners, penitent women,* and *women in childbirth.* Her attribute, a maiden standing on a dragon, or leading it on a chain. Her special day, July 20.

MARGUERITE

(See daisy)

MARIGOLD

Flower of the aster family, referred to as *mystic gold of Mary,* symbol of *remembrance, gratitude.*

MARJORAM

Fragrant garden herb used by both the early Greeks and Romans in wreaths for crowning married couples as a symbol of *good wishes for happiness.*

SAINT MARK, THE EVANGELIST

Patron saint of *Venice,* and of *glaziers,* and *notaries.* His festival day, April 25. In his character as the writer of the Gospel of Mark, his emblem is a book and scroll, and a winged lion, emphasizing the fact that his gospel reveals the royal dignity of Christ, the Lion of Judah. Illustration, p. 10:9.

In his character as an evangelist, his emblem is a pen and the book of his Gospel.

MARS

Roman deity, originally having various functions, particularly as god of *fertility*. Later, as he became identified with Greek, Ares, he became god of *war, tumult, disorder*.

MARSYAS

In literature, featured as a lover of rustic life. As a young Greek shepherd lad he rescued Minerva's flute from the sea where she had thrown it when she saw the reflection of her face, less beautiful than she wanted it to be. The boy, becoming skilful in playing the flute, challenged Apollo in a contest — flute against the lyre. Apollo won only by adding his voice to the lyre music, and Marsyas was banished; later, flayed alive.

SAINT MARTHA OF BETHANY

Patroness of *cooks, housewives, innkeepers*. In Biblical narrative she devoted herself to domestic affairs and the running of the home. She is usually shown with a ladle in her hand, or with a dragon at her feet as she holds an aspergillum. Her special day is July 29.

SAINT MARTIN OF TOURS

Patron saint of *Tours, France*, and of *penitent drunkards*. He cut his cloak in two to give half to a beggar, and that night had a vision of Christ appearing to commend him for his act of beneficence. His chief attribute is a *goose*, a fowl whose loud quacking disclosed his hiding place when he had in modesty secluded himself to withstay a call to become a bishop. His special day, November 11.

MASKS

A mask in early classical plays was a figure of a head worn on the stage to identify a character and to aid in projecting the voice. The denotations were dependent upon the expression of the face, whether of *despair, rage, remorse, terror*.

MATCH

Symbol of *uprightness*.

SAINT MATTHEW, APOSTLE AND EVANGELIST

Patron of *bankers* and tax collectors. His special day, September 21. His attribute is a *winged man* in reference to his detailed account of the incarnation of Christ in the Gospel of Saint Matthew. An axe, instrument of his martyrdom in Ethiopia is sometimes shown. Illustration, p. 10:8.

MATZOTH or MATZA

Jewish unleavened bread eaten at the Passover, with signification of *affliction.*

MAULSTICK

Stick used by painters as a rest for the hand while working. With palette and brush, the emblem of *artists.*

SAINT MAURICE

Patron of Austria, of *foot soldiers, dyers, coppersmiths, hatters,* and *knifegrinders.* His special day, February 21. Pictured as a moorish warrior with lance and trefoil cross on his shield or banner.

MAUT, or MUT

In early Egyptian religion, deity worshiped as *mother nature.* Pictured or sculptured as a draped woman, vulture-headed.

MAYFLOWER

(See arbutus.)

MAYPOLE or MAYTREE

In early German lore, a Maypole stood for *generative power, fertility, productiveness.* In more recent times, with changed customs of the festival with which it is associated, the denotation of *rebirth* has been interpreted to mean *rejuvenation, spring gaiety.*

In ancient India and Egypt, a phallus was used as the object around which maidens danced as a *remedy for sterility.*

MEDEA

In Greek mythology, *the dawn,* an enchantress who aided Jason in gaining possession of the Golden Fleece.

MEDUSA'S HEAD

(See Gorgon.) Illustration, p. 7:10.

MELOPOMENE

In Greek mythology, one of the nine Muses, daughter of Zeus and Mnemosyne. She presided over *tragedy*. Her attributes, a mask with crown of gold enwreathed with laurel.

MENORAH

In liturgical symbolism, a seven-branched candelabrum signifying the seven gifts of the Holy Spirit as enumerated in Revelations Chapter XII.

Power

Riches

Wisdom

Strength

Honor

Glory, Blessing. Illustration p. 11:10.

MERCURY

In early Roman religion, *god of commerce, gain,* and *eloquence,* identified with Greek Hermes. A carrier of messages to and from the gods, and conductor of souls to the lower world.

MERMAID

A fabulous nymph, pictured with body of a woman, and with tail of a fish, and, in Syrian religion *goddess of regeneration.* In Greek myth known as *mother of the world, dispenser of wisdom.*

In Mediaeval Christian religion, sometimes signifies the *dual nature* of *Christ.*

METIS

In Greek mythology, divinity of the *spiritual faculties, prudence, wisdom, skill.* One of the Titans, first wife of Jupiter. She administered a draught to Saturnus which caused him to disgorge his own children whom he had swallowed.

MI

In the Japanese zodiac, a *serpent.*

MICE

(See mouse.)

SAINT MICHAEL, ARCHANGEL

Prince of the Heavenly Host, protector of the Hebrews. His attribute, pictured in *armor with sword and scales.* His special day, September 29.

MICROPHONE

In modern picture language a popular signification for *communication, inquiry, investigation.*

MICROSCOPE

In commercial art, *critical inquiry.*

MIDAS

In Greek mythology, King of Phrygia, featured in two episodes, the one in which his ears were changed to ass's ears when he favored Pan instead of Apollo in judging a contest of music; the other when even his food was changed to gold after Dionysus granted his wish that everything around him might be changed into gold. He was compelled to ask that his favor might be remanded.

MILK

General symbolism, *innocence,* from the implication that milk is the food of babes.

MILL

From the Middle Ages, a religious implication of the *Gospel,* with reference to feeding the soul.

MILLSTONE

Circular stone used for grinding grains, signifies *martyrdom,* since the stone was used to crush a victim, or fastened to his body when he was to be thrown into the waters.

MIMIR

In Norse mythology, deity of *wisdom* and *knowledge*. He drank daily from a babbling well which gave him magic power to discern both the past and the future.

MIMOSA

Also known as a wattle. Symbol of *immortality, fecundity, Platonic love,* in association with natural characteristics of the tree to spread rapidly, and continue growth for a number of years.

MINERVA

(See Pallas Athene.)

MING TREE

Symbol of *long life* and *strength of character.* Carried over from Chinese legend which reveals that the trees were handed down traditionally from generation to generation. Widely used as an expression of *happy birthday.*

MINT

Symbol of *good luck,* from early stories of magic where sprigs of mint were placed in boats about to be launched in the South Pacific, as an assurance of safety.

MIRROR

Symbol of *truth, retrospection, vanity,* from its use as a device of reflection.

In China, a mirror signifies *unbroken conjugal happiness.*

An old Persian marriage custom, still upheld by many persons, wherein there is a symbol of *joy.* The bride and groom sit in front of a mirror as marriage verses are read from the Koran.

MISTLETOE

Ancient pagans believed mistletoe was a sacred plant with miraculous *powers of healing.* Rivals who met under it in a forest laid down their fighting weapons for a day. Legends of early Germans, and of Druids of England, likewise held the plant to be a symbol of *healing.* At their winter ceremonial festivities, it was honored as an emblem of *peace, light, revival of nature.* By the Celts, mistletoe was credited with magical power, since without roots in the earth, its evergreen branches can renew its leaves in winter.

According to Norse legend, mistletoe is sacred and must not touch earth. From this belief comes the modern custom of hanging it high. Today, the plant signifies *peace* and *good will,* and for lovers who kiss under a suspended branch, they are assured a *happy life together.*

In Christendom, the white berries are said to be rays caught from the star which led the Wise Men to the Christ Child; hence the symbolism *purity, peace.*

From a combination of these early significations of the mistletoe, have arisen the modern denotations, *purification, healing, togetherness* when sprigs are used at Christmas or New Year's festivities.

MITRE

An ecclesiastical headdress, symbolic of *authority* and carried over into heraldry with the same denotation. The material and style of the mitre have changed from century to century. In the headdress of Moses, the two horns stand for the two rays of light that issued from his head when he received the ten commandments. When two flaps are attached to the mitre, they designate the *spirit and letter of the law.*

Three styles of mitres are still in use: the simple, illustrated page 14:6; the orphreyed, ornamented with embroidered bands or cloth of gold; and the precious, where there is rich adornment.

MNEMOSYNE

In Greek mythology, goddess of *memory,* daughter of Heaven and Earth.

MOCCASIN FLOWER

Same symbolism as for lady's slipper, *stability.* Emblematic flower of the state of Minnesota.

MOCKING BIRD

Remarkable for its exact imitations of songs of other birds.

Emblematic bird of Florida since 1907; of Texas since 1927; of Arkansas, since 1929; of Tennessee, since 1933; also emblematic bird of Mississippi and South Carolina.

MOCK ORANGE

Flower of the hydrangea family and emblem of the state of Idaho.

In Greek religion, the three Fates — Klotho, Lachesis, and Atropos, who spin, twist, and cut the thread of life.

MOLE

A small burrowing animal that lives almost solely under the ground, symbol of *blindness, timidity.*

MONUS

In Greek mythology, *ridicule,* personified as a mocking, censorious god.

In U.S.A., grotesque leader of the annual New Year's mummer's parade, such as the traditional one in Philadelphia.

SAINT MONICA

Mother of Saint Augustine, pictured as a Roman matron with scarf in her hand. Her special day, May 4.

MONKEY

Symbol of *mischief, imitativeness, malice.*

In Nikko, Japan, of significance are the three monkeys:

Mi-Zara, he who *sees* no evil.

Kiki-Zara, he who *hears* no evil.

Iwa - Zara, he who *speaks* no evil.

MONSTER

Any one of a number of mythical chimeras. Those emitting flames from wide open jaws, or holding human beings between jaws, signify *Hell.*

MOON

In Greek mythology, the attribute of Selene, with the denotation of *receptivity.*

A full moon signifies *harvest, victory, good fortune.*

A crescent moon is symbol of *night, sleep, virginity, glorified womanhood.*

In Biblical symbolism, a moon denotes subordinate ruling power, Revelations 12:1.

MOONSTONE

Gem of *health, longevity, conjugal happiness.*

With the pearl, one of the emblematic birthstones for the month of June. Among some Orientals, the belief exists that a moonstone can banish fears and nightmare.

MORNING GLORY

As for most clinging vines, the symbol of this flowering plant is *affection, humility.* In Japan, the denotation is *transiency of life.*

MORPHEUS

In Greek mythology, *god of dreams,* son of Erebus and Night. Called the *fashioner or molder* because of the shapes he conjures up before the sleepers. Pictured as a chubby child with wings. In casting his spells, he held in one hand a vase and in the other, poppies which he wafted gently to bring on a drowsiness, and then full sleep.

MORS

In Roman myth, Mors stands for *Death* as a personification.

MORTAR AND PESTLE

Symbol of *tribulation.* Emblem of *apothecaries* and *drug dispensers.*

MORTAR BOARD

An academic cap with broad projecting square top. Symbol of *dignity, honor, learning.*

MOSQUITO

Insect signifying *minor troubles.*

MOUNTAIN

Mountains symbolize, *strength, firmness, constancy,* and also, in another vein, *meditation.*

In Biblical symbolism, mountains denote *spiritual strength,* or *eternal righteousness,* in reference to Isaiah 2:12-14; Daniel 2:35.

MOUSE

Because of the destructiveness of this small animal, it has become a symbol for *destruction, poverty, evil, silent activity.* A black mouse and a white one together stand for *night and day.*

MUDEVI

Early Hindu goddess of *war.*

MULBERRY

Symbol of *tragic love* from the Greek Pyramus and Thisbe legend where the white mulberry tree of their secret meeting place turned to red by the blood of Pyramus, and then purple with the blood of Thisbe. A mulberry tree also stands for *wisdom.* In Japan it is said to be a *protection against lightning.* In China, it is an attribute of the *silk goddess.*

MULE

A long ago established symbol of *obstinacy, stubbornness, bastardy.* The term, mule, often used synonymously with donkey, emblematic figure for the *Democratic Party in U.S.A.*

MUNIN, THE RAVEN

In Scandinavian lore the raven of Odin, chief god of the Eddas, symbol of *memory.* When together with Odin, *thought.*

MUSES

The nine muses, daughters of Jupiter and Mnemosyne, patroness of poetry and music are:

Kalliope, the sweet voiced one, who presided over the heroic epic, her attribute, a writing tablet and crown of laurel.

Kleio, meaning *praise* presided over historical epic; her attribute, a scroll and crown of laurel.

Ourania, the heavenly one, presided over the astronomical epic; her attribute, a globe with crown of stars.

Erato, the lovely one, presided over the *love-lyric;* her attribute, a zither and crown of myrtle and roses.

Terpsichore whose delight was in the dance, presided over the *choral lyric;* her attribute, a lyre with crown of palms.

Euterpe, who stands for delight, presided over *flute music;* her attribute, a flute and crown of flowers.

Melpomene, stands for song, presided over *tragic drama;* her attribute, a tragic mask with crown of laurel.

Thaleia, example of luxuriant beauty, presided over *comic plays;* her attribute, a comic mask with crown of ivy.

Polymnia, stood for delight in many hymns, presided over *religious hymns and pantomime;* her attribute, a crown of pearls.

MUSIC

Many objects and figures are brought into use as symbols of music. Among them: any musical instrument such as the lyre, violin, harp, organ, piano, a shepherd's pipe, a psaltery; a printed musical score, notes on a staff, birds, singing, angels, youths singing, a figure playing upon a musical instrument; Apollo with a lyre; Orpheus with a lyre; Pan with a shepherd's pipe.

MUSICAL INSTRUMENT

Any stringed musical instrument signifies *joy.*

MYRRH

In Biblical narratives of the gifts of the Magi, myrrh signifies *wealth, humanity, holiness, monastic chastity.*

When the reference is to myrrh with a bitter taste, the denotation is *remorse, sorrow, bitterness.*

MYRTLE

In Roman mythology, the myrtle plant was sacred to Venus; hence the symbolic meaning it conveys: *love, beauty, youth,* and, with the advancement of time *maidenhood, virginity.*

For the ancient Hebrews, myrtle meant *peace, justice, joy.*

In early England, the implications were *home, restfulness.*

Now, generally, as a nuptial plant, a sprig added to a bride's bouquet bears the message *happiness, long life.* Illustration, p. 22:5.

N

NAIADS

In classical mythology, the water nymphs, patrons of *poetry and song,* and, more particularly of *lakes, rivers, springs,* and *fountains,* places of their abode.

NAIL

In Christian significance, one of the thirteen symbols of the Crucifixion; hence the meaning, *Christ's Passion.* Usually there are three in number. Illustration, p. 13:5.

NANTEEN

Both plant and berries signify *rising fortunes.*

NAPAEA

In Greek mythology, wood nymphs, patrons of *valleys* and *flocks.*

NAPKIN OF VERONICA

One of the thirteen symbols of the Crucifixion; hence denotes *Christ's Passion.* John 20:7. (See Veronica's napkin.)

NARCISSUS

Beautiful youth in Greek myth, son of a river god, symbol of *self-love, vanity, selfishness, coldness, indifference.* In the story, Narcissus spurns the love of a Greek maiden, Echo, whose love had been so deep that she pined away to her death at the youth's inattentiveness. Nemesis, goddess of vengeance cast a spell over Narcissus, causing him to fall in love with his own image when he saw it reflected in the water, and he drowned while trying to embrace it. After his death, he was changed into the lovely narcissus, and the Greeks then gave us a starting point for the symbol of the flower, *devotion,* and it has been accepted as the emblematic flower of December with that denotation.

The narcissus has become the national flower of China, though tea is often listed as such. The signification here is *benevolence, prosperity,* and when used in special New Year's festivity, the meaning is *happiness.* When used as a decorative flower in Christendom, the denotation is *devotion.* Illustration p. 21:12.

NASTURTIUM

Symbol of *patriotism*. In reference to shield-shaped leaves standing out like a banner or flag.

NAVE

The Latin term means *ship* to which the church has often been likened; hence in church architecture the nave is the symbol of the *ark* in which people found refuge during the great flood of Noah's time.

NEB-THET

Early Egyptian god of the *family*.

NEEDLE, THREAD, AND THIMBLE

Symbol of *household art, feminine industry*.

NEITH

In early Egyptian religion, goddess of the upper heaven, or *ether*, whereas Sati is goddess of the lower heaven, *air*. Much like the Greek Athene who stood for the first *light of dawn*, and then, in later Greek implications, *intellectual light;* hence Neith became a deity of *wisdom*.

NEKHEBET

Vulture goddess of upper Egypt, protector of the king. Her attribute is a vulture holding a ring or other royal symbol.

NEMESIS

In Greek mythology, goddess of *revenge*, noted for her hard heart. She was especially hostile to wealthy persons. Pictured as a hag with a scourge.

SAINT NEOT OF CORNWALL

His special day, July 31. He was a kinsman and preceptor of Alfred the Great. In art he is pictured with palmer's hat and crossed staff, or plowing with four stags fastened to the plow.

NEPH

Egyptian god corresponding to Norse Woden or Greek Zeus. Pictured as having a ram's head with curved horns.

NEPHTHYS

Egyptian goddess, mistress of the temple. Queen of the *night,* and patroness of the *dead.* Pictured with horns and a solar disc.

NEPTUNE

In classical mythology, known in the earlier part of his life as the *earthshaker,* because of his grasping desires to gain the powers rightfully belonging to others. Later, he is identified with Poseidon, god of the sea, and rules from his palace under the waters. His attributes, dolphins, horses, and a trident with which he is always pictured.

NEREIDS

In Greek mythology, sea nymphs, attendants upon Neptune, god of the sea. Daughters of Nereus and Doris, one hundred in number, pictured as riding seahorses, and usually having human form.

NEREUS

In Greek mythology, nymph representing the *pleasant aspects of the sea.* Father of the Nereids. Pictured as an old man with a thick beard of matted hair, holding a trident.

NESSUS

In Greek mythology, known as the *abductor,* for having carried the wife of Hercules across the river to claim her as his own. Met his death from poisoned arrow from a shot from Hercules' bow.

NESTOR

Counselor of the Greeks in the Trojan War, known for *justice, eloquence, wisdom.*

NET

Early Egyptian god of the *hunt.* In the Japanese zodiac, the rat.

NETTLE

From natural characteristics of the plant, *annoyance, distress.*

SAINT NICHOLAS OF MYRA

Chief *patron saint of Russia*. Also saint of *boys, sailors, merchants, bankers, captives, pawnbrokers, travelers*. A great lover of children, and presented them often with gifts. Legendary stories reveal that he is the original Saint Nicholas, modern Santa Claus. His attributes, three purses or three balls in reference to his charities. His special day, December 6.

NIGHT (NYX or NOX)

In Roman mythology, goddess of *night*, mother of *day* and *light*. Represented in art with black robes or draped in dark blue, powdered with stars. Her attributes, *bats, black mice, a poppy*.

NIGHTINGALE

Symbol of *passion, unrequited love*, and sometimes *purity*. In an old Persian nuptial ceremonial, the bride sets nightingales free to fly over the countryside as symbols of *happiness* and *joy*.

NIGHT-RAVEN

From its cries late at night, symbol of *solitude*.

NIKE

In Greek mythology, goddess of victory, symbol of *strength, progress, freedom, triumph, courage*. Represented as a winged woman, carrying a laurel wreath, and bearing palms and a trumpet. She was an attendant of Jupiter, father of all gods, who, it is said, held her in such high repute that he usually held an image of her in his hand.

NILE-GOD

In early Egyptian religion, *bestower of life, fidelity*, and *fertility*.

NIMBUS

A pictured circle of light surrounding the head of distinguished personages, used even in pagan times as a symbol of *power, honor*, and lent itself readily to the suggestion of *spiritual glory*, or *sanctification* when early in Christendom it was used to surround *Christ, His Saints*, or *the Virgin*.

Some authorities make a distinction of employing a square or rectangular nimbus for a living person, and the circular one for the deceased or divine. (See, also, aureole.)

As a representation of the Holy Trinity, there are three radiating rays of light.

NIMROD

Among the Babylonians, a *mighty hunter*. Genesis 10:8-10.

NINE

The number nine, being a multiple of three, is regarded as a sacred number with those persons who see implications of the *Holy Trinity* in any picturing of three like objects.

The nine Worthies, the personages rated in the Middle Ages as most worthy of note, and represented as such in the writings of the day:

Three Gentiles — Hector, Alexander the Great, Julius Caesar.

Three Jews — Joshua, David, Judas Maccabeus.

Three Christians — King Arthur, Charlemagne, Godfrey of Bouillon.

NIOBE

In Greek mythology, daughter of Tantalus and Amphion, has become in literature a personification of *the clouds*. She had great pride in letting the world know about her twelve children, and to punish her, when she derided Leto for having only two, Apollo and Artemis, the two children of Leto, slew all of Niobe's twelve. At her great loss, Niobe's tears turned to ice on the mountain tops, her home, and she became a symbol of *winter*.

NOOSE

Symbol of knowledge, in that learning enables one to get a firm hold on matters of life value, in the same way that a lasso serves in a useful way the needs of the hunter in catching wild animals.

NORNS, THE THREE

In Scandinavian mythology, the three Fates, identity with those of the Greeks:

Urdus represents the *past*.

Skuld, the *future*.

Verdande, the *present*.

NOX

(See Night.)

NUPTE, also NEPTE

Egyptian divinity, mother of Isis and Osiris, called the *mother of the gods*. She presided over births and nursing.

NUTMEG

Emblematic tree of the state of Connecticut.

NUU

Egyptian divinity, god of the *abyss,* called "Father of the mysterious gods," oldest and wisest deity. Pictured either as a normal human being or with head of a frog.

NYMPHS

Minor divinities in classical mythology, represented as beautiful maidens living in the mountains, in the forests, meadows, or waters.

When pictured gathering flowers, they are symbols of *spring*.

Twelve nymphs, hand in hand, are symbols of the *year*.

NYX

In Roman mythology, *mother of day and light*. From legends we learn that she laid her silver egg in the lap of darkness from which hatching came the whole world. She is the goddess of *night*.

OAK

From its physical appearance or its habits of growth, the oak reflects these symbolisms: *strength, might, sturdiness, endurance, durability.* It was a tree sacred to Greek Zeus. The ancient Druids worshiped it as a higher being, and from their veneration, it was absorbed readily into Christian symbolism as *adoration of Christ or the Virgin.* Tradition has it, that the oak was the tree from which the Crucifixion Cross was made, though several trees have that distinction.

In church architecture, the oak leaf of eight lobes is a symbol of *regeneration.*

OANNES

Ancient Babylonian god of *science* and *letters.* Pictured as half man and half fish.

OAR

Punishment, in association with its use as an implement of discipline upon early galley slaves.

OBELISK

When an ancient Egyptian deity stands between two obelisks, the signification is *time, eternity, fertility.*

OBERON

Husband of Titania, who in Ovid is an identity of Diana. In mediaeval folk lore, Oberon is *king of the fairies,* and has become a favorite character for modern artists and poets.

OCEANID

An ocean nymph, in Greek mythology one of the 3000 daughters of Oceanus and Tethys. In myths, she represents *the winds.*

OCEANUS (Also OKEANOS)

In Greek mythology god of the *sea encircling the entire world.* Son of Ouranos and Gaia. His wife, Tethys, his counterpart. Together they were parents of the rivers, brooks, and springs of the earth, and of 3000 divine daughters called Oceanides, and 3000 divine sons.

ODIN

A significant deity in Norse mythology, *the father of saga, god of war, poetry, wisdom*. As sky-god he governed the sunlight, the rainclouds, and the dispensation of darkness. His attributes are two ravens Hunin (thought) and Munin (memory).

ODYSSEUS (See also Ulysses)

One of the Greek chieftans of the Trojan War, famed for his craft, wisdom and eloquence. In literary allusions he stands for *cleverness, versatility, perseverance*.

OEDIPUS

Son of Laius and Jocasta, and legendary king of Thebes. Doomed through an oracle to kill his father, he was given at birth to a herdsman to "expose unto death." His life was spared, however, and he was adopted by the king of Corinth, where he learned through prophecy that he would put his father to death and then marry his own mother. The prophecy was fulfilled. OEdipus is known in story for his having solved the riddle of the Great Sphinx of Thebes which passers-by were challenged to solve; if unsuccessful, their lives were at stake.

OENONE

Beautiful nymph on Mount Ida and wife of Paris until he abandoned her for Helen of Troy. She threw herself upon the burning pyre of Paris, in resentfulness that she had not come to offer remedies for wounds which caused his death.

OIL

As an element of consecration, oil signifies *peace, plenty, health*.

In church sacraments of baptism, confirmation, ordination, and unction it is the symbol of the *Grace of God*. When used in anointing the breast and back of a child in the rite of baptism, an additional meaning is intended, *fortitude, gladness*.

In modern commercial art, oil stands for *property, plenty*.

OLIVE

Tree, branch, and fruit, each has a significance of its own including:

A gnarled olive tree in Christian symbolism signifies the *Passion of Christ, Gethsemane.* Also a denotation of *source* of *spiritual supplies,* in reference to its rich production of fruit and oil.

An olive tree in general symbolism, means *eternity,* from the length of its life.

An olive branch, generally, stands for *peace, concord, healing, faith, wisdom.* Illustration, p. 22:4.

A crown or wreath of olive leaves signify *victory.* With this implication, it was used early as an award in the Olympian games.

A dove with olive branch in its mouth sculptured on olden tombstones indicates that the souls of the departed left this world in the Grace of God.

OLYMPUS

Famous mountain in Thessaly, home of the gods. In poetry, the significance is *high point of inspiration.*

OMER

The Hebrew cup of *manna,* or *sacrificial blood.*

ONION

From Egypt comes the symbolism, *unfolding, primal cause,* seemingly from the layer arrangement of the skin tissues of the bulb.

ONYX

Gem of *dignity, dominion, authority.* In old England said to be the talisman of *victory* over one's enemy. Set in a ring or other piece of jewelry, the symbolism is sincerity.

It is the birthstone for August.

OPAL

Gem of *hope* and *happiness,* but in early times considered to be unlucky, and still a prejudice with some people.

OPEN BIBLE

See Bible. Illustration, p. 16:3.

OR (GOLD)

Symbol of *honor, glory, loyalty.*

ORANGE

For the color, the symbolism is *strength, endurance, joy, benevolence,* a reflection of the symbolisms for red and for yellow.

The orange tree is a symbol of *useful beauty, generosity;* the fruit, *celestial food, wisdom,* from its similarity in color to the golden apple of Hesperides, of classical mythology.

In China, the presentation of ripe oranges on New Year's Day extends the wish that the recipient may enjoy *happiness* throughout the year.

The orange was believed to have originated in southeast Asia, where it soon became a part of legend and folk lore. One legend of the Temple says it came from the garden of an ancient Chinese temple of love, and granted *fertility* to childless couples who ate it there.

The orange blossom symbolizes *purity, chastity, conjugal* love; hence it has become a popular nuptial flower, sometimes referred to as the *Virgin's flower.*

In art, an orange tree is sometimes depicted instead of an apple or fig tree in scenes showing the fall of man. When found in scenes of Paradise, it alludes to the fall of man and his *redemption.*

ORANTE

In ancient Greek art, a female figure with arms extended upward in the attitude of prayer. It has a history dating back from the catacombs into its more modern use on church frescoes and on sarcophagi.

The symbolic meaning is the *Kingdom of God,* the *Church,* or, *Communion of Saints.*

ORB

An orb signifies the *world.* In Christian symbolism, *Christian extension over the world.* When an orb is surmounted by a cross or crown, held in the left hand of a monarch, *power.*

ORCHID

Because of its soft lines and delicate hues, an orchid signifies *modesty, purity, humility, feminine charm.* The larger species stand for *true nobility.* Illustration, p. 22:2.

The cattelaya orchid is the emblematic flower of Brazil; the lycaste variety, of Guatemala; and the dove, or Holy Ghost orchid of Panama.

ORGAN

When pictured as a church instrument, the symbolism is *holiness*.

ORIOLE

Since 1947 the emblematic bird of Maryland, named for Lord Baltimore whose colors were black and gold, the striking combination of colors of the oriole.

ORMAZD

In ancient Zorastrianism the supreme deity, *creator of the world, guardian of mankind, and principle of good.* He created man to help him fight against the hosts of evil.

ORPHEUS

In Greek mythology, a Thracian poet and musician, widely known in the literatures of all time and all countries for his ability to charm, even Pluto, in the Orpheus-Eurifice episode. Variously used as a personification of *winds*, of *morning*, and the *sun*.

An early Christian symbol of *Christ* who had power to tame the deep passions of sinful man.

OSIRIS

Great deity of early Egyptian religion, god of the *underworld, judge of the dead.* He is identified with the *sun or sunlight,* or the *vivifying powers in nature,* the brother and husband of Isis, goddess of motherhood and fertility. Pictured of human form with headdress composed of the white crown of upper Egypt, the horns of a bull, and feathers. Sometimes goes by the name of Serapis. Illustration, p. 7:4.

OSTRICH

Symbol of shamefacedness, from habit of hiding its face in the sand. Illustration, p. 18:9.

OTUS

Gigantic son of Neptune, having special power to rule over *winds* and *hurricanes.*

OURANIA

Known as the *heavenly one* among the nine Muses, daughters of Zeus and Mnemosyne. She presided over the *astronomical epic,* and in art is pictured with a globe and a crown of stars.

OWL

Since an owl can see in the darkness, ancient Greeks adopted the bird as a symbol of *learning* or *wisdom,* accomplishments that penetrate obscurity. In later times these two significations have been expanded to include *sagacity, diligence,* and *meditation.*

A horned owl festooned with flowers, a rare religious symbol denotes *death in life.*

In Chinese art, an owl may signify *longevity, fidelity, happiness.*

In Japan, *filial ingratitude.*

The chariot of Pallas Athene was drawn by an owl. Illustration p. 18:1.

OX

Because of his physical make-up, the ox denotes *strength, endurance, labor.* In that an ox was a common animal to be burned on the altar he signifies *sacrifice.* A winged ox becomes the emblem of Saint Luke because in his gospel we have a lengthy description of the sacrificial death of Christ. Illustration p. 10:10.

An ox without wings sometimes represents *Christ, the supreme sacrifice.*

A lion-headed ox represents *earthly power, abundance.*

Yoked oxen, attached to a wain serve as a modern symbol of *agriculture.*

When hitched to a prairie schooner, *emigration.*

An ox-goad in religious symbolism stands for *promptings of the conscience* with reference to Acts 9:5.

OYSTER

In association with the secluded life of an oyster within its shell, it has become the symbol of *silence, stupidity.*

PADLOCK

In picture language a padlock signifies *security, silence.*

PALETTE

A palette with brush and maulstick is the emblem of *artists.*

PALL

A cloth covering for a coffin, usually black or violet, used instead of the customary wreath, signifies that in *death all are equal in the sight of God.*

PALLADIUM

In Greek mythology a palladium refers to an image of Pallas Athene which was supposed to have fallen from heaven. Then the term was used for any statue of the Greek goddess, and more especially to the one in which the safety of Troy was involved, until the symbolic interpretation now for palladium is *protection, safety.*

PALLAS ATHENE

In Greek mythology, daughter of Zeus and Metis. Goddess of *wisdom* and the *finer arts of war.* Patroness of the *domestic arts* and *crafts.* Pictured wearing a helmet of fantastic design, accompanied by one or more of her attributes — an owl, a snake, a horse, or a griffin. Pictured p. 7:2, with owl as attribute.

PALM

The palm tree, leaf, or branch, all offer numerous possibilities for symbolisms, among which are:

With ancient Romans and Greeks when given as a prize or mark of distinction to the winner of a contest of strength or skill, a palm branch meant *victory, honor, triumph, dignity.*

The leaf and branches were regarded as sacred among the early Jews, and when carried by them the signification was *triumphant rejoicing.* Illustration, p. 22:3.

In Christendom, the palm branch reflects two contrasting symbolisms; one, *martyrdom,* in reference to those who gave up their lives for their faith. In early gravestone markings, the palm branch is still to be seen, signifying *martyrs to the cause of Christ,* or *joys of Paradise.*

Secondly, and more generally, the symbol of a branch stands for *joy, triumph,* in reference to the triumphal entry of Christ into Jerusalem in Matthew 21:8. Further meanings of *justice, righteousness* are also suggested.

PALMER'S STAFF
Symbol of *pilgrimage.* Illustration, p. 15:11.

PALMETTO
State emblematic tree of South Carolina, adopted in 1939.

PALO VERDE
State tree of Arizona since 1949.

PAN
Greek *divinity of nature,* more particularly, god of *flocks and pastures, forests* and their wild life, the *hills,* the *weather and mirage.* Patron of hunters and shepherds.

In early art, shown as man with legs and thighs of a goat, and with furry ears, but later with the pointed ears of a faun, and with less evidence of his bestial characteristics.

Pan with his shepherd's pipe is a symbol for *music.*

PANDORA
In Greek mythology, symbol of *hope,* a woman created in heaven and sent to earth by Zeus to bring misery to man as a revenge, and a punishment of Prometheus for having stolen fire from heaven for the benefit of mankind.

From a box given to her by Zeus (Pandora's Box) all human beings, except Hope, escaped, as some authorities tell us.

PANSY
Symbol of *remembrance, thought, meditation, circumspection.* In church symbolism, the Holy Trinity, from the three large petals of the flower. Illustration, p. 20:7.

PANTALOON

Nickname for Saint Pantaleon. With Pierrot, as harlequins, the two depict a *carnival spirit*. In literature they frequently denote *disillusionment, old age*.

PANTHER

As an attribute of the god Bacchus, symbol of *evil, luxury, dissipation*.

PANURGIO

As one of the nine spirits of intelligence, in Zoroaster's Oracle, the symbol of *wit* and *vitality*.

PAPYRUS

One of emblems of the *printing industry* in association with the material from which paper was first made the papyrus of Egypt.

PARCAE

In Roman religion, the three fates. (See Moira.)

PARIS

Son of Priam and Hecuba, personification of the *sun* in the sun-myths. Seducer of Helen the beautiful, indirectly the cause of the Trojan War. Pictured as a youth wearing a phrygian cap presenting an apple to Aphrodite, goddess of love and beauty, who was judged by Paris to be more beautiful than Hera or Pallas Athene.

PARNASSUS

In Greek mythology, famous mountain in Phocis, sacred to Apollo and the Muses. In literature stands for a collection of literary works of *mountain-high excellence*.

PARROT

Symbol of *prophecy*, their ability to mimic leads them to carry the sounds of the present on to the language of the future.

PARSLEY

Aromatic garden herb of the carrot family, signifies *victory*, from its use in the crowns of the victorious athletes in the early Nemean Games.

PARTRIDGE

The bird has symbolisms of contrasting implications when used in Christian depictions. On one hand the *Church* and *truth;* on the other, *deceit* and *theft,* in reference to Jeremiah 17:11.

PASHT — (Same as BAST)

In early Egyptian religion, the *cat goddess,* of human form, but with head of a lioness, wearing the sun-disc and uraeus.

PASIPHAE

In Greek mythology, wife of Minos. She became enamored of a large white bull belonging to Minos, and gave birth to the minotaur, fabulous beast which ruthlessly devoured the youths of Athens.

PASQUE FLOWER

Also known as wild crocus, state flower of South Dakota since 1903. Also province flower of Manitoba since 1906.

PASSION FLOWER

Early state flower of Tennessee, but the iris was given official adoption in 1933.

The flower is symbol of *Christ's suffering, His Passion.* The central column is representative of the *scourging;* the ovary, the *hammer* used in driving the nails; the five stamens, the *five wounds;* the ten petals, the *ten apostles* who fled from the Crucifixion scene. Close observers also point out in the markings of the flower, the cross, the crown, the nails, and the cords that bound Christ to the column. Illustration, p. 20:11.

PASSOVER

Annual sacrificial feast of Jewish religion, symbolizing the *special grace,* as well as the *special burden* of Holy service, given by the Lord to Israel. It is commemorative of the sparing of the Hebrews in Egypt when God smote the first born. Exodus Chapter XII.

SAINT PATRICK

The apostle of Christianity to the Irish people in the fifth century. Patron saint of Ireland, represented in art as a bishop with serpents at his feet or holding a shamrock. A small fire burns before him. His special day, March 17.

PATROCHUS

In literature, he is often personified as a *feeble reflection of the sun's splendor,* in reference to the characterization of him as a friend of Achilles. Fighting in the guise of Achilles, he was slain by Hector.

SAINT PAUL, THE APOSTLE

Patron of *missionaries* and *ropemakers.* His attributes are a sword, weapon with which he presumably was slain, and a scroll of the Epistles which he wrote.

Known in New Testament narrative as Saul of Tarsus whose conversion to Christianity was attended by a great vision, impelling him to take up the life of a missionary. Spoken of as the greatest missionary among the apostles, having made three extensive journeys throughout Greece and Asia Minor. His special day, June 29.

PAVEMENT

In church architecture symbolizes the *foundation of faith,* and the *humility of the lowly,* or poor.

PEACH

As a symbol of *longevity* has come to us from early China where the tree was an attribute of Shon Hsing, the Taoist god of long life.

The fruit, also, in China denotes *long life,* or *immortality.*

In Christian symbolism, the fruit symbolizes the *fruit of salvation,* and with this denotation, a peach sometimes takes the place of the apple in pictures of the Madonna and Child.

The blossoms in U.S.A. signify *congeniality, domesticity, purity of heart, and prosperity.*

The peach blossom by common consent became the flower of Delaware, through the wide cultivation of the fruit in that state.

PEACOCK

The best known symbolisms of the peacock are *ostentation, pride, vanity, magnificence* and *majesty* from the natural characteristics of the fowl, his flaunting tail, and strutting display of feathers. Illustration, p. 11:9.

From Greek mythology, comes the denotation of *omniscience* in connection with the story of Argus, the hundred-eyed monster which was set to watch over Io, maiden beloved of Zeus, whom Hera, through jealousy had changed into a heifer. After the death of Argus, Juno placed his eyes in the tail of the peacock.

In the catacombs of Soteris, there is a beautifully colored peacock, in gold, blue, and green which Christians have taken to symbolize *heavenly glory* or *immortality*, and later as the symbol of the *resurrection*. When the fowl molts, he grows new feathers, seemingly more beautiful than those he lost, from which renewed beauty has grown the implication of the *beauty of the soul bestowed by baptism;* hence he symbolizes the *many graces baptism bestows.*

One further symbol of Christendom, *incorruptibility,* stems from a belief that a peacock's flesh will not decompose within a year. Also to be found in Christian symbolism is the significance of the eyes in the tail feathers, as the *all-seeing church.*

In Christian art, a peacock is widely used in stained windows, and as an altar and baptismal font imprint.

PEAR

Stemming from China, the symbol of a pear tree with the meaning *benevolent justice* has evolved from the traditional story that Lord Shao dispensed justice under a pear tree. Likewise from China comes the symbolism of a pear blossom, *delicate feminine beauty, purity.* Frequently appears with this denotation in Christian art, with the signification of the *Incarnate Christ,* an allusion to His purity, and His love for mankind.

PEARL

Birthstone for the month of June, with the general meaning of *purity, innocence, humility, rare value, self-sacrifice, health, long life.*

In church symbolism the denotation is *salvation,* Matthew 13:15; and *word of God,* Matthew 7:6.

From China come the implications *perfection, wisdom, riches.*

In Greek mythology, a crown of pearls was an emblem for personages connected with *hymns* or *pantomime,* presided over by the Muse, Polymnia.

194

PEAS

From Japan comes the symbolism *strength, health,* or *good luck* from the characteristics of the garden variety black-eyed peas. In Southern U.S.A. a New Year's *good luck* viand.

PECAN

Emblematic tree of the state of Texas since 1919. The significance is that of *stateliness,* in reference to the natural growth of the tree.

PEGASUS

In Greek mythology, a winged horse which sprang from drops of blood issued from the head of Medusa. With a blow of his hoof he caused Hippocrene (fabulous fountain on Mount Helicon) to spring forth. He was then given into the care of the Nine Muses, nymphs who preside over prophecy and song. From these episodes, Pegasus has become the symbolic representation of *poesy,* and *imagination.* Illustration, p. 8:9.

PELICAN

In Christian symbolism, a pelican may serve as a representation of *benevolence, charity, redemption through the blood of Christ, piety, sacrifice,* or *atonement.* It was an early belief that the pelican pierced her breast, that her young might get sustainment from the blood of her body. This act has long since been disproved, yet the symbolic interpretation of *sacrifice* still remains. The pelican mother opens her bill for the young to reach into her mouth to get at the supply of food accumulated in the large pouch beneath the lower half of her beak.

The pelican is widely used as a symbolic representation on church altars, in decorative Christian literature, and even (though rarely) nesting atop a cross. P. 11:7.

In general symbolism, the fowl may stand for *filial ingratitude, parental self-sacrifice.*

It is the state bird of Louisiana.

PELOPS

In Greek mythology, son of Tantalus, (wealthy king, son of Zeus). His father served him up to the gods for food, but the gods restored him back to life. Demeter, goddess of agriculture, gave him an ivory shoulder in the place of the one she had eaten. Pelops in literature sometimes suggests *withered fruits,* in reference to the punishment placed upon his father, Tantalus, for having attempted to destroy his son. In the lower regions, Tantalus was caused to suffer for want of food and drink, with tantalizing fruit and drink placed just outside his reach.

PEN

A pen symbolizes *literature, authorship.*

A pen and scroll, *poetry.*

A pen with inkwell, or inkhorn and blotter, *eminence in literature.*

PENDULUM

Symbol of *time.*

PENELOPE

In classical mythology, wife of Odysseus, who learned that during his long absences from home, Penelope was receiving implorations of love from many different suitors. She postponed her decision to accept one of the offers until she had finished weaving a funeral pall for her husband's father, Laertes. To lengthen the procedure, every night she unraveled what she had woven during the day, until Odysseus, returning ended the amorous implorations of the suitors by killing the most ardent lover.

In literature, Penelope stands for the *weaver of bright evening clouds.*

PENTAGON

A pentagonal star is the symbol of *heavenly wisdom, guidance.*

PEONY

The symbolisms, *regal power, affluence, prosperity, stability* reflect the natural characteristics of the flower, these meanings having reached us through Oriental influence. Illustration, p. 20:10.

PERIDOT

Symbol of *happiness,* especially *conjugal happiness.* According to some authorities, with the sardonix, the August birthstone, though significations vary in different regional areas.

PERIWINKLE

As for most trailing plants, *affection.*

PERSEPHONE

In Greek mythology, goddess of *vegetation,* especially of *flowers.* In literature, frequently a personification of *young, blooming life.* In myths, she appeared in the light of the upper world; in autumn, she disappeared, while in the winter, she dwelled in the underworld, as do seeds at rest.

PERSEUS

In literature, personification of the *early morning sun.* In Greek mythology, golden-haired son of Zeus and Danae, who like other solar heroes was cast adrift at birth. In early manhood he travels through the land of the mists, and conquers Medusa, whose head he presents to Athene.

PERSIMMON

The fruit of the persimmon tree is a symbol of *wisdom,* drawn from certain likenesses to the golden apples of Hesperides.

SAINT PETER, THE APOSTLE

Sometimes referred to as the *impetuous apostle.* Has many attributes, referring to various episodes in his religious experiences. When seen with keys, the reference is to Matthew 16:15-20; when the fish is seen, the denotation is *Peter the fisher of men,* suggesting the facts that he was a fisherman before he became a disciple of Christ, and that afterwards he became searcher of the souls of men, having served twenty-five years as a mission preacher; when pictured with a cock, the reference is to his denial of Christ. Persecuted for his strong Christian stand, he was in the end crucified, head downward. His special day, August 1. Illustration of crossed keys, p. 10:7.

PHAEDRA

In Greek myths, character of many tragedies, variously depicted by Euripides, Seneca, and Racine. She was the daughter of Minos, and wife of Theseus. Said to have ended her life by hanging, as an act of remorse when she relented having deceived Theseus.

197

PHAETHON

In Greek mythology, son of the sun god, Helios. He was allowed for one day to guide the chariot of the sun, and so reckless was he that he would have set the whole world afire had not Zeus with a thunderbolt killed him as he approached the Po river.

PHALLUS

Symbol of *fertility, life,* and *regeneration.* In rites of ancient Egypt and India, maidens danced around the phallus, as an assurance against sterility. A representation of the phallus is still observable in some shrines of Thailand where women, unable to produce children, perform rites which are held to cure sterility. The phallus also served as an object of renewal of the fertility of the earth. In ancient times man was skeptical as to whether each year there would be a renewal of life in nature after the long months of cold winters. Whereupon he planned a spring festival, with dance around a phallus, to encourage bountiful soil production. It is said our modern Maypole ceremony comes from this early festival custom.

PHEASANT

The ring-necked pheasant is the emblematic fowl of South Dakota.

From early China come these symbolisms: *happiness, beauty, good fortune, long life, happy home life.*

PHILOMELA

In Greek mythology, a young maiden of noble birth, who, according to Ovid was turned into a *nightingale* as a protection against the pursuit of her sister's husband who had in an earlier tragedy silenced Philomela by cutting out her tongue. In poetical allusion, she is a *nightingale.*

SAINT PHILIP, THE APOSTLE

Patron saint of *hatters* and of *pastry cooks.* His special day, May 1. His chief attribute is a dragon, in remembrance of a miracle he performed at Hierapolis, Scythia, where, when he found the people worshipping a serpent, aided by the cross, he caused the serpent to disappear. There was left, however, an unbearable stench which caused the death of the king's son. Again, with the help of the cross, Saint Philip's great power was brought into use, and he restored the life of the son. This act enraged the more the priests of the serpent when their god was overthrown, that they put the saint to death. Usually in art, Philip is represented bearing a Latin cross fastened to the top of a staff or reed.

PHOBOS

Divinity of the state of the mind, that of *fear*. One of the attendants of Mars, said by some, to be son and brother of Deimos, divinity of *panic*.

SAINT PHOCAS

Patron saint of *gardens* and of *gardeners*. His special day, July 3. His attribute, a layman holding a shovel or of one working among the garden plants.

PHOEBE

(See Diana).

PHOEBUS

In Roman mythology, god of the *sun*, and of *medicine*. In literary allusion, he represents the *sun* personified.

PHOENIX

A mythical bird, which from an early Arabian story, at death bursts into flames, only to appear again after a great length of time, again to begin a cycle of death and rejuvenation. We are told that the phoenix, having somewhat the appearance of an eagle, after having lived from three to five hundred years, gathered for its nest twigs of aromatic plants or branches from an ash tree. Then both bird and nest were consumed by the heat of the sun. Out of the ashes another bird came forth, recreated for another cycle of time, and so on throughout endless ages the process of death and rejuvenation continues, with symbolic implications of *immortality, resurrection*.

The phoenix became an early symbol of *resurrection, immortality*, among Christians of Rome, and representations of the bird were found in the catacombs, with those denotations, and is still a favorite decorative design in symbolic Church decorative art. Illustration, p. 9:2.

PHORMINX

Ancient Greek musical instrument, similar to a modern lyre, symbol of *music*, or *concert*, a representation widely used as a decorative design on concert programs.

PIANO

In commercial art, symbol of music, especially *classical music*.

PICK

In modern picture language a pick and shovel are emblematic of the *mining industry*.

PIERROT, (See Pantaloon)

Feminine mate of the harlequin Pierrot. Together they depict a *carnival spirit*. In old French pantomime, Pierrot was a jester dressed in pure white with white skullcap as a personification of *man in a state of innocence;* with a black skullcap, *man after the fall*.

PIG

From natural habits of the animal, *gluttony*.

PIGEON

(See, also, dove)
When represented with envelope in its beak, the pigeon is a symbol of communication.

PILLAR

In church architecture, one massive pillar signifies *Christ's Passion;* two stand for *strength and beauty;* four, for *stability*. (See *columns*.)

PINCERS

One of the thirteen symbols of the Crucifixion referring to the act of lowering Christ's body from the cross. Illustration, p. 13:11.

PINE

The pine tree is the object of many symbolisms, among them:
> The tree itself signifies *immortality, strength, hardihood, wisdom gained through experience*.
> In Japan, both red and black pine trees denote *endurance, con-*

stancy. The branches, pairs of growing needles, used as wedding pieces, express a wish for a *life of harmony*, and that *one will not long survive the other*.

In the early Isthmic games pine twigs and wreaths were symbols of *victory*.

In the U.S.A. pine branches have become a popular Christmas festivity decoration, with the meaning of *good will*.

The white pine tree, with its cone and tassel, is emblematic of Maine. Adopted in 1925.

PINK

The color, from a combination of the symbolisms for red and white, is symbolic of *romance, charm, sweetness*.

Pink is the emblematic color for an infant girl.

The garden flower, pink, is one of the Virgin's flowers, with the denotation of *humility*.

There is an ancient Flemish marriage custom, where, on the wedding day, the bride conceals a pink somewhere upon her garments, and the groom must make a playful search for it. The symbolism here is *love, affection*.

PINON

A species of pine, the state tree of New Mexico.

PIPE

The pipe of Pan (syrinx) is a symbol of *music, alluring melody*. The peace pipe of the American Indians, a *promise, oath*.

PITCH

A tarlike substance symbolic of *evil* from its color and tenacious clinging quality.

PITCHER

In Biblical picture language a pitcher above a basin signifies Pilate's washing of hands to declare his belief in the innocence of Christ.

PLANE TREE

Symbol of *firmness of character, moral superiority*, from the manner of the tree to spread its branches high and wide. In church symbolism, specifically the *charity of Christ*.

PLANTAIN

In Biblical symbolism, the *path of Christ,* spoken of as *"the way bread."* Plantain is a short-stemmed grass, commonly seen along the roadside in Palestine.

PLATTER

(See dish.)

PLEIADES

In Greek mythology, the seven daughters of Atlas — Alcyone, Celaeno, Electra, Mais, Merope, Asterope, and Taygeta. Only six of them are to be seen in the constellation Tauris, because Merope concealed herself for having fallen in love with a mortal. Her sisters, pursued by Orion were changed into the stars seen in Tauris.

PLOW

In early Roman mythology, the plow was considered to be the symbol of the silver age of the world, with Jupiter the ruler. In modern symbolism, the emblem for *agriculture, pioneer service.*

In Biblical symbolism, *spiritual labor.* Luke 9:62.

PLUM

With the plum, there are these symbolisms:

The fruit signifies *fidelity, independence, virtue, tender sorrow, sweetness.*

The tree, from Chinese symbolism denotes *good fortune, success, longevity.* Also *hardiness, courage,* from the fact that the tree sends forth blossoms before the leaves appear.

White blossoms, generally, are symbols of *purity of character,* and the emblem of the *spirit of womanhood.* A snarled blossoming branch is indicative of *vitality in old age.*

A withered plum symbolizes *bastardy.*

PLUTO

In classical mythology, god of the infernal regions. Shown as the *bestower of plenty,* with a horn of plenty in his hand, and an eagle perched on his scepter or head. He has a heavy mass of hair which usually falls over his eyes. (See, also, Hades.)

POINSETTIA

Called by some the *Christmas rose*. Widely used as a Christmas flower, with the signification *Christmas joy, good will*. In Christian symbolism, our *Lord's Nativity*. Illustration, p. 22:7.

In Mexico, called the flower of the *Holy Night*, stemming from a folktale of a poor girl, who, having no present to lay at the foot of the Virgin on Christmas Eve, gathered an armful of poinsettia twigs, in which, following her prayer, the upper leaves turned red.

POISON

A cup with poison label signifies *execution*.

POLE

A barber pole striped with red and white, serves as an emblem for *barbers* in wide areas of the world. This symbol has been handed down from the Mediaeval Ages, when the barber was also the surgeon who "let blood."

POLYMNIA

In Greek mythology, one of the nine muses, daughter of Zeus and Mnemosyne. She presided over *religious hymns* and *pantomime*. Her attribute is a crown of pearls.

POLYPHEMES

In Homer's Odyssey, symbol of *remorse, punishment*. He was the one-eyed giant who imprisoned Ulysses, and devoured two of his companions each day until Odysseus made him drunk and they put out his one eye with a heated club. Usually pictured chained to a rock, a vulture attacking him.

POMEGRANATE

The pomegranate has provided us with a wide area of symbolisms, among which are:

In classical mythology associated with Proserpina, symbol of a *new life*, from her recurrent return to the earth each spring from her home in the underworld.

In older days when it was used to adorn the robe of the Jewish High Priest, the significance was *respect for authority, piety*. Illustration, p. 20:5.

In Christian symbolism, a bursting pomegranate denotes, *resurrection of the Lord,* and also of *His faithful followers.* It signifies the hope of a new life because it is split by the pressure of many seeds, suggesting the power to reproduce life, *fecundity.* In much use as ornamental design in church architecture, or coverings of altar or lectern. In general symbolism, a pomegranate signifies *brotherhood, fraternity, future success.*

POMONA

In Roman mythology, goddess of *horticulture, orchards,* and *gardens,* wife of Vertumnus, god of the changing season. She is represented as a youthful matron in short tunic and cloak, bearing a pruning hook and basket of fruit.

POND LILY

Symbol of *companionship, companionability,* from natural growth habits of the plant.

POPLAR

The Lombardy poplar tree is a symbol of *aspiration,* from its high upward growth.

Poplar leaves are pictured in the crown of Hercules, indicative of *strength, ambition.*

POPPY

Among the symbolisms of the poppy are:

From its narcotic properties, *oblivion, death, forgetfulness, enchantment, sleep, rest, sloth,* and even *witchcraft.*

From its profusion of small seeds, *fertility.*

In Christian symbolism sometimes alludes to *Christ's Passion* from its bold-red color, and its significance as to *death.* The golden poppy since 1903 has been adopted as the emblematic flower of California.

PORTCULLIS

In architecture, *defense, protection, security,* from the purpose this iron grating serves in buildings where security is an objective.

POSEIDON

In Greek mythology, god of the *sea, large inland waters,* and of *horses and horsemanship.* (See Neptune.) Illustration of Poseidon and his chief attribute, a *dolphin,* p. 7:1.

POTATOES

Humorously spoken of as the symbol of Ireland. In general symbolism, *tranquility* from the belief that potatoes have a distinct tendency to calm the nerves.

POTHOS

In classical mythology, god of *peace* and *friendship.* One of the many attendants of Venus.

POTTERY

Pieces of broken pottery symbolize, *precious things of the past.*

PRAIRIE ROSE

Emblematic flower of the state of North Dakota.

PRIAM

In Greek mythology, last king of Troy, father of Hector and Paris. Slain in the sacking of Troy.

PRIAPUS

In classical mythology, rural deity of *horticulture, shade, vineyard-growing, procreative power.*

PRIMROSE

As a flower of early spring, signifies *youth, gaeity, dalliance.*

PRINCE'S FEATHERS

Like the amaranth, of which it is a species, *immortality.*

PRINTING PRESS

In commercial art, symbol of *communication,* the *art* of *printing.* When a human figure is seated at a press, with lithographic sheet in hand, *lithography.* Illustration, p. 19:4.

PROMETHEUS

In early Greek religion regarded as the *founder of civilization* and *benefactor of mankind*. In literary allusion, he has become a symbol of *prophecy, magnanimous endurance of unmerited suffering*, and of *strength of will to resist oppression*. He stole fire from heaven to bring down to earth as a benefit to mankind. For this act he was chained to a rock on Mount Caucasus where a vulture daily fed upon his liver, yet which organ each night grew again to normalcy. Hercules slays the vulture and Prometheus is released.

PROSERPINA

(See Diana.)

PROTEA

National flower of South Africa.

PROTEUS

In Greek mythology, prophetic sea god in the services of his father Poseidon. In literary allusion he characterizes one who *easily changes his mind*, from the fact that Proteus, when attacked in his sea exploits, had the power to assume different shapes, thereby deceiving his opponents.

PRTHIVI

Early Hindu earth goddess, pictured in the form of a variegated cow yielding both milk and honey; hence suggestive of *abundance, resourcefulness*.

PSYCHE

Emblem of the *soul*, the *mind*. In classical mythology a beautiful princess of whom Venus became very jealous. When Cupid, the son of Venus fell in love with Psyche, his mother impended many hardships upon the two, but in the end they were united and became immortal.

PSYKELIA

In Zoroaster's *Oracle*, as one of the nine spirits of intelligence, stands for *good fortune, success*.

PSYKOMENA

In Zoroaster's *Oracle* as one of the nine spirits of intelligence represents *folly* and *ridicule*.

PTAH

In early Egyptian religion, the first of the seven great gods; hence regarded as the *father of beginnings of the world.* Spoken of as the opener, creator of the egg, of the sun and the moon. He is patron of *artificers.*

He appears as a mummy, shaped as a male or as a pigmy god, symbol of *creation* and *resurrection.*

PTARMIGAN

Together with the Steller's jay, is the emblematic bird of Alaska.

PULPIT

In Christian symbolism, symbol of *Christian instruction, the preaching of God's word, the primacy of the word of God.*

PUMPKIN

When represented in autumn scenes, symbol of *harvest.* In wide use as a Thanksgiving Day, or Halloween festival decoration.

PURPLE

In Old Testament symbolism, purple was the distinguishing mark of *royalty, dignity, honor, power, glory* or *purification from sin.*

Throughout Christendom, for many churches, purple is the liturgical color during the Lenten season, except for Good Friday.

As a color of *mourning,* not considered as deep as is black.

In fashions, purple is symbolic of *elegance, regality, gentility.*

In church symbolism, deep purple is symbolic of *penitence, suffering, loyalty, love of truth.*

PURSE

Dependent upon the accompanying surroundings, a purse may symbolize *charity, philanthropy,* or, *penury, avarice.*

A purse has become the emblem of *bankers* and *merchants.* It is one of the attributes of Saint Matthew, when he is represented as a tax-gatherer.

PYGMALION

In classical mythology a great sculptor, and king of Cyprus. He fell in love with an ivory statue he had made of a maiden, and in answer to his prayers, Aphrodite gave life to the prized figure.

PYRAMID

Symbol of *firmness, strength, stability, lasting qualities,* because of the heavy foundation of the structure.

In Japan, a pyramid stands for *fervor, spiritual power.*

The broken or unfinished pyramid on the back side of the U.S.A. dollar bill represents *building for the future with strength and assurance.*

PYRAMUS

Pyramus and Thisbe, legendary lovers of ancient Babylon, whose secret courtship formed the basic plot for Shakespeare's *Midsummer Night's Dream.* According to Ovid, Pyramus, finding a veil smeared with blood, and recognizing it as a part of Thisbe's garment, drew a swift conclusion that she had been killed by a wild animal. He took his life, and when Thisbe returned to their accustomed meeting place, finding Pyramus dead, killed herself beside her lover.

On many tombs in ancient European cemeteries, the figures of Pyramus and Thisbe have been sculptured as a touching symbol of *perfect love.*

PYTHEUS

Surname given to Apollo, as *python slayer.*

PYTHON

In literary allusion implies a *demon* or *soothsayer,* from a monstrous serpent in Greek legend which arose from the mud left by the deluge. The serpent was known to deliver prophecies in Delphi, and was eventually slain by Apollo.

Q

QEB (SEB)

In early Egyptian religion, the *earth god,* father of *all gods* and deity of *vegetation.* Pictured as a human being with a goose on his head, or, as resting on his side with plants springing from his body.

QUAIL

From Biblical references symbolizes *food sent from heaven.* Exodus 16:12, 13.

Since 1931, emblematic bird of California.

QUATREFOILS

In church architecture there are many designs of four parts with implications of the four *Evangelists — Matthew, Mark, Luke* and *John.* There may be groupings of four scrolls, four open books, four streams of water issuing from a rock, or perhaps a four-leaved clover. The general symbolism of a quatrefoil when applied to a deity is *perfection.*

QUEEN

A queen, symbolically, means *royalty.* The three queens of Arthurian legend represent *good thought, good word, good deed.*

QUILL

A goose quill shaped to a nib symbolizes *literature.*

QUINCE

In ancient Greece, a quince was a symbol of *fertility,* and the fruit was always among the foods at wedding feasts.

In modern floral symbolism, a spring of quince blossom added to the bridal flowers signifies *good luck.*

The quince is often thought of as the *fruit of redemption,* and legend has it that the tree of knowledge of good and evil was a quince tree.

RA

Egyptian deity identified with the Greek god of the *sun*, Helios. He is represented as a human being with the head of a hawk.

RABBIT

(See also, hare, bunny)

Symbol of *resourcefulness*. A common decorative design for Easter festivities.

RAIN

In church symbolism, signifies *impartial goodness of God*, or *heavenly blessing*. Hebrew 6:7.

RAINBOW

In general, symbolism expresses *hope, protection, covenant, good luck.*

Biblical denotations are, *God's mercy and faithfulness, pledge of promise,* in reference to Genesis 9:16.

RAKE

A rake in Bunyan's *Pilgrim's Progress* stands for *avarice.* A hayrake in industrial pictures denotes *thrift.*

RAM

A ram in ancient Egyptian and Roman religions was a symbol of *fertility, procreation.*

In general symbolism, stemming from the ram as being leader of the flock, the symbolism is *guidance, spiritual leadership, creative powers.*

The ram's horn or shofar in Hebrew practices serves as a means of calling the congregation to *atonement;* it is also a proclamation of *liberty.*

RAN

In Teutonic mythology, wife of Aegis, god of the sea. She draws drowning men to their death in the bottom of the deep.

SAINT RAPHAEL, ARCHANGEL

Guardian of *travelers*, patron of *apothecaries*. Special day, October 24. Attribute, a jar of ointment, or a fish or fish's gall attached to a staff.

RASPBERRY

Symbol of *kindly feelings, gentle heartedness*, from the juice of the fruit which is of the color of blood which flows from the heart.

RAT

Symbol of *enmity, major troubles, evil*, because of the destructiveness of the small rodent.

RATTLESNAKE

Symbol of *virulence, malignity*. When coiled and with the motto "Noli me tangere" signifies *independence*.

RAVANA

Symbol of *lust* in the famous Indian epic of *Ramayana*.

RAVEN

As the bird sacred to Minerva, *wisdom*.

In Jewish legend, the raven, originally white, turned to black when it failed to return to Noah's ark; then from Greek mythology, the bird was turned black when it bore bad news to Apollo.

The black plumage makes the raven a symbol of *evil, bad tidings, disaster, ill-omen, sin*. Illustration, p. 18:6.

A night raven denotes *solitude*.

RECTANGLE

Denotes *opposition*, opposite sides being equal.

RED

The symbolism of this color is dependent somewhat upon the shade, but in general it denotes *courage, strength, vibrancy of life, love, valor, patriotism, creative power, hardiness, royalty, youth*.

In church symbolism it depicts *Christian zeal*, the *work and ministry of the church, fervor*, and also stands for *sin and atonement*. In churches of high ritual, it is the liturgical color for special festivals of the church, for the special days of the apostles, evangelists, and those early Christians who suffered martyrdom. The list includes:

Saint Matthew — an evangelist
Saint Mark — an evangelist
Saint Luke — an evangelist
Saint John — an evangelist
Saint Andrew — an apostle
Saint Bartholomew — an apostle
Saint James, the Elder — an apostle
Saint Thomas — an apostle
Saint Philip and Saint James, Less — apostles
Saint Mathias — an apostle
Saint Simon and Saint Jude — apostles
Saint Stephen — a martyr

Red is also the color for Pentecost, All Saints Day, Thanksgiving Day, Festival of the Harvest, Nativity Day of John the Baptist, and for all church anniversaries and for dedication services.

REDBUD TREE

One specie is called the *Judas tree* in that it is thought Judas hanged himself of this tree.

Official emblematic tree of Oklahoma since 1937.

REED

One of the thirteen symbols of the Crucifixion, in association with the rod used in offering vinegar on a sponge to the three men on the cross. Illustration, p. 13:10.

A reed and hyssop with bowl underneath, used by Jews in a traditional rite, symbolizes *cleansing, purification.*

SAINT REPARATA

Special day, October 8. One of the patron saints of the *City of Florence,* martyred as a Christian at the age of twelve. Represented with a dove flying from her mouth, in that it is said her soul was seen rising to Heaven in the form of a dove.

RHADAMANTHUS

In Greek mythology, son of Zeus and Europa, who after his death became one of the judges in the lower world.

RHEA

Called the *mother of the gods* in that she bore Zeus, Hera, Poseidon, Hades, Demeter and Hestia.

Represented as a matronly figure, crowned and riding in a chariot drawn by lions.

RHINOCEROS

Symbol of all *cultures,* of *art,* in particular. The horn represents *bravery, victory.*

RHODODENDRON (See azalea)

Western rhododendron is emblematic flower of the state of Washington; Eastern variety, since 1903, state flower of West Virginia.

RIBBONS

Waving ribbons denote *pleasure.* The ribbons of the Maypole are representative of the rays of the sun. Ribbons with knots tied at the ends signify *friendly associations, agreement, fraternity.*

When nuptial bouquets have ribbons with knotted ends, *deep love, marriage;* when used on gift packages, *devotion, true friendship, remembrance.*

RICE

An ancient symbol of *fertility* and *productiveness.* When thrown at bridal couples, *good wishes for a life of rich abundance.* Green and growing rice, in the East Indian Islands used in decoration for Christmas festivities has the same symbolism as holly, *good will, eternal life.*

RING

In general, the symbolism of a ring is the same as for any circular object — *perfection, continuity, eternity, unity.*

Wedding rings have a long history. We are told that they became customary, back in caveman days when the rings were made of plaited grass or rushes, and placed around the chosen bride's wrists or ankles, and only much later around her finger. In modern symbolism, an engagement ring signifies, *deep affection, continuing love.* The wedding ring stands for *conjugal loyalty, and love, a covenant and promise, faithfulness throughout life.* Early, a plain band of gold, it merely signified *matrimony.* The Egyptians are believed to have made the first metal finger rings, probably of gold. In the ninth century Christians began using the rings as wedding bands.

A signet ring, used also as a seal, is a sign of *authority,* and in early times served a most valuable purpose as an identification in business transactions, or to show that the wearer was a property owner.

In church symbolism, when the right to wear a special type of ring is earned, the denotation is a *marriage with Christ, chastity.* The pontifical ring is usually one of great beauty, and significations. Called the fisherman's ring in reference to Luke 5:10, the band must be large enough to permit its being slipped on over a glove. It must be broken after the death of the Pope to prevent the sealing of any document during the vacancy of the papal see.

RIVER

A river in art depicts *peace, refreshment.*

In Greek mythology, the River Lethe in Hades stands for *forgetfulness, oblivion.* The River Styx which encircled Hades seven times signified *death.*

ROAD RUNNERS

Also called chaparral of the cuckoo family, since 1949 has been the emblematic bird of New Mexico.

ROBE

A flowing robe covering the whole body is symbol of *righteousness.*

Rich robes and jewels, *worldly pomp and vanities;* a white robe, *innocence.*

With crown and scepter, the robe denotes *royal dignity.*

ROBIN

Symbol of *friendliness,* and with this signification in mind was chosen as emblematic bird of the British Commonwealth. Also the state bird of Connecticut, Michigan, and Wisconsin.

SAINT ROCHE OF MONTPELLIER

Patron saint of those suffering from the plague. While giving aid to plague victims, he, himself became stricken and retired into the woods where his dog daily brought him a loaf of bread. Returning to his native town after a fair recovery, he was unrecognized and thrown into prison as a spy. He died there. His special day is August 16. He is represented in paintings as a pilgrim with cockleshell, wallet and staff, lifting his robe to show a plague spot on his thigh. Usually his dog accompanies him.

ROCK

Symbol of *firmness, stability, primal cause,* a *foundation.*
In Biblical symbolism, *place of safety, firm foundation,* Psalm 18:2.
A rock as the symbol of the *Lord,* Psalm 28:1; as name of *Saint Peter,* Matthew 16:18.

ROD

Thought of in Old Testament symbolism as *authority, instrument* of *chastisement* or *correction,* Job 9:34. Aaron's flowering rod is a symbol of the *tree of life.*

ROLL

Any material in a roll, from Japanese symbolism, *prophecy, wisdom.*

ROPE

Symbol of *bondage, enslavement.* With noose, *threat of hanging.* In Biblical symbolism, emblem of the *betrayal and arrest of Jesus,* John 18:12.

ROSARY

Symbol of *devotion, prayer,* consisting of a certain number of beads, used as a counting device by Buddhists, Mohammedans, and some Christian bodies.

ROSE

Flower of many symbolical meanings, dependent upon the variety, the color, the occasion of use, or the objects which accompany it. As Gertrude Stein has said, "A rose is a rose is a rose." Illustration, p. 21:6.
In Roman mythology, at the marriage of Cupid and Psyche, roses were strewn on the ground before the couple as a symbol *of beauty and sweetness of young love.*

215

In Greek mythology, the roses in the crown of the Muse Erato stood for *loveliness*.

In general symbolism, a rose denotes *regal beauty, love, wisdom, charm, grace, fidelity*.

A wreath of roses, *joy, remembrance*.

A rosebud, *hope*. Illustration, p. 20:8.

A white rose, sometimes denotes *silence;* a red rose, *martyrdom,* or, more frequently, *deep love*.

As a flower of the Virgin, the rose signifies, *divine love, purity, righteousness*. As a nuptial flower, *joy, happiness*.

In church architecture, a conventionalized rose provides an ornamental design for windows, moldings, ends of pews, and church school classrooms, with the implications of *beauty, Messianic hope,* the *Nativity of the Lord, paradise, promise* of *eternal life,* but above all *love* — love of God for man, and love of man for man. Illustration, p. 11:8.

The Christmas rose, or starwort, with touch of pink denotes *heavenly grace, divine love, Christ's nativity*.

A yellow rose, on occasion denotes *jealousy, infidelity*.

The golden rose, gift of the Pope to communities and persons of distinction carries with it a message of *joy,* and *blessing of the church*.

The American Beauty rose, by sanction of the Board of Commissioners, became the emblematic flower of the District of Columbia.

The Cherokee rose is the state flower of Georgia.

The wild rose is emblematic flower of Iowa, New York, and North Dakota.

ROSEMARY

Symbol of *remembrance, healing*. It was in early use in England as a Christmas flower recalling the *Nativity of Christ*.

Rosemary has significances with bridal customs. Entwined in wreaths of bouquets, it denotes *constancy, fidelity*. In early days of England, sprigs of rosemary, sometimes perfumed or gilded, and combined with bay leaves, when carried in a wedding procession, signified *fidelity, a long life of happiness* and *prosperity*.

RUBY

Birthstone for the month of July. Symbol of *deep love, contentment, passion*.

Favorite gem of adornment of royal crowns, symbolizing *power, dignity*.

In Christian symbolism, burning *zeal, ardent love*. Stone of the tribe of Judah.

RUDBECKIA

Commonly known as black-eyed Susan, symbolic flower of Maryland since 1915.

RUE

Symbol of *regret, repentance, mourning, grief,* in association with the bitter taste of the leaves of the herb.

RUINS

When pictured in art, *mortality, destruction,* even *death.*

SACK

A sack showing money, jewels or other objects of value, from Oriental symbolism, signifies *wealth, good fortune, contentment.*

SACKCLOTH

A black drapery fabric indicative of *sorrow, bereavement, mourning.* Often associated with ashes, likewise a symbol of *sorrow.*

SAFE

In commercial art, symbol of *security.*

SAFFLOWER

In India, garlands of safflower, or marigolds, serve as an emblem of *welcome;* also used as a shrine offering, with the meaning of *adoration, devotion.*

SAFFRON

Same symbolism as for crocus, of which family it is a kin. Denotes *charity, illicit love.*

Saffron color in early Greek times was considered a royal color. Streets of Rome were sprinkled with saffron when Nero made his entrance to the city.

SAG

A chimera of early Egypt with the head of a hawk, body of a lioness, and tail ending in a lotus blossom, having powers as a *generator, preserver,* or *destroyer.* Illustration. p. 9:6.

SAGA

In Norse mythology, wife of Odin, goddess of *history* and *poetry.* She harbored near the streams of time and events, taking notes of all she observed. She is identical with Clio, the Greek muse of history whom Apollo sought beside the inspiring fountain of Helican.

SAGE

Common name for a genus of salvia. Symbol of *longevity, immortality,* from the hardiness of the plant. Held by ancients to have strong healing powers.

SAGEBRUSH

Symbol of *good luck*, from its wealth of yellow flowers suggestive of gold.

The blossom was adopted as the state flower of Nevada in 1917.

SAIL

Symbol of *venture*, and when extended with the wind, *spirit and breath of life*.

SAKE

A rice wine, in Japan signifying *friendliness, good cheer, a hearty welcome*. When provided at wedding ceremonies, the symbolism is *future happiness*.

SALAMANDER

A mythical creature having the power to endure fire or intense heat without harm, which capacity, coupled with its pairing practices, has given rise to the symbolism, *ardent lover*.

SALLAK

In Zoroaster's *Oracle*, the *lucky genius*.

SALMON

Symbol of *knowledge* stemming from the wisdom shown in seeking a spawning area of water.

SALOME

In literary allusion, woman of *wantonness, pleasure*, drawn from the New Testament narrative in Matthew 14:6-12.

SALT

Many symbols and figurative expressions have been derived from the natural qualities of salt.

In general symbolism, *friendliness, wisdom, purity, good counsel*.

In Biblical allusion, *strength, superiority,* from Matthew 5:13.

From early Middle European church rite of cleansing a child's mouth with salt before the baptismal ceremony, the symbolism is *protection against evil, wholesome living.*

SAMARITAN

In Biblical allusion, a *benefactor, one ready and generous in helping beings in distress.*

SAMSON

Distinguished Israelite judge, symbol of *strength,* hero of many early Hebrew folk tales. His attribute, the jawbone of an ass. His story in Judges Chapters XIII-XVI.

SANGUINE

A color symbolizing *sacrifice, patriotism* from a combination of the symbolism of *red* and *blue* the basic colors of the purplish-red tone of sanguine.

SANTA CLAUS

(See Saint Nicholas of Myra.)

SAPPHIRE

Birthstone for September, this gem of rich-blue color is symbol of *hope, heavenly wisdom, heavenly reward, truth, virtue, constancy,* and *contemplation.*

Set into a ring, it is a stone of good omen, with symbolic meaning, *hope.*

The color of the sky, it signifies that while yet on earth, mankind should set its *affection on things above.*

The star sapphire is a Christmas stone, combining the blue with the sentiments of "the moving star of the East."

SARASVATI

Wife of the Hindu, Brahma, goddess of *poetry, fine arts, wisdom, eloquence.* Pictured usually as riding on a peacock.

SARDIUS

Deep orange-red variety of the chalcedomy stone, symbol of *martyrs* who poured forth their blood for the cause of Christ.

SARDONIX

With the peridot, birthstone for August, symbol of *marital or family happiness.*

In Christian symbolism, there are two contrasting meanings, dependent upon the predominating layer of color observable. If the middle is white with red above, the denotation is, *suffering for Christ's sake;* if there is black below the white, the reference is to *those who in their own eyes appear to be deeply sinful.*

SARU

In Japanese zodiac, the *monkey.*

SATI

In early Egyptian religion, goddess of the *lower heaven,* or *air.*

SATURN

Roman identity of Greek Cronus, father of the gods. In his honor, the great annual feast of the Saturnalia was established. Festivities began on December 17, when a general spirit of carnival prevailed. Masters were made to serve the slaves, and by lot a king was chosen to preside over the feast. Some say that the modern idea of gift exchange at Christmas time is an outgrowth of the Saturnalia, as are other winter festivals the world over, such as Mardi Gras.

SATYRS

In Greek mythology, male deities of the woods, half man, half goat, given to *riotous music, dancing* and *revelry.* Sometimes pictured with tail and ears of a horse, pursuing the wood nymphs and striking terror to man.

SAVORY

An European mint, symbol of *stimulation.*

SAW

Implement of *martyrdom*. Attribute of James, the Less apostle.

SCALES

As for balances, symbol of *equity*, Emblem of an *apothecary*. In Biblical symbolism, when scales are out of balance, they signify Christ's *unjust trial under Pontius Pilate; when balanced, justice, equality.* Illustration, p. 15:3.

SCALLOP (See also shell)

A scallop denotes a *pilgrimage;* three scallops, a *long journey.*

A scallop is an attribute of Saint James, the Greater, and when accompanied with a sword, it reflects his beheading.

SCAPEGOAT

Symbol of *imposed responsibility for guilt,* stemming from a practice in Jewish antiquity which, after the sins of the people were placed upon a goat, it was allowed to escape to the wilderness.

SCARAB

Dark-colored beetle, attribute of the Egyptian sun god Chapers, symbolic of *immortality, resurrection,* and often with these significations, it is placed upon their mummies.

In modern times often seen in a conventionalized form, with or without wings, as a gem or ornament with the symbolic meaning of *good fortune, long life, success.*

Behind the signification of the scarab as a symbol of *immortality* or *eternal life,* lies a story beautifully told in Egyptian literature. When the sacred cow eliminates, the beetle digs under the dung from west to east, making a ball from the mixture of soil and dung, then, after coming out of the east with the ball at the rising of the sun, and his returning again to the west at eventide, the movement continues and we get an endless "circle of *eternal life.*" Illustration, p. 17:9.

SCARLET

General symbolism, *courage, zeal, mutual love,* as for all colors allied with basic red. With certain associations, scarlet denotes *lasciviousness,* as for scarlet woman.

SCAPULA

In ecclesiastical vestment, a narrow length of cloth placed over the shoulder and extending to the hem of the garment both in front and in the back. Symbol of the *yoke of Christ*.

SCEPTER

A staff borne by a sovereign as an emblem of *authority, power*. From China has come an additional meaning, *longevity*.

SAINT SCHOLASTICA

Twin sister of Saint Benedict, and the chief female saint of the Benedictine Order. Patroness of *Monte Cassino*, Italy. Her festival day, February 10. Represented holding a lily or crucifix with a dove, either at her feet, pressed to her bosom, or flying toward Heaven.

SCISSORS

Emblem of Kali, evil genius of Hindu myth who held in her right hand, a shears or scissors with which she severed the thread of life; hence symbol of *physical extermination*.

Also symbol of *spiritual decision*, it can cut through error and ignorance, the veil of individual consciousness. (See also shears.)

SCORPION

Dreaded reptile of *torture, rebuke, evil*. Has taken on the symbolism of *beguilement, flattery*, from the action of the scorpion to flatter with its face, while it stings with its tail.

In Christian art often seen on the flags or shields of the soldiers who assisted at the Crucifixion of Christ, with the signification, *treachery*. Later, became an *attribute of Judas*, the betrayer.

SCOURGE

One of the thirteen symbols of the Crucifixion.

Two scourges crossed, in Christian symbolism denote *Christ's Passion*.

When one is held in the hands of a saint, the meaning is *penance, self mortification*. If the lashes are detached from the handle, the signification is *of sins already forgiven*. Illustration, p. 13:3.

SCRIP

As for wallet or bag, symbol of *forethought*. Also the emblem of a *pilgrim*.

SCROLL

In Greek mythology, symbol of the *historical epic* presided over by the muse Kleio.

In church symbolism, a scroll denotes *Christ's ministry of the word of God; ministry of teaching*. Also stands for the *gospel*, a *petition*, a *prophecy*.

In U.S.A. when a scroll and pen are held in a hand, the implication is *emancipation proclamation*.

SCYLLA

In classical mythology, symbol of *danger*. A female monster, partly human, but with heads of fierce dogs growing about the waist. She inhabited a rock in the Strait of Messina, and was a great menace to seafarers.

SCYTHE (or sickle)

In the hands of Father Time, symbol of *mortality*. In general symbolism, *inevitableness of death*.

SEA

A calm sea, symbol of *refreshment, abundance;* a turbulent sea, *evil*. Isaiah 57:20.

SEA GULLS

Known as a *sailor's friend,* following a ship on the ocean until met by a ship coming in the opposite direction, and then returning with the incoming vessel.

State emblematic bird of Utah.

SEA HORSE

In classical mythology, a fabulous creature, half horse and half fish, driven by. seagods or ridden by the Nereids. Attribute of Neptune. Illustration, p. 8:5.

224

SEAL

Symbol of *security, secrecy.*

SEAMLESS GARMENT

One of the thirteen symbols of the Crucifixion. Illustration, p. 13:8.

SEAWEED

From natural characteristics, *everlasting, eternal life.*

From Japan, comes the symbolism *pleasure, joy.* The seaweed in that country is an emblem of the New Year.

SEB

(See Qeb.)

SAINT SEBASTIAN

Patron of *archers, armorers, bookbinders, burial societies, arrowsmiths, corn-chandlers, gardeners, ironmongers, lead founders, needlemakers, racquet-makers, stone masons, prisoners,* and of those suffering from the plague. His special day, January 20. Represented in art as a young man whose body is pierced by many arrows. Often bound to a tree or stake. At his death, his body was thrown into a Rome sewer, but recovered and buried at the feet of Saints Peter and Paul in the catacombs.

SEBEK

In ancient Egyptian religion, the *destroying power of the sun.*

SECHMET

In ancient Egyptian religion, goddess of *war.*

SEGO LILY

Same as mariposa, a flower belonging to the tulip family, symbol of *constancy.*

Since 1911 emblematic state flower of Utah.

SELENE

In Greek mythology, a *moon goddess,* same as Diana. In literature,

Selene is known as having thrown Endymion into a deep sleep that he might be unconscious of her affectionate caresses.

SENEMIRA

In Zoroaster's *Oracle*, the *principle of evil*.

SERAPHIM

Symbols of *eternal youth*. An order of celestial beings, ranked as the highest among angels, immediately above the cherubim. They excel in *wisdom* and *zeal* in the service of God.

SERPENT

From the serpent we get a great variety of symbolisms, among them:
In general symbolism, *good, evil, wisdom, power, eternity,* everything that is base, dark, low, depending upon the circumstances into which the reptile is drawn.
From Matthew 10:16, symbol of *wisdom*.
Serpent surrounding a tree, *fall of man*.
Serpent wrapped around a globe, *spread of sin*.
A serpent coiled when held aloft upon a staff, *regeneration*.
Coiled with head erect, *defiance*.
With tail in its mouth, *eternity*, or *temptation*.
Man-headed with double tail, *fraud*.
Serpent drinking from a kantharos in hand of a maiden, (Hygeia) *health*.

SET

In early Egyptian religion, deity of *war* and *evil*. Brother and enemy of Osiris. Manifest in thunderstorms. A chimera with body of an ass, muzzle and ears of a jackal, and tail of a lion.

SEVEN

Usually referred to as the *perfect number*, having innumerable categories among which are:
The seven virtues (all females)— *faith, hope, charity, temperance, prudence, fortitude, justice*.

The seven vices — *pride, covetousness, lust, anger, gluttony, envy, sloth.*

The seven sacraments, (when spoken of as the mysteries) — *baptism, confirmation,* the *Eucharist, penance, extreme unction, holy orders,* and *matrimony.*

The seven gifts of the Holy Spirit according to Isaiah, *Saprentia, Intellectus, Consiluim, Fortitudo, Scienta, Pietas, Timor.*

The seven liberal arts — *grammar, logic, rhetoric, arithmetic, music, geometry, astronomy.*

The seven wonders of the world at the time of Alexander the Great — *Pyramids of Egypt, Hanging Gardens of Babylon, Temple of Diana at Ephesus, Statue of Jupiter at Athens, Mausoleum at Halicarnassus, Colossus of Rhodes, Pharos of Alexandria.*

The seven penitential Psalms — 6, 32, 38, 51, 102, 130, 143.

The seven corporal works of mercy — to *feed and give drink,* to *clothe the needy,* to *shelter the stranger,* to *visit the sick,* to *minister unto captives and prisoners,* to *visit the fatherless and widows,* to *bury the dead.*

The seven words on the cross — "Today shalt thou be with me in Paradise," "Woman, behold thy son," "I thirst," "My God, why hast thou forsaken me?", "Father, into thy hands I commend my spirit," "It is finished."

The seven candles of the menorah.

The seven flames, signifying the gifts of the Holy Spirit. Illustration, p. 16:5.

SHAFT

When of classic design, one of the symbols of *architecture.*

A broken shaft, symbol of *unfinished work,* seen on gravestones, and in floral arrangements of funeral sprays.

SHAMROCK

Same as three-leaved clover, symbol of the *Holy Trinity.* From Saint Patrick's use of the tri-part leaf of this plant to illustrate the three persons of the Trinity — the One-God for the people of Ireland whom he was attempting to convert to Christianity. Much later, the shamrock was adopted as the emblem of Ireland and all loyal sons and daughters of the country still wear a shamrock on Saint Patrick's Day, March 17. Illustration as for the three-leaved clover, p. 10:5.

SHANGRI-LA

Fanciful name for a Utopian spot, thought of as La Mountain Pass in Tibet. In general symbolism, *ideal beauty* or *dream-life pleasures*.

SHEAF

A Roman sheaf of pale, golden grain is symbol of *fertility*.

As a funeral memorial piece, symbol of a *life well-spent*.

In Biblical symbolism, a sheaf refers to the Eucharist — the *bread* made from wheat. When heavy grains are predominant in the sheaf, the meaning is the *rich blessings* which flow from the sacraments.

SHEARS

In general symbolism, *foreseen and foreordained end*, stemming from the cutting aspects of the shears.

As an instrument of torture, *martyrdom*. Emblem for *tailors*.

An attribute of Saint Agatha, alluding to the tragic experience of having her breasts torn with a shears when she would not deny Christ.

SHEEP

In Christian symbolism, *man who has become lamb-like* in his need for the loving care of a Shepherd (Christ). Illustration, p. 17:8.

In early English *Bestiaries*, a sheep is thought of as the *soul* of an individual, or a *believer*.

SHELL (See also scallop)

A conch shell is one of the eight Buddhist symbols, and from Buddhism we get the shell as a *talisman of mariners*.

A cowry shell in Japan signifies *wealth*.

In general symbolism, a shell is a symbol of a *pilgrimage*, from an early crusader who picked up a shell on his way to the Holy Land and used it as an adornment on his garment.

Sometimes in Christendom art, a shell dripping water, signifies the *Baptism of Jesus*.

SHEPHERD

Frequent Biblical allusion to *Christ the Good Shepherd*.

In general, a shepherd symbolizes a *guardian, leader, protector*.

A shepherd's crook denotes *spiritual guidance*.

SHIBBOLETH

Denotes a *test,* from an account in Judges Chapter XII, wherein the Gileadites were able to identify the Ephriamites by their pronunciation of this word.

SHIELD

Symbol of *trust, protection, faith, defense, peace and tranquility.* Trust and faith drawn from Ephesians 6:16; and protection and defense from Genesis 15:1.

SHIP

In early days, the church, symbolically speaking, was the ark or ship of the Lord. The nave, the main body of the church proper is from Latin *navis,* a ship. Illustration, p. 22:11. The ship represents the *life voyage of the Christian to the port of salvation.* In early Christian funeral sculpture, a ship traversing the sea was used to denote the *course of life,* and this representation is still to be seen in cemeteries of Rome. A ship, in general symbolism denotes *exploration, adventure, travel, enterprise, the State.*

A ship is the symbol of the *tribe of Zebulum* in the bronze door of the Baptistry of Florence.

SHIPWRECK

A representation of a shipwreck signifies *misfortune, tragic death.*

SHIRT

In Greek mythology, the shirt of Nessus is symbol of *treachery, burning pain,* from the tragic story of Hercules who suffered such intense agony from a shirt steeped in the poison blood of the Centaur Nessus, he ended his own life because of the torturing pain.

SHIVA (Also Siva)

Hindu god of the *universe;* also of *destruction,* and *reproductive,* and *restorative power.* He holds the key of salvation. He rides on a white bull, a trident in one hand and in the other a rope with which he and his wife Kali strangle evil doers. He wears a necklace made of human skulls; his earrings are serpents; his loins wrapped in tiger skins. From his head springs the River Ganga.

SHOES

A pair of shoes signify *usefulness, utility.* Removing shoes before entering a holy place denotes *reverence, respect.*

SHOFAR

A horn, as of a ram, used as a trumpet by the ancient Hebrews, in battle or in sacred festivals. Still used in synagogues on the Day of Atonement. Illustration, p. 16:7.

SHUTTLE

In commercial art, emblem of *textile manufacturers.*

SIBYL

In classical mythology, one of a goodly number of women reputed to have power of *prophecy, divination.* The most famous one was the Cumaean sibyl who led Aeneas down to Hades.

SICKLE

Symbol of *harvest.* In Biblical symbolism, *reaper of God.*

A sickle and bundle of wheat in commercial art, one of the symbols of *agriculture.* Illustration, p. 19:5.

A sickle and hammer, emblem of the *Soviets* or *Sovietism.*

SILENUS

In Greek mythology, tutor of Bacchus. He was the eldest of the satyrs, and said to have been the inventor of Pan's pipes. Fond of music, dancing, and sleep, commonly pictured as a tipsy, jovial, bald old man, riding an ass, a winebag in his hand.

SILO

In industrial art, symbol of *nourishment, fruitfulness of the soil.*

SILVER

The metal, silver, is symbol of *purity, chastity,* from its color, and from the fact that it can stand the test of fire. The color, silver, denotes *faith, truth.*

SIMITAR

Symbol of *valor, power.* Illustration, p. 15:5.

SAINT SIMON ZELOTES, APOSTLE

His special day, October 28. Famous as a preacher throughout Syria and Mesopotamia. His attributes, a large *saw and book,* or an *axe and a cross.*

SIRENS

Symbols of *voluptuousness, deceit, insidiousness.* In Greek mythology, female divinities of alluring charms and bewitching wiles. They are represented as birds with great talons, but with heads and breasts of beautiful women. They allured mariners by their songs until they turned their vessels from the right course, and they were dashed to pieces on the rocks.

SISAMORA

In Zoroaster's *Oracle,* the principle of *good.*

SISTRUM

In Egyptian religion, symbol of *joy, worship, religious ecstasy.* A musical instrument made of metal frame and metal rods, to be shaken. They resound with a loud metallic sound, and were useful in frightening away the evil spirits. Seen always in processions honoring Isis, goddess of *motherhood and fertility.*

SIX

In Christian symbolism considered to be an imperfect number — one less than seven, the perfect number; the beast 666 in Revelations held to be the depth of imperfection.

Six attributes of a deity are held to be: *power, majesty, wisdom, love, mercy, justice.*

SKELETON

Symbol of *death.* When a skeleton of human being bears in hand a scythe, the denotation is, *shortness of life;* when holding an hourglass, the *swift passage of life;* when winged and holding a scythe, *pestilence.*

SKULL

In church symbolism, *Christ's Passion,* also, a *warning of death,* or *the passing of precious time.*

The skull is a very old and much used symbol of *death, mortality, penance,* besides its popularity as a symbol of *medicine.* It serves as an attribute of numerous saints, including Mary Magdalene, Saint Paul, Saint Jerome, and Saint Francis of Assisi.

SKULL AND CROSSBONES

Symbol of *death, danger, piracy, poison, warning of death.*

A cross with skull and crossbones at its base, signifies *Golgotha,* or *thoughts on life after death.*

SKULLCAP

In ecclesiastical symbolism, the zucchetto, a mark of *distinction, dignity, office.* The color is in accord with the rank of the wearer.

SMILAX

As a funeral remembrance plant, symbol of *hope, resurrection.* As an addition to floral beauty at festal occasions, including weddings, *devotion.*

SMOCK

With a biretta, in commercial art, emblem of an *artist.*

SMOKE

In general symbolism, *vanity,* in that it rises into the air, only to disappear.

In Christian symbolism, a reminder of the *shortness of life,* and the *futility of seeking earthly glory.*

SNAIL

Symbol of *slowness,* of *humility* (it crawls on the ground); *frugality, contentment with one's lot,* (makes no effort to seek food, eating that which is at hand).

In Christian art, seen in Easter scenes with the implication of *resurrection,* in that the snail bursts open its shell when the warm sun in spring warms all nature. When placed at the right in Crucifixion scenes, the denotation is *late conversion of the thief*.

SNAKE

Symbol of the *tribe of Dan* in the bronze door of the Baptistry of Florence.

Snake with head erect, symbol of *fascination, wisdom*.

When coiled with "Noli me tangere," *independence*.

Circled with tail in its mouth, *eternity*, or *sin encircling the world*.

SNOOD

A head covering or ornament, which in ancient Scotland was an emblem of *exemplary maidenhood*.

SNOW

Obviously, symbol of *purity*. From Japan, the symbolism of snowflakes is *material wealth*.

A snowman, widely used as a Christmas symbol.

SNUFF-BOTTLES

From China, we get the symbolisms, *scholarliness, learning*.

SOCK

In early drama, sign of *comedy*, from the thin-soled *soccus* worn by classical actors in comedies.

The sock, or stocking, has become a popular Christmas symbol.

SODOM AND GOMORRAH

Symbols of *carnal passions*. In Biblical literary allusions, *spiritually reprobate people*. Revelations 11:8.

SOKAK

In Zoroaster's *Oracle, unlucky genius*.

SOMNUS

In Greek mythology, god of sleep, son of Erebus and Night. Father of Morpheus. Pictured as a drowsy god, asleep in a dark cave, lying on an ebony couch ornamented with black feathers.

SOPHROSYNE

Greek divinity of *temperance.*

SORREL

Symbol of *bitterness, sorrow,* from the pungent taste of the juice. In Christian symbolism represents the *sorrows of the Virgin,* or, the *Passions of Christ.*

SOW

Symbol of *fecundity.*

SPADE

When appearing in representations of Adam, the first man, the denotation is *primitive occupations.* In commercial art, emblem of *gardening.*

SPARROW

From Japan we get the symbolism *friendliness, gentleness.* In Biblical literary allusion, *lowly life, God's protective care.* Matthew 10:31; Luke 12:7.

SPEAR

Symbol of *valor, supreme honor, war or intimation of war.*
A spearhead in Christian symbolism denotes *Christ's Passion.*

SPHERE

Emblem of the *people of the world, creative motion,* in that the manifesting force is rotary.

SPHINX

In Greek mythology, goddess of the *rising sun.* A winged monster having a woman's head and lion's body. In Egypt, a beneficent being who personified the fruit-bearing earth, and, like the sun deities, was goddess of *wisdom* and *knowledge*. The figure is often seen at entrance steps of museums or libraries. The Great Sphinx of Egypt, now somewhat mutilated, is a good example of a conventionalized form of the god of the rising sun, the human head, symbolizing *wisdom;* the body of a lion, *strength*. Illustration, p. 8:4.

SPICES

Spices denote *heavenly delight, holiness,* in association with the pleasing flavor they give as an additive to common viands.

SPIDER

Symbol of *industry, ambition, presumption, cunning, temptation, envy.* When pictured in the center of its web, *perseverance*. The symbolism *envy* stems from a Greek myth in which a maiden, Arachne, was changed into a spider by Athene who envied Arachne's superior skill as a weaver.

SPIKENARD

Fragrant ointment of the ancients, with symbolic implication of *holiness,* mentioned in the Bible as being precious or costly.

SPINDLE

Common Greek symbol of *fertility*. In commercial art, emblem of *textile manufacturing*.

SPIRAL

With allusion to early architectural design, symbol of *magnificence*. In Christian symbolism, *ascending growth in Christian service*.

SPIRE

In church architecture, as for a tower or a steeple, the symbolism is *aspiration, hope, faith*.

SPONGE

One of the thirteen symbols of the Crucifixion in reference to the drink offered Christ on the Cross. Illustration, p. 13:9.

SQUARE

From the square as a geometrical figure, symbol of *equality, firmness, stability.* A carpenter's square and compass denotes *skilled craftsmanship.*

SQUIRREL

Symbol of *forethought,* a squirrel stores food for winter consumption.
A squirrel cracking a nut implies that one should *pierce below the husk of the external, deep thought, meditation.*

SPRINGBOK

Rare gazelle-like animal, national emblem of *Africa.* Noted for its grace, and for its habit of springing suddenly into the air.

SPUR

Emblem of *knighthood, honor.* When winged, a *special messenger.* The rowels of a knight's spur stand for *deeds of honor, chivalry, virtue.*

STABLE

In Christmas scenes, symbol of *Nativity of Christ.*

STAFF

The staff of Hermes (Mercury) called the caduceus, symbol of a *physician* or of the *medical corps.* In modern times the staff of caduceus has been adopted as a symbol of *commerce* since Mercury is the god of commerce.

In Christian symbolism, a shepherd's staff is symbol of *Christ's ministry* of service — the Shepherd who guides and guards His flock.

STAG

Symbol of *purity,* and *solitary life, fleetness,* and, from Japan, *longevity.*
In Christian art, Christ is often pictured as a white stag with a cross between the antlers.

A stag with crucifix between the horns, attribute of *Saint Eustace,* and *Saint Hubert;* without the crucifix, *Saint Julian.*

STAIRS

A winding stairs denotes *aspiration, self-improvement.*

STAKE

A stake with iron collar hanging by a chain, symbol of *torture, martyr-dom.*

STAR

Because of the position of stars in the universe, there has arisen the symbolism, high ideals, lofty sentiments, directive leaders. Special significations are dependent upon the number of points of the star, or its position with accompanying objects. Among these meanings are:

Four-pointed star — A cross, with pointed ends of the cross-beams and the upright post, is sometimes spoken of as a four-pointed star, with symbolisms usually given to a cross.

Five-pointed star, which with imagination suggests the figure of a man with head, two arms, and two legs, has been given various names — Star of Jacob, Star of Jesse, Star of Bethlehem, Star of Epiphany (associated with the Incarnation), and Pentagonal Star. Symbolisms are *guidance, merit, protection, morning.* In Christian symbolism the denotation is *Christ, divine guidance.*

A six-pointed star, called the Star of Creation, Star of David (symbol of Zionism). In the six points there is implication of the creation of the world in six days. When thought of as an emblem of *God the Father,* the points refer to His attributes — *power, wisdom, majesty, love, mercy, justice.* Illustration, p. 16:9.

The seven-pointed star, called the Mystic Star, reflects the seven gifts of the Holy Spirit, *power, riches, wisdom, strength, honor, glory* and *blessing.* Revelation 5:12. Latin words for the gifts are: Virtus, Divinitas, Sapientia, Fortitudo, Honor, Gloria, Benedictio.

Eight-pointed star, called Star of Regeneration or Star of Baptism, symbolizes *regeneration* because the number eight is symbolically, *rebirth.* Baptismal fonts and baptistries are frequently octagonal in shape, with origin not fully established, some say representative of the eight souls saved in the ark, some maintain it stands for a new creation, a divine octave of the seven days plus the time of rest afterwards.

The nine-pointed star denotes the nine fruits of the Holy Spirits, Galatians 5:22,23 — *love joy, peace, longsuffering, gentleness, goodness, faith, meekness, temperance.*

The ten-pointed star refers to the ten continuing disciples, counting out Judas who betrayed, and Simon Peter who denied Christ.

The twelve-pointed star, stands for the twelve tribes of Israel, the twelve apostles. The large silver star still seen in the Nativity Church of Bethlehem has twelve points. Tradition associates that number with close relationship between the human and the divine. The fifty stars on the flag of the United States of America are of five points, white on a blue background, each one representing one state. See illustration, p. 22:9.

A star and crescent is emblem of *Turkey,* and of *Mohammedanism.*

STARWORT

Sometimes called the Christmas rose or Christmas aster. The flower is a symbol of Christ's Nativity.

STATUE OF LIBERTY

Generally thought of as the huge statue in New York Harbor, true symbol of *human freedom.* One hundred fifty-one feet high, copper sheathed, statue of Miss Liberty with torch held high.

STEAM

Symbol of power.

STEAMSHIP

In commercial art, *commerce, navigation.*

STEEPLE

Steeple with weathervane, *challenge to face difficulties,* and, a warning to *beware of changing with every wind.*

In church architecture, when topped with any pointed ornamentation, *one true God whom people come to worship.* When topped with a cross, *God's love for the world, His reconciliation of the world with Himself through the worship, prayers, and meditations and hymns in the church below the steeple.*

STEPHANOTIS

The word means, *fit for a crown* as used by the Greek poets; hence when used in formal arrangements for debutante or bridal festivities it signifies, *high honors, virtue*.

SAINT STEPHEN

First Christian martyr. Stoned for having been accused of blasphemous words against Moses and against God. His attributes *stones,* as instruments of martyrdom. His special day December 26.

STEPS

In church architecture, when there are three steps, the signification is *faith, hope,* and *charity.* This number is not unusual for a base for a cross, or for an ascent to the pulpit; here the denotation is the *Holy Trinity*.

STIGMATA

Phenomenal appearance of five marks on hands, feet or on the side of devout persons, as representations of the *five wounds of Christ on the Cross.*

STILETTO

Symbol of *assassin* or *assassination*.

STOCK

A new name for ancient gilly-flower, symbol of *fidelity in misfortune*.

STOLE

In clerical vestment, symbol of *willingness to serve God.* A reminder of the yoke which Christ took to the Cross for the sins of the people. Illustration, p. 14:5.

When worn as a mass vestment, it is the sign of *priestly dignity* and *power,* and usually bears as symbolic ornamentation a cross, a triangle and three circles (signifying three persons, yet one God), often enriched with embroideries, monograms, or even jewels. The color should match that of the chasuble and maniple.

STONE

In church architecture, because of its durability, the symbolism is *eternal values, eternal truth;* also *consecration, sacrifice.*

From Japan comes the symbol of a rounded stone, *peace;* of a rectangular one, *labor* and *usefulness;* from one wider at the base, *constancy, strength, stability of character;* if balanced but wider at the top, *dynamic force of character;* water stones, *serenity.*

In general symbolism, a stone is the symbol of *firmness.* It is an attribute of Saint Stephen, the first Christian martyr who met death from stoning; also of Saint Jerome, who is frequently represented at prayer, beating his breast with a stone.

STONEHENGE

Famous stone of Salisbury, England, popularly called the "Altar Stone" is symbol of *time* stemming from the fact that it possibly dates back to the neolithic or early bronze age.

STORK

Symbol of *maternity, longevity, good fortune, parental piety, affection, vigilance, prudence,* and *chastity.* Illustration, p. 18:5.

There is a North European explanation of the traditional belief that the stork is bearer of a newly born child. The connection lies with Saint Anne, who announced to Mary, the coming of the Christ Child. As the stork, harbinger of spring announces the approaching vernal season, so Saint Anne made her announcement to Mary.

STRAWBERRY

When pictured with fruit and flower, in Christian symbolism, the meaning is *good works of the righteous,* or *fruits of the spirit.*

STREAM

Calm or slow moving waters denote, *peace, righteousness.*

STURGEON

Symbol of *preservation, security,* in association with the tough, protective covering of the fish.

STYLUS

From Egypt, symbol of a *scribe*.

STYX

In Greek mythology, a fabulous river of the underworld over which all newcomers were ferried by Charon, son of Erebus.

SUADELA

In Roman mythology, god of the *soft speech of love*, one of the huge train of attendants upon Venus.

SUBRAMANJI

Early Hindu god of *victory*.

SUGAR

Signifies a *plea for happiness*, in association with an ancient Persian wedding rite where sugar was sprinkled over a bride to bring her happiness.

SUM

In Zoroaster's *Oracle*, the *I Am*.

SUMAC

The North American laurel sumac, symbol of *resoluteness*, from the sturdiness of the shrub.

SUN

In Egypt, symbol of Ra, the sun god, identified with Greek Helios, with the general implication of *protection, life-giving*. In general symbolism, these denotations are found: *creation, fecundity, good fortune, enterprise* and for a rising sun, *progress, increasing knowledge*. In Christian symbolism, *eternal life, regeneration of the soul, Christ the sun of the universe*. Illustration, p. 9:8.

SUNDIAL

Symbol of *time* in the same sense as for a scythe or an hourglass.

When used as an ornamentation in ancient gardens, a sundial served as a reminder that *life is brief.*

SUN-DISC

A disc with conventionalized wings, in Egypt, the symbol of Ra, the sun god who offered *divine protection.* In the royal headdress of Ra the sun is seen between the two attributes of the god, motion, and life. See illustration, p. 9:1.

SUNFLOWER

Emblematic flower of the state of Kansas, adopted by legislation in 1903. Also national flower of Peru. Illustration, p. 20:12.

In church symbolism, the sunflower denotes *religious obedience,* the *soul turning to Christ* (as the sunflower follows the sun).

In general symbolism, the meaning is *glory, gratitude, remembrance.*

SURPLICE

As a clerical vestment, the white surplice, symbol of *purity,* covers the black cassock, the complete signification being, the gospel (white) covers sin (the black).

SURYA

Early Hindu sun-god. Represented, four-armed, driving a chariot drawn by numberless horses harnessed abreast. He, in a way, corresponds to Greek Helios, not so much as the god of light as the special god who lived in the body of the sun.

SWALLOW

Symbol of *speed,* the forked tail of the bird an aid in gaining rapid flight; *wandering spirit,* from the peculiar circling movement when catching insects for food. Illustration, p. 18:10.

In religious symbolism, *diligence, filial piety,* from the way the swallow trains its young.

SWAN

Symbol of *grace, purity,* and of *poetry and music.* In early art, *solitude, retirement.* Has been called a hypocrite because of its black flesh beneath the white plumage. Illustration, p. 18:11.

Swans and dolphins, in conventionalized design are often seen as symbols of the *opera*.

The epithet "swan song" springs from the belief that the fowl, having no distinct song in normal life, utters a peculiar murmur as death approaches.

SWASTIKA

A cross made of two capital Greek gammas crossed, a very ancient symbol of unknown origin. In pre-Christian times connected with sun worship and the origin of fire; used in the catacombs, doubtless with reference to Christ as the *Sun of Righteousness*. Illustration, p. 12:11.

In India still, when used in Hindu marriage rites, the swastika bears the wish that the best blessings may rest upon the bride and groom.

Before the political implication of *conformity* was fixed for the swastika, the general symbolic denotations were *pleasure, good luck, activity*.

SWEET PEA

Symbol of *youthfulness, versatility* in association with the great variety of colors, and freshness of fragrance. Illustration, p. 21:4.

SWORD

Dependent upon the circumstances into which the sword is thrust, symbolisms are *valor, authority, power, conflict, execution*.

In religious symbolism, a flaming sword signifies *authority of God, expulsion from Garden of Eden;* when the sword points to the naked heart, the implication is *divine justice which overcomes all who have sinned*.

A double edged sword is symbol of *destruction*.

SYCAMORE

In early Greek mythology called the *world tree,* having broad shade from lengthy branches. In Biblical symbolism, the denotation of the *opportunities God provides,* grew out of the story of Zacchaeus in Luke 19:2-9.

Sometimes a symbol of *greed* and *cupidity,* from the habits of growth (reaching out).

SYRINGA

Also called mock orange, symbol of *fraternal love,* stemming from its having been the favorite flower of Ptolemy Philadelphia, King of Egypt, known in history for the close affection he held for his brother.

The syringa is emblematic flower of Idaho.

SYRINX

In Greek mythology, a nymph who was pursued by Pan, and who was changed into a reed out of which Pan formed his musical pipes.

TABLE

In Christian representative symbolism, *fellowship, communion.*

TABLET

From Greek mythology, a writing tablet crowned with laurel is a symbol of *heroic epic,* the form of poetry presided over by the muse, sweet-voiced Calliope.

Two tablets of stone in church symbolism stand for the *ten commandments of Moses, the law.*

TABOR

Same as for tambourine, signifies *joy, worship, religious ecstasy.* An instrument related to the Egyptian sistrum used in the religious ceremonies of Isis, goddess of motherhood and fertility. The small type, used by Salvation Army members in U.S.A., signifies a *call to Christian service.*

TAMBOURINE

(See TABOR.)

TANAGER (Scarlet)

Emblematic bird of Minnesota.

TANIT

In classical mythology, goddess of the *moon at full;* symbol of *motherhood.* Patroness of Carthage.

TANSY

From the Greek word *athanasia,* a plant early believed to live forever; hence symbol of *immortality, deathlessness.* Also used in literature as a symbol of *hostility.*

TANTALUS

In Greek mythology, wealthy king who, for betraying secrets of the gods, was punished in the lower world by being placed in water up to his chin, but which receded when he attempted to take a drink. In literary allusion, reference is to one who is *doomed to hunger, and to torturing thirst.*

TARES

In religious symbolism, *worthless pretenders*, Matthew 13:24-30.

TARRAGON

An herb which gets its name from the Latin word for dragon (its roots coil like a dragon); hence the symbolism, *sin, enemy of truth, bitterness.*

TASSELS

In religious symbolism, when a tassel appears on each of four corners of a scarf or other fabric covering, the denotations are, *justice, fortitude, prudence, temperance.*

TATU

In Japanese zodiac, the *dragon.*

TEA

Often thought of in literature to be the national emblem of China, but the narcissus is the legally adopted flower.

TEETH

(See dragon's teeth.)

TEFNUT

In early Egyptian religion, *goddess of rain.* Represented as a human being with a lion's head. Holds a sundial and an asp.

TELEGRAPH POLES AND WIRES

In commercial art, symbol of *electricity, commerce, communication.*

TELEMACHUS

Son of Odysseus and Penelope. In literary tragedies slew the suitors of Penelope while his father was away from home.

TELLUS

A Roman goddess, identical with Greek Gaea and Rhea. In literary allusions stands for a personification of the *fields* or the *earth.*

TEMPLE

Representations of a temple, symbol of *Christ's ministry of teaching*.

A temple facade has become an emblematic figure for *architecture*.

TEN

Ten is considered the complete number. In the ten commandments, man is given his whole duty toward God and toward man.

Ten, the number of faithful apostles. The twelve minus Judas, who betrayed, and Peter who denied Christ.

SAINT TERESA OF AVILA

Patroness of *lacemakers,* and of Spain. Founder of the Reformed Carmelites. Her special day, October 15. Her attribute, an angel holding a flame-tipped arrow.

TERPSICHORE

In Greek mythology, one of the nine muses, daughter of Zeus and Mnemosyne. She presides over the *choral lyric* and *the dance.* Her attributes, a *lyre* and *crown of palms.*

TEST-TUBE

In scientific picture language, *inquiry*.

SAINT THAIS PENITENT

Patroness of *fallen women*. Represented in art as destroying her jewels and as doing penance in a prison cell. Her special day, October 8.

THALEIA

Symbol of luxuriant beauty. One of the nine muses, daughter of Zeus and Mnemosyne who inspired gaiety and favored rural pursuits. She presided over *comedy*. Her attributes, a *comic mask*, and a *crown of ivy*.

THANOTOS

The same as Roman Mors. In Greek mythology, personification of *Death*, brother of Hypnos (sleep) and son of Nyx (night). His habitation was in the lower regions.

THEMIS

In Greek mythology, wife of Zeus and goddess of *law* and *justice*. Her attributes a horn of plenty in one hand and scales in the other.

SAINT THEODOTUS

Patron of *innkeepers*. His special day, May 18.

THESEUS

In Greek mythology, chief Attic hero, son of Aegeus, King of Athens. He drove away the evil doers from Athens, slew the minotaur, and carried away the queen of the Amazons. Later he became one of the Argonauts and took part in the Calydonian boar hunt.

THETIS

Chief of the Nereids, mother of Achilles and his instructor.

THIMBLE

In commercial art, symbol for *feminine industry, household arts* and *needlework*.

THIRTEEN

The superstition of thirteen as an unlucky number, is said to stem from Judas as the thirteenth man in the Biblical account of the Last Supper. This superstition is disregarded in the emblem of U.S.A., for there are:

Thirteen stripes on the American flag.
Thirteen olives and leaves on the branch in the seal.
Thirteen arrows held by the eagle.
Thirteen stars in the crest.

All are representations of the thirteen original colonies on the eastern border of the nation.

In Christian symbolism, there are thirteen representations for the Crucifixion:

The whipping post
A scourge
A hammer
Pincers
Sponge
Reed
Lance

Seamless garment
Napkin of Saint Veronica
A ladder
The nails, three usually given as the number
A crown of thorns
A cross

THIRTY

In journalism usage denotes *completion, finis.*

When seen on clerical vestments, thirty-three ornaments of the same design, stand for the thirty-three years of the earthly life of Christ.

THISBE

(See PYRAMIS.)

THISTLE

The thistle is the emblematic flower of Scotland, with the implication "None offend me with impunity." Illustration, p. 20:4.

In Christian symbolism, the denotation is *sin,* the *fall of man, austerity.*

As a thorny plant, the thistle has become one of the symbols for the *Passion of Christ,* and particularly of His *crowning of thorns.* Because of the curse pronounced against Adam in Genesis 3:17,18, there has arisen the symbolism, *earthly sorrow and sin.* When the blossom, and not the prickly portions of the plant is referred to, the symbolism is *redemption.*

SAINT THOMAS à BECKET, OF CANTERBURY

The "hooly, blisful martir," whose shrine the pilgrims of Chaucer's *Canterbury Tales* were seeking to visit, was murdered on December 29, 1170 in the cathedral at Canterbury. He is represented as a Benedictine bishop, usually as receiving a red chasuble from the Virgin Mary, blood flowing from his head.

SAINT THOMAS AQUINAS

Patron of *booksellers, pencil-makers, scholars,* and all *students.* His special day, March 7. He has numerous attributes symbolizing his great learning, among them: a chalice (because of his Eucharistic writings) a book, a star, and an ox for which he was nicknamed by companions at the monastery who thought him dull and dumb.

SAINT THOMAS DIDYMUS, THE APOSTLE

Known as doubting Thomas. Patron of *architects, carpenters, masons, geometricians, theologians*. His special day December 21. His usual attribute a builder's rule or square or a spear and book.

THOR

In Scandinavian mythology, the great god of thunder, fire, and war. Patron of *farmers* and *thralls*. Always represented carrying a hammer, even when driving his cart drawn by goats.

In literary allusion, Thor denotes *fierce courage, colossal might and strength*.

THORNS

Symbol of the *flesh, suffering, grief, tribulation*, all reflective of natural characteristics of thorny plants.

Branches of thorns denote *minor sins*. A crown of thorns is one of the thirteen symbols of the Crucifixion. Illustration, p. 13:4.

THOTH

In early Egyptian religion, *scribe of the gods*, inventor of numbers, measurer of time, and keeper of records for Osiris. Known as the god of wisdom, learning and magic. Represented with the head of an ibis, and bearing in his hands a tablet, pen, palette, and palm branch.

THRASHER

Bird with song much like that of the mockingbird. Emblematic bird of Georgia.

THREE

In church symbolism, three objects of any kind usually refer to the Holy Trinity — three candles, three panels of the altar, three columns, three steps to the pulpit, etc.

Three golden balls, emblem of *pawnbrokers*, in some way connected with the coat of arms of the noted Medici family of Florence.

THRIFT

An herb, denoting *sympathy*, in association with the pink or white flower heads, traditionally signifying remembrance.

THRONE

Symbol of *highest power, authority, government.*

In Christian symbolism, *Christ's ministry of intercession,* the *World's True King.*

THRUSH

Called the *hermit,* because he becomes silent when he is conscious of a listener.

Hermit thrush, emblematic bird of Vermont.

Wood thrush, bird of the District of Columbia.

THRYSUS

Vine encircled wand with point protected by a pine cone, borne by the followers of Dionysus in special ceremonial rites. The attribute of Dionysus (Bacchus), and the satyrs.

THUNDERBIRD

In general symbolism, *liberty,* a conventionalized form of an eagle. Among North American Indians a mythical bird supposed to cause thunder and lightning, and, for them, has the same significance as the eagle has for *freedom, liberty.* Illustration, p. 9:10.

THYME

Herb of the mint family, symbol of *bravery, activity,* handed down from ancient days in Greece where fine flavor of honey of Mount Hymettus was attributed to the thyme which covered it. Supposed to provide energy for those who ate the honey.

TIARA

As ecclesiastical vestment, a circular headpiece, sometimes plain, sometimes ornamented, consisting of three crowns one above the other, surmounted by a cross. Symbolic of the *Holy Trinity,* worn only by a Pope. Also alludes to the *three estates of the Kingdom of God.*

TIGER

From natural physical characteristics of the beast, *ferocity, greed, extreme cruelty, treacherous.* In church symbolism, the *wrath of God, evil forces in the world.*

A tiger skin is an attribute of Bacchus (Dionysus), god of wine.

TIGER LILY

Symbol of *fertility* same as for pomegranate or flowers with many seeds. The lily has many spots.

TI LEAVES

When used as background in floral arrangements, *hope*.

TIME

Father Time, in art and literature a personification of the *passing year*. Represented usually as a man of extreme age, holding a scythe or an hourglass. Sometimes, the representation accompanying Father Time is a snake or dragon biting its own tail.

TITANS

In Greek mythology, twelve in number, primeval deities, representative of *powerful obstructive forces* rather than contributors to the appreciation of beauty, intelligence, or light. They are children of Uranus and Gaea, with these descendants:

> Cronus and Rhea, who bore Zeus and the Olympians.
> Coeus and Phoebe, parents of Leto.
> Japetus and Themis, whose offsprings are Atlas, Epimetheus, Prometheus, Dione, Maia.
> Oceanus and Tethys.
> Hyperion and Theia.
> Creus and Mnemosyne.

TOADSTONE

A stone or stony substance said to have formed in the head or body of a toad. Symbol of *health, witchcraft,* and early held as a charm to ward off poison.

TONGUE

In general symbolic denotation, *gossip, malicious talk.* In Christian symbolism, tongues of flame signify the *Holy Spirit,* and thus become an emblem of the Day of Pentecost. When there are seven flames, they stand for the seven gifts of the Holy Spirit, *wisdom, understanding, counsel, might, knowledge, fear, delight.*

252

TONSURE

A custom (among both secular clergy and monastic orders since the seventh century) of clipping or shaving the crown of the head. The three significations of this practice are:

A remembrance of the crown of thorns.
Rejection of temporal things.
A reminder of the perfect life.

TOPAZ

A precious gem, symbol of *friendship, fidelity, fruitfulness, longevity.* In early times held to be a charm for happiness.

In religious decorative art, *goodness of God, love toward God, faithfulness in God's service.*

Emblematic birthstone for November.

TOPE

A round bubble-topped Buddhist shrine, signifying the *hollowness of the world.*

TORA

In Japanese zodiac, the *tiger.*

TORCH

Dependent upon its surroundings, a burning torch signifies, *progress, education, increasing knowledge, light, wisdom, leadership, enlightenment, research.*

A torch when burned out, or when reversed denotes *death.*

In religious symbolism, the *witnessing of Christians.*

The torch in the hand of the Statue of Liberty in New York Harbor signifies *enlightenment.* Atop the dome of the Library of Congress, *science ever-burning, research.*

TORII

In Japanese zodiac, the *cock.*

As a gateway or perch, thought of as *gateway of the dawn; perch for the birds which greet the sunrise.* Commonly seen at an approach to a Shinto temple.

TORNADO

Symbol of *invincible power, destructiveness.*

TORTOISE

Symbol of *immortality, longevity, strength, sloth, sagacity, endurance, slowness,* depending upon the surroundings of the tortoise. When used as a Christian symbol, the implication is *courier of heavenly blessings.* In Chinese art, *virility, fruitful marriage, happiness, good luck.* When a tortoise is pictured with a crane on its back, the denotation is *strength, longevity.*

TOUCHSTONE

A flint-like stone, symbol of *veracity, truthfulness, purity,* stemming from an early use of the stone to test the purity of gold and silver by the streak left on it when rubbed by the metal.

TOURMALINE

Gem of great beauty found in colors of pink, red, yellow, blue, and primarily, green. Symbol of *hope, elegance.*
With the opal, birthstone for October.

TOWER

Early associated with the worship of a supreme sun-god, symbol of *defense, safety.*
In church architecture, symbol of *protection, strength, spiritual uplift.*
(See, also, steeple, spire.)

TRAGEDY

Illustration, p. 19:3. The emblem is a masked face with agitated expression.

TREE

The symbolism of a tree or trees in art or literature is, as a rule, easy to decipher, reflecting the characteristics of growth, as to height, spread of branches, or age. In general, a tree stands for *vigor, productiveness, prosperity, aspirations, diffused knowledge, progressiveness.*
A gnarled, age-worn tree trunk stands for *barrenness, unproductiveness.*

When a gnarled tree is decorated with vines or fresh flowers, the implication is *victory of hope over despair*.

A Christmas tree, idea of which started with the Germans, originally signified *enduring life*. Has more recently taken on the meaning of *sharing the fruit of the tree with others*, or, if an evergreen tree, *everlasting joy*.

In art, the stump of a tree signifies, *farewell to the past*.

TREFOIL

Three overlapping circles of equal size, a commonly used symbolic figure in Christendom for the *Holy Trinity*. Illustration, p. 10:1. The trefoil in plant life is the name given to any three-lobed leaf such as the shamrock or three leaved clover. Used by Saint Patrick in Ireland as a pattern for explaining the three-fold Godhead to the people he wished to convert to Christianity.

TRIAD

Any group of three elements, symbol of *good luck*, and in Christian symbolism, the *Holy Trinity*.

TRIANGLE

This geometrical figure, see p. 10:3, has many features which lend themselves to symbolic meanings — the three lines of equal length; the point extending up, or pointing down, and it can readily be combined with other figures, or formed from various materials. Among the significances are:

In general symbolism, *equality, democratic thinking, perfection*. The watchword of the French Revolution, *Liberty, Equality, Fraternity*.

In Christian symbolism represented in the catacombs as the *Trinity*. When pictured with divergent rays, *eternity*, the rays indicative of *glory and brightness*. Sometimes made of two fishes with meaning of *Trinity*. When within a circle, *divine Triplicity*.

When triangle is red, with apex down, on white background, symbol of Y.M.C.A., Young Men's Christian Association.

When triangle is blue, apex down, and name bar in center, symbol of Y.W.C.A., Young Women's Christian Association.

In art and architecture, in designs with apex pointing upward, the symbolism is *heaven*.

Two interwoven triangles to form six-pointed star, *Star of David, creation.*

Triangle with hand, in church symbolism, *Hand of God.*

In flower arrangement — triangular form lying on long side, *repose;* standing on the acute angle, *stateliness* and *power;* standing in an inclined position, *dynamic force.*

TRIDENT

A three-tined fork, when seen in representations of Neptune, the denotation is *sea-power.*

TRINITY

Illustration, p. 10:4, Symbol for *Father, Son, and Holy Spirit.*

TRIPOD

From ancient Greek times, *symbol of achievement* in dance or song.

TRIQUETRA

Of frequent use in church architecture, the three equal arcs symbolizing the equality of the *three Persons of the Godhead.* When the lines run continuously from one arc to another, *eternal existence;* when interwoven and inside another triangle, the meaning is *unity, eternity, glory, equality.* Illustration, p. 10:2.

TRITON

In Greek mythology, son of Poseidon and Amphritrite. Represented as human, with lower part of the body a fish. He drives a chariot drawn by seahorses. His attribute a trumpet made of a conch shell. Personification of the *roaring sea,* and the *larger bodies of fresh water.*

TROMBONE

Powerful brass wind instrument, symbol of *voluptuousness.*

TRUCK

In modern commercial art, symbol of *industry, commerce.*

TRUMPET

In general religious symbolism denotes a *call to worship, day of judgment, resurrection.*

As an orchestra instrument, *glorification.*

TSAO CHUN

In China, the *kitchen god.*

TS'AO KUO-CHIN

In Taoism, patron of the *theatrical arts.*

TULIP

Symbol of *constancy, good wishes for many happy years.* The denotation of constancy is said to have stemmed from an old Persian traditional story wherein red tulips sprang from the blood of a ruler who had jumped to death from a cliff in despondency over the loss of his beloved wife. The flower was the shape of his *turban,* the word from which *tulip* was derived.

In Victorian days in England, a red tulip was a *declaration of love* when sent from a fair youth to a shy damsel.

The tulip tree is emblematic of the state of Indiana.

TUNICLE

A short, close-fitting ecclesiastical garment, symbol of *joy* and *contentment,* worn under the dalmatic.

TUNNY-FISH

Large mackerel-like fish, symbol of *wisdom* and *sagacity,* suggestive of the wiles of the fish in an escape from its captors.

TURKEY

From the proud strutting of the male fowl, *ostentation, vainglory.*

TURQUOISE

Birthstone for December. Symbol of *prosperity, success, courage,* perhaps an outgrowth of early superstitions wherein the gem gave to its owner good fortune, or special health cures.

TURTLE

With Japanese influence, the symbol of *longevity*. (See, also, tortoise.)

TURTLE DOVE

A bird noted for its plaintive cooing, basis for these symbolisms, *constancy, affection, loyalty to a mate, chastity*.

A pair of turtle doves denotes, *conjugal love*.

TWELVE

A universal number showing closeness of group membership.

The twelve tribes represent *all Israel*.

The twelve apostles indicate the *church universal*.

The twelve fruits of the spirit are, *love, joy, peace, long suffering, gentleness, goodness, faith, meekness, patience, modesty, temperance*, and *chastity*.

The twelve Apostles are, Peter, Andrew, James the Great, John, Philip, Bartholomew, Thomas, Matthew, James the Less, Jude, Simon, and Judas Iscariot.

For twelve signs of the zodiac see, *zodiac*.

Objects frequently seen as representations of the twelve apostles: twelve bunches of grapes, twelve columns; twelve sheep.

TWO

In Christian symbolism, two as a symbol means *incarnation*, Christ as God and man.

Duads of literature, *goodness and knowledge; heaven and earth; day and night*.

TYCHE

In Greek religion, goddess of *fortune, chance, risk*. As time went on, each city of importance had its own Tyche, in whose predictions the people placed great confidence.

TYPEWRITER

In commercial art, symbol of *literature, authorship, commerce*.

TYPHAEUS

In classical mythology, a giant monster created by Tellos, having one hundred heads with fearful eyes and voices. Some gods in fear of the monster, fled to Egypt, some assumed the forms of animals to escape his wrath. Jupiter became a ram; Juno, a cow. Soon, however, Jupiter ashamed of his cowardice, returned and slew Typhaeus with his thunderbolts.

TYR

In Norse mythology, son of Odin. He was god of *war* and *athletic sports*. He had but one hand, the other having been bitten off by the wolf Fenrir.

Our word *Tuesday* is a memorial to his name.

U

In Japanese zodiac, sign for the *hare.*

UBASTI

Worshipped in early Egypt as goddess of *wild nature.* To her the cat was the sacred animal and she is figured with the head of a cat or lion. Same as Greek Artemis.

ULLE

In Norse mythology, god of the *chase.* He was a speedy runner on stilts, and a skilled archer. Stepson of Thor, god of thunder.

ULYSSES

(See Odysseus.)

UMA

In the Japanese zodiac, the *horse.*

UMBRELLA

Symbol of *sovereignty, official authority.* One of the eight symbols of Buddhism.

UNICORN

Fabulous beast with head and body of a horse, legs of an antelope, tail of a lion or of a horse, beard of a goat, and with only one horn. It is the symbol of *strength, swiftness, ferocity.* The beast was early accepted as a symbol for *feminine chastity,* from the myth that no hunter could capture a unicorn by force, but when they led a virgin to the point of capture, it would lay its head in her lap and fall asleep.

With the denotation of *chastity,* the unicorn has become an attribute of the Virgin Mary, and the one horn signifies the *Cross.*

In Chinese art, it signifies *virility, fruitful marriage.* It is the symbol of the Tribe of *Ephriam* in the bronze door of the Baptistry of Florence. Illustration, p. 8:8.

UNIFORM

In U.S.A. a soldier's uniform is symbol of the *strength of the country.*

UNKATAHE

Among American Indians, goddess of *protection against disease.*

UNKNOWN SOLDIER

In all countries a symbol representing those *who have died in a struggle for the best interests of their country.*

URAEUS

From early Egyptian religion, the uraeus is a representation of the sacred asp, now widely seen in Persia, Egypt, and Mexico as a symbol of *sovereignty* when it is used on the headdress of an important person. The circle stands for the *sun, outermost manifestation of the Divine;* the wings denote the *active, moving presence of God's love;* and the serpent implies the *quickening quality of Divine life.*

URANUS

In Greek mythology, a personification of the *Heavens*, which spread out like a veil, and cover all the earth.

SAINT URBAN

Patron of *vintners* and *vinedressers.* His special day is May 25.

URN

An urn signifies *plenty*, in the supposition that it is filled with wine, oil, or cereals.
    A draped urn reflects *death, mortality.*
    A tilted urn dripping clear oil, is symbolic of a *Holy life.*

SAINT URSULA

Patroness of *schoolmistresses, maidens, drapers.* She was martyred by three arrows through her body, by Huns in Cologne. Her attribute, a crowned princess holding an arrow and white banner with a red cross, symbolic of *mercy.* Her special day, October 21.

USHAS

In Hindu mythology, goddess of *wisdom*, and the *dawn.* Identical with Greek Eos.

V

This letter when made or pictured with first two fingers upraised, is a symbol of *peace, victory.* Popularly known as the Churchillian V-sign, in honor of the great Winston Churchill.

VALERIAN

A perennial herb, symbol of *readiness,* from the quickening effect of the drug made from its roots.

VAMPIRES

Fictitious night birds, reanimated bodies of persons long dead, who return to suck blood from persons asleep. Symbols of *evil.*

VARUNA

In early Hindu myth, the *all-seeing night god,* co-ruler of the world with Mitra, the sun god. He bestows rain when it is needed, and punishes offenders of the law. Represented as riding a monster, holding in his hands a noose or fetters with which to bind violators of social and moral laws.

VASE

Same symbolisms as for urn.

VAULTING

In ancient church architecture, the vaulting signified *those ministers of the Word that bore heavenward the infirmities of their parishioners.*

VAYU

In ancient Hindu myth, god of the *winds* or the *air.*

VEIL

As a piece of wearing apparel with religious associations, the symbolism is *modesty, mystery, bondage, renunciation of the world,* dependent upon the circumstances and occasions for wearing the veil

The bridal veil, now usually white, or, at least a delicate shade of color, earlier implied *submission;* now merely *marriage,* or *high romance.* In art, a veiled figure represents the *inscrutable, unfathomable.*

VENUS

Symbol of *grace, charm, amiability, love, admiration,* from the Roman goddess of bloom and beauty, protectress of gardens and flowers. Same as Greek Aphrodite.

VERBENA

Symbol of *peace,* good *fortune.* Sprigs of verbena were used by ancient Greeks and Romans as an emblem of peace in the signing of treaties. In the Middle Ages, verbena flowers were braided into bridal wreaths to bring good fortune and enduring affection.

SAINT VERONICA

In Apocryphal gospels, Veronica is mentioned as wiping the sweat from the brow of Jesus at the Crucifixion, and that miraculously the cloth retained the likeness of Christ. She has become patroness of *laundressers* and *linendrapers.* Her special day is March 25.

VERONICA

The flower veronica is symbol of *fidelity,* from Saint Veronica, *always faithful.*

VERONICA'S NAPKIN

Illustration, p. 13:7. One of the thirteen symbols of the Crucifixion.

VERTUMNUS

In Roman religion, god of the *orchards,* of the *development* of *vegetation,* and of the *changing seasons.* Patron of agriculture.

VESTA

In Roman mythology, goddess of the *family hearth* and its fire. Her temple symbolized the hearth of the city of Rome where on the beginning of the New Year (March) the vestal virgins rekindled a fire to be kept burning throughout the entire year. She is identified with Greek Hestia.

263

VICTORIA

Roman goddess, identical with Greek Nike, *goddess of victory.*

SAINT VINCENT OF SARAGOSSA

Patron saint of Lisbon and Milan. Also of *vintners* and *vinedressers.* Persecuted for his faith, he was thrown into the sea with a millstone around his neck and the waves hollowed out a suitable grave as his body was washed. ashore. His special day, January 22.

VINE

From its growing habits as a twining plant, a vine denotes *affection.*

One of the most vivid symbols in the Bible representative of the relationship between God and man. Isaiah 5:7. As an emblem of *Christ,* John 15:1, 5, 8. As symbol of the *Church* or the *Eucharist,* a vine, with or without grapes, is frequently carved on or about the altar, sometimes the branches bearing shields of the apostles. An arrangement of a vine, wheat, bread, and wine denotes a *close unity of Christ and His followers.*

A vine, in architecture, stands for *beauty.* In association with Bacchus, it denotes *riotousness.* A vine leaf implies, *first fruits.*

VIOLET

As a color, see liturgical colors. In general, violet denotes *loyalty, humility, watchfulness, resignation, sympathy, penitence, fasting, mourning,* depending upon the occasion of its use, or its surroundings.

Violet, the flower, foremost, is symbol of *humility, modesty, innocence, meditation,* in connection with the natural haunts of the flower — usually beneath hedges or in the shadow of larger plants.

The symbolisms, *suffering* and *mourning* are said to be an outgrowth of an old Christian legend which relates that the flower drooped in the shadow of the cross as Christ died. Illustration, p. 21:2.

A white violet signifies the *innocence of youth,* or *shy modesty.* It is a striking *attribute of Saint Fina,* whose grave soon after her burial was found covered profusely with the flower.

The violet is popular as an emblematic state or national flower. With the daisy and the lily, one of the three national flowers of Italy, and national flower of Greece. The woodviolet is state flower of Illinois. Other states who have adopted the violet are: Wisconsin, New Jersey, Rhode Island.

VIPER

In Biblical symbolism, *poisonous doctrines,* in reference to Matthew 3:17, and 12:34.

A viper and lamprey entwined, from Mediaeval times, have been strong symbols of *adultery.*

VISHVAKARAMAN

Ancient Hindu god of the *arts and crafts.*

VISHNU

The second god of the Hindu Trimurti composed of Brahma, the creator; Vishnu, the preserver; and Shiva, the destroyer. He has many incarnations, among them: Matrya, a *fish;* Kurma, a *tortoise;* Varaha, a *boar;* Narasingha, a *male lion;* Rama, a *dwarf.* His chief avatar is Krishna, most loved god of the Hindus, under whom Vishnu has many worshippers. On his standard, is a garuda. Most usually, he rides upon a tortoise. In his four hands he holds a shell, a quoit, a club, and a lotus.

VITHAR

Norse deity, next to Thor in strength. God of *twilight* and *silence.* Known for having silenced the treacherous Fenrir wolf, devourer of the gods.

SAINT VITUS

Patron saint of Saxony, Bohemia, and Sicily; also of *actors, dancers,* and *those who find it hard to rise in the morning.* His attributes, a boy bearing a palm; boy accompanied by a cock; wolf, or lion; boy holding a dog in leash, or a caldron of oil. His day, June 15.

VULCAN

Roman god of the *forge,* and all *working metals,* but more especially of *fire* in its fearful aspects.

The head of Vulcan, in modern times has often been seen as an emblem of *commerce.*

VULTURE

Bird of ill-omen, symbol of *punishment, death, remorse, major troubles* and a *portent of evil tidings.*

WAGONS

In U.S.A., a train of covered wagons with their teams, either of horses or oxens, is symbol of *westward trend of civilization.*

WAIN

A loaded wain or rick in agricultural picture language is symbol of *harvest.*

WA-HUN-TE-DAN

In American Indian myth, is a *goddess of war.*

WALLFLOWER

The same as a gilly-flower, symbol of *fidelity in misfortune,* in association with the clinging of the plant to old European building walls.

WALLS

In Old Testament Biblical art, *security,* from Isaiah 26:1.

WALSEROBIN

Since 1937 the adopted emblematic flower of Ontario.

WAND

The winged staff of the Roman god Mercury has become a symbol of *equality, cooperation, coordination of effort, healing, harmony,* and with these implications has become the adopted symbol in U.S.A. health programs.

WASSAIL

Both wassail, the beverage, and the wassail bowl, ancient expressions of *good wishes* when used upon festive occasions, especially at Christmas when one drinks to the health of a friend.

WATCHDOG

A popular symbolic figure for *vigilance, the dawn, watchfulness.*

WATER

In general symbolism, as waters of the sea, rivers, fountains, wells, rain, or dew, the implications are, *invigorating qualities of the spirit, refreshment, cleansing.*

Troubled waters denote, *affliction, tribulations, destruction.*

In reference to the baptismal rite in religion, *rebirth, regeneration, grace, purification, sanctifying power.*

WATER LILY

Symbol of *beneficence, charity,* in that the flower shares its place in the pool with others.

In Biblical symbolism, *regeneration,* or *purity* through the rite of baptism.

WATTLE TREE

The wattle tree, or yellow mimosa, is symbol of *immortality, fecundity, Platonic love* in reference to its growth habits — the abundance of seeds readily take root in shallow soil, assuring continuity of the original stock.

WAVES

In Christian art, rolling waves imply *refreshment, renewed spiritual power.*

WEAPONS

Generally are employed as *trophies of victory,* but when reversed, *death, mourning.*

WEATHERCOCK

When, in earlier times, a weathercock was placed atop the steeple of a church, aside from the practical purpose of indicating the direction of the wind, it also served as a challenge to viewers to *face difficulties and warnings,* and to *beware of changing with every wind of doctrine.*

WEDDING RING

(See ring or circle.)

WELL

A well or flowing fountain in religious decorative art implies *divine grace, waters of eternal life, a rebirth through baptism.*

WHALE

Symbol of *violent passion,* the *Devil and his cunning means of destruction.* Associated with an ancient legend where marines mistook the huge body of a whale for an island. Their ship which had been anchored to the animal was suddenly dragged to destruction at a jerking plunge of the whale.

WHEAT

Wheat lends itself to numerous symbolisms:

Wheat heads symbolize *fertility, productivity,* from the many grains in each head.

Wheat heads with grapes, or grapevines, *the bread and wine of the Eucharist.*

Sprays of wheat, indicate the *Bread of Life.*

Wheat arranged as a sheaf, symbol of *hope* and *resurrection,* and as such, used by florists in funeral displays.

A sheaf with sickle, denotes *God's bounty, harvest,* and, together with wheat in the stack or in a shock form an emblem for *agriculture.* Illustration, p. 19:5.

WHEEL

A wheel has a variety of significations, among them:

In general symbolism, *movement, cooperation, power* of *locomotion, the universe, impartiality, divine reunion.*

A winged wheel, denotes *progress.* Illustration, p. 22:10.

Fortuna's wheel (young woman with revolving wheel), *fortune.*

A cogwheel, *full cooperation.*

A broken wheel, *unfinished life work,* when used in a funeral spray.

Wheel of the law, in Buddhism, the eight spokes denote the noble eight-fold path of: *right knowledge, right intentions, right speech, right conduct, right means of livelihood, right effort, right mindfulness,* and *concentration.* Illustration, p. 14:10.

WHIP

A whip, attribute of taskmasters, stands for *compulsion, punishment, tyranny.* Two crossed whips symbolize *hunting.*

WHIPPING POST

One of the thirteen symbolisms of the *Crucifixion,* or the *Passion of Christ.* Illustration, p. 13:1.

WHIRLWIND

In general symbolism, *invincible power;* in religious implication, *irresistible force of the might of God.*

WHITE

Symbol of *purity, joy, rejoicing, innocence, glory, simplicity, perfection, divine wisdom, faith.*

For Christian symbolism, see liturgical colors.

In art, for angels, saints in Heaven, and the Virgin Mary, white has been the favored color. In pagan times, maidens chose white for their wedding gowns.

WILLOW

Usually called weeping willow from its natural characteristics of growth. The symbols are *grief, mourning, desperation.*

Willow branches, are symbols of *grace, friendship, mercy, welcome,* in association with their movement with a slight wind.

In Christian symbolism, from the fact that the willow continues to flourish, no matter how many shoots have been cut off, there has arisen the denotation, *the gospel of Christ remains intact no matter how widely it is distributed among peoples of the world.*

WINDING SHEET

Symbol of *Christ's Passion.*

WINDLASS

In association with its use as a hoisting device, symbol of *compulsion.*

WINDOWS

Light radiating from windows of a home at night, denotes *good cheer.*

In church symbolism, windows reflect the *Christian life;* when open, *good thoughts;* when closed, *things that harm.*

WINDS

Zephyrus is the gentle wind of the west which gives *strength to plants.*

In Christian religion, the denotations are: *operation of the spirit, fickleness, vain hope.* Hosea 12:1; Acts 2:2; James 1:6.

From Egyptian religion, the gods of the four winds are:

North wind — Qehui, the ram-headed god.
South wind — Shehbui, the leopard-headed god.
East wind — Henk-Hisesui, the cow-headed god.
West wind — Hutchaiui, the asp-headed god.

In classical mythology: Boreas represents the north wind; Aquilo, the north-by-east wind; Eurus, the southeast wind; Notus, the south wind; Zephyrus, the west wind, and Corus (Caurus) the northwest wind.

WINE

As an element of consecration in the Eucharist, *refreshment, blood of Christ, remembrance.*

The significance of Jewish consecrated wine, *joy;* additionally, when administered in the marriage rite, *true partnership.*

A wine cup or glass, signifies, *revelry, orgy.*

WINGS

In general symbolism, *speed, aspiration, protection, swiftness of thought, omnipresence, activity.*

With the symbolic meaning of *diligence and activity,* seen on the caduceus. Illustration, p. 19:9.

With the symbolic meaning of *protection, quick action,* seen on the emblems of the four evangelists: on the winged man of Saint Matthew, Illustration, p. 10:8; on the winged lion of Saint Mark, Illustration, p. 10:9; on the winged ox of Saint Luke, Illustration, p. 10:10; on the winged eagle of Saint John, Illustration, p. 10:11.

With the symbolic meaning of *quick responsiveness,* attribute of Hermes.

WISHBONE

Symbol of *fulfilled desires.*

WISTERIA

Symbol of *gentleness and devotion of womanhood.*

WITCH

As an outgrowth of an old pagan cult to whom the devil gave supernatural power, we get the symbolisms, *enchantment, black magic,
power of prophecy, evil.*

WOLF

In Biblical symbolism, a *furious ungodly person,* Isaiah 11:6, and 65:25.
And from John 10:12, *destroyer of God's elect.*

In general symbolism, *famine, major troubles, relentlessness.*

The symbol of the *tribe of Benjamin* on the bronze door of the
Baptistry at Florence.

WOMAN

The symbolisms are varied, among them:

Woman with child in her arms – *motherhood.*

Draped in dark blue, dotted with stars – *night.*

Giving alms, or protecting children – *charity, pity, the Good
Samaritan.*

Mature woman holding grain or fruit, *autumn.*

Woman storing money in a safe – *avarice.*

Woman with book in hand, measuring a sphere with compass –
science.

A veiled woman – *modesty.*

Veiled, and with bowed head, hands crossed in prayer – *piety.*

Blindfolded, a sword in her left hand and holding aloft a balanced scale with her right hand – *justice.*

Women representations of the five senses:

Sight – woman gazing into a mirror.

Hearing – woman listening to music of a lute played by an
attendant.

Smell – woman inhaling the fragrance of a rose.

Touch – woman repulsing a cupid who touches her with the
point of an arrow.

Taste – woman crushing grapes, and drinking the juice.

WOODPECKER

In Greek mythology, a bird sacred to Ares, god of *war.* Symbolic meaning, *perseverant action.*

In church symbolism, usually a woodpecker is thought of as the
Devil, or as *heresy.* In its swift movements to find insects for food,

there is an association with Satan probing the hearts of men to lead them to condemnation.

WOODRUFF

An aromatic herb, also called our Lady's Strawbed, from the legend that sweet woodruff was found amid the straw of the manger birthplace of Christ. Its symbolic meaning is *sweet-flavor*.

WOODTHRUSH

Accepted as the emblematic bird of the District of Columbia.

WORLD

(See globe, orb.)

WORM

From early Christian era, *Satan*, a creature that will never die. Isaiah 66:24; also *hell* from Mark 9:44.

WORMWOOD

Symbol of *calamity, sorrow, displeasure, extreme penitence, humility*, in association with the bitter oil which the herb exudes, an over-use of which is said to lead to mental derangement.

WREATH

An ancient Greece, symbol of *allegiance, dedication, victory*. A laurel wreath was the prize in the Pythian games; a pine wreath in Isthmian games, and an ivy wreath in Nemean games. Funeral wreaths were of roses, narcissus, marjoram. In many countries, a wreath of flowers denotes *death, mourning*, when fastened to the door of the residence, or place of business of the deceased.

Wreaths when used as a church adornment, signify *heavenly joy;* when a decorative element in nuptial festivities, *happiness, lasting joy.*

WREN

The Carolina wren became the emblematic bird of South Carolina in 1948; the Cactus wren for Arizona in 1931.

X

XOCHIPILLI AND XOCHIQUETZAL

The Aztec American deities of *flowers, love,* and *art.*

X.P. (Greek CHI-RHO)

Illustration, p. 11:12, the first two letters in the Greek spelling of the word *Christ.* A Christian symbol widely used as a monogram in embroideries, painting, and printing.

YEAR

Symbolisms of the church hold a special place in the devotions of those Christian denominations whose members observe the nine seasonal divisions of their church calendar. The number of days in each season is fixed, yet the beginning date is not the same year after year, in that Easter, a movable festival is the determining factor for the establishment of the time of the church events which follow. Easter is always the first Sunday after the full moon which happens upon, or next after, the twenty-first of March. If, however, the full moon happens on a Sunday, Easter is observed on the following Sunday.

For each calendar season, to lend atmosphere or create a devotional mood, there is a special symbolic color (described under liturgical colors). There is likewise a distinctive, meaningful symbol for each season or special festival. These divisions of the church calendar, with their respective symbolisms follow:

Advent — This is the first season of the church year, beginning on the Sunday nearest November 30. Its symbol is the Greek Alpha and Omega, with the signification of a *preparation for the coming of a Redeemer*. The special color is violet, symbol of *thoughtfulness and penitence*.

Christmastide, extending from Christmas Eve (December 24) to Epiphany (January 6), has for its symbol the monogram IHS, standing for *rejoicing*. The seasonal color is white, which is used for all occasions closely connected with Christ.

Epiphany — Begins with January 6, the "twelfth night" after Christmas. Its symbol is the star, as it celebrates the visit of the Wise Men to the manger scene. The color, white, continues until the last four days when the green of *new life and hope* is used.

Lent — Begins with Ash Wednesday, forty days before Holy Week. It is therefore not a fixed date. The symbolic color is violet, with implication of *penitence*. The *cross* is the symbolic figure for this season.

Season of Christ's Passion — commonly known as Holy Week. Since it comes within Lent, the symbol is the *cross,* which until Easter day, denotes the *Crucifixion*. On Easter day, the empty cross, *Resurrection*. The color for the week is red, except for Friday, which is black.

Easter — White is the symbolic color, and a *circle* the representing figure, signifying for this occasion, *God's eternal power over death*.

Ascension — is Thursday, forty days after Easter, Its symbol is a *crown*, depicting *Christ's victorious kingship*. White is the symbolic color, denoting *the hope of eternal life with God*.

Pentecost — also called Whitsuntide, is the seventh Sunday after Easter. Its symbols are the *dove and tongues of flame* that symbolize the *Holy Spirit*. The symbolic color is red, with a message of *action, witnessing*.

Trinity is a long season, extending from Pentecost to Advent. Its symbol is the *triangle or trefoil*, illustration, p. 10:1. Its color is the green of *renewal*.

Within these seasonal periods are many special festival days, symbolic colors for which are to be found under liturgical colors.

YELLOW

Yellow is a color of many variant hues, and it is difficult to determine the source of the traditional symbolism which has attached itself to the different degrees of intensity of the color. Among them are:

Those radiating from yellow, the color of the sun — *goodness, enlightenment, inspiration, supreme wisdom*.

Those reflecting the color of gold — *benevolence, fruitfulness, joy, faith, the goodness of God*.

A dingy yellow, *faithlessness, deceit, jealousy*.

Pale yellow, *anguish, treachery*.

A deep orange-yellow — *hospitality, revealed faith*.

Saffron yellow — *debauchery, malevolence, impure love*.

In fashions, yellow is the color of *gaiety, brilliance, imagination*.

YELLOWHAMMER

Thought of also as a golden-winged woodpecker, since 1927 the emblematic state bird of Alabama.

YO-HE-WAH

In American Indian legend the spirit of *the grass*.

YOKE

Symbol of the *law, slavery, restraint, service, labor*.

YEW

Symbol of *resilience*, from the natural growth of the branches which aids them to spring back to original shape after having been bent. A yew branch suggests the *ability of a person to recover after dire misfortune.*

A yew tree planted on graves of early Celts symbolized *immortality* and Christians have continued the same practice with the same symbolic implications.

YMIS

In Norse mythology, the giant from whose body the gods created the world.

YOGI

A follower of yoga philosophy, and physical practices, symbol of *self-control* and *mental discipline.*

YUCCA

Hardy plant of warm, dry regions, also called the Joshua tree. Since 1927 the adopted state plant of New Mexico. Also national plant for Salvador.

YULE LOGS

Symbols of *happiness* and *long life,* based on an old belief that in saving charred pieces of the Christmas log of one year to be used the next in starting the traditional festival fire, one could prolong both life and happiness.

SAINT ZENO

Patron saint of *Verona*, Italy, a fisherman who became a bishop. His special day, April 12. Represented in art in the costume of a bishop, with fish hanging from his crosier.

ZEPHYRUS

In Roman mythology, son of AEolus (god of storm and the winds) and of Eos (Aurora, goddess of the dawn). In the literature of England, Zephyrus has become the personification of the *west wind*, a gentle, beneficent wind, tempered by the warmer air from the Gulf Stream not so far away from the western coast of Britain.

ZEUS

Greek *father of all gods and men, ruler and preserver of Heavens and earth,* and *god of fertility.* His wife is Hera, queen of heaven, and goddess of marriage. Zeus is pictured as a man of great dignity and power, with long beard and with crown of oak leaves. He is either seated or standing, in his hands a thunderbolt, ruler's staff, and an image of Nike, goddess of victory. By his side, an eagle, one of his most representative attributes. Illustration, p. 7:11.

ZINNIA

Symbol of *charming beauty,* from the profusion of color in beds of blooming zinnias, and, *longevity,* from the long blossoming period of this sturdy flower.

ZIRCON

The reddish-colored variety of this gem is also called hyacinth, with symbolical implications of *constancy,* and *prosperity,* symbolisms for the flower from which the gem took its name. With the turquoise, and lapis lazuli, featured as birthstone of December.

ZITHER

In Greek mythology, symbol of the *love-lyric* presided over by the muse Erato who stood for *loveliness.*

ZODIAC

Referred to as *The House of Life,* the zodiac is an imaginary belt encircling the Heavens, containing twelve important constellations associated with twelve months of the year. Symbols as representations of human or animal life for the different months are:

January — Aquarius, the *water-carrier*.
February — Pisces, *the fishes*.
March — Aries, *the ram*.
April — Taurus, *the bull*.
May — Gemini, *the twins*.
June — Cancer, *the crab*.
July — Leo, *the lion*.
August — Virgo, *the virgin*.
September — Libra, *the scales*.
October — Scorpio, *the scorpion*.
November — Sagittarius, *the archer*.
December — Capricornus, *the goat*.

ZUCCHETTO

A close-fitting cap which, when worn by the clergy, signifies *dignity*, the color of which is definitive of the rank of the church official — for the Pope, white; for a bishop, purple; for a cardinal, red.

HONORED PATRONS, GUARDIANS, AND PROTECTORS

A representative list of sainted personages who have become recognized at patrons, guardians or supporters of the various occupations of man and his allied interests — past and present:

ACTORS — St. Genesius, St. Vitus.

ANIMALS — St. Francis of Assisi.

APOTHECARIES — Sts. Comas and Damian, St. Raphael, archangel.

ARCHERS — St. Sebastian.

ARCHITECTS — St. Barbara, St. Thomas Didymus, apostle.

ARMIES — St. Maurice.

ARMORERS — St. Barbara, St. Laurence, St. George of Cappadonia.

ART DEALERS — St. John, apostle.

ARTILLERYMEN — St. Barbara, St. George of Cappadonia.

BAKERS — St. Ambrose, St. Elisabeth of Hungary, St. Honorius.

BANKERS — St. Matthew, apostle.

BARBERS — Sts. Comas and Damian.

BASKET-MAKERS — St. Anthony, abbot.

BEEKEEPERS — St. Ambrose.

BEGGARS — St. Alexis, St. Elisabeth of Hungary.

BOATSMEN — St. Julian, hospitator.

BOOKBINDERS — St. Bartholomew, St. John, apostle, St. Luke, apostle.

BOOKSELLERS — St. John, apostle, St. Thomas Aquinas.

BOXMAKERS — St. Fiacre of Breuil.

BOYS — St. Nicholas.

BRASSBEATERS — St. Fiacre of Breuil.

BREWERS — St. Adrian, St. Arnold, St. Boniface, St. Dorothea, St. Laurence.

BRIDES — St. Dorothea.

BUILDERS — St. Barbara, St. Thomas, apostle.

BURIAL SOCIETIES — St. Sebastian.

CABINET MAKERS — St. Anne.

CAPTIVE SLAVES — St. Leonard of Limoges.

CARPENTERS — St. Joseph, husband of Mary, St. Laurence.

CHAMPIONS — St. Drasius.

CHARITABLE ORGANIZATIONS — St. Elisabeth of Hungary.

CHILDREN'S NURSES — St. Lambert of Maestricht.

CHOIRMASTERS — St. Gregory the Great.

COBBLERS — St. Crispin.

COMPOSITORS — St. John, apostle.

CONFECTIONERS — St. Joseph, husband of Mary, St. Laurence.

COOKS — St. Laurence, St. Martha of Bethany.

COPPERSMITHS — St. Benedict, St. Fiacre of Breuil, St. Maurice.

CORN CHANDLERS — St. Bartholomew, St. Sebastian.

CUTLERS — St. John, the Baptist, St. Laurence, St. Lucy of Syracuse.

DANCERS — St. Vitus.

DENTISTS — St. Apollonia of Alexander.

THE DYING — St. Joseph, husband of Mary.

DOCTORS — St. Luke, the apostle.

DOMESTIC ANIMALS — St. Ambrose.

DRAPERS — St. Ursula.

DYERS — St. Bartholomew, St. Helena, St. Maurice

EMBROIDERERS — St. Clara of Assisi.

ENGINEERS — St. Joseph, husband of Mary.

ENGRAVERS — St. John, apostle.

FALLEN WOMEN — St. Thais, Penitent.

FARRIERS — St. Eligius, St. John the Baptist.

FERRYMEN — St. Julian, hospitator.

FIREFIGHTERS — St. Barbara.

FIREWORKS MAKERS — St. Barbara.

FISHERMEN — St. Andrew, apostle.

FISHMONGER — St. Andrew, apostle, St. Magnus.

FLORENCE — St. Reparta.

FLORISTS — St. Fiacre of Breuil.

FRANCE — St. Joan of Arc, St. Louis of Toulouse.

FRINGEMAKERS — St. Gregory, the Great.

FRUITERERS — St. Leonard of Limoges.

FURRIERS — St. Bartholomew.

GARDENERS — St. Dorothea, St. Fiacre of Breuil, St. Phocas.

GARDENS — St. Fiacre of Breuil.

GEOMETRICIANS — St. Thomas Didymus, apostle.

GLAZIERS — St. Laurence, St. Lucy of Syracuse, St. Mark, apostle, St. James of Ulm.

GLOVEMAKERS — St. Bartholomew, St. Maglorious of Dol.

GOLDSMITHS — St. Eligius of Noyon, St. Luke, apostle.

GRAVEDIGGERS — St. Joseph of Arimathea.

GREENGROCERS — St. Leonard of Limoges.

GUNSMITHS — St. Barbara.

HAIRDRESSERS — St. Louis of Toulouse.

HATTERS — St. Clement of Rome, St. Maurice, St. Philip, apostle.

HEALTH — St. Geminianus.

HELPLESS — St. Jude, apostle.

HORSEMEN — St. George of Cappadonia.

HOSIERS — St. Fiacre of Breuil.

HOSPITALITY — St. Julian, hospitator.

HOUSEHUNTING — St. Joseph, husband of Mary.

HOUSEWIVES — St. Martha of Bethany.

HUNTSMEN — St. Eustace of Rome, St. Hubert.

INN KEEPERS — St. Martha of Bethany, St. Theodotus.

IRELAND — St. Patrick.

IRONMONGERS — St. Sebastian.

JUDGES — St. Ives.

KNIFEGRINDERS — St. Maurice.

KNIGHTS — St. George of Cappadonia.

LABORERS — St. Isadore.

LACEMAKERS — St. Elisabeth of Hungary, St. Teresa of Avila.

LAUNDRESSES — St. Veronica.

LAWYERS — St. Ives.

LEADFOUNDERS — St. Fiacre of Breuil, St. Sebastian.

LEATHERWORKERS — St. Bartholomew.

LINENDRAPERS — St. Veronica.

LITHOGRAPHERS — St. John the Baptist.

MAIDENS — St. Catherine of Siena, St. Ursula.

MARRIED COUPLES — St. Joseph, husband of Mary.

MASONS — St. Peter, St. Thomas Didymus, apostle.

MATHEMATICIANS — St. Hubert.

MEDICINE — Sts. Comas and Damian.

MERCHANTS — St. Nicholas.

METALWORKERS — St. Eligius, St. Hubert.

MIDWIVES — St. Dorothea.

MILLERS — St. James the Elder.

MINERS — St. Barbara.

MINSTRELS — St. Julian, hospitator.

MISSIONARIES — St. Paul, apostle.

MORNING RISING — St. Vitus.

MUSIC — St. Cecelia.

MUSICIANS — St. Cecelia.

NAILSMITHS — St. Chlodulf of Metz, St. Helena.

NAVIGATORS — St. Christopher.

NEEDLEMAKERS — St. Fiacre of Breuil, St. Helena, St. Sebastian.

NOTARIES — St. Ives, St. Lucy, St. Luke, apostle, St. Mark, apostle.

PAINTERS — St. John, apostle, St. Luke, apostle.

PAPERMAKERS — St. John, apostle.

PASTRY COOKS — St. Philip, apostle.

PAWNBROKERS — St. Nicholas.

PEDLARS — St. Lucy of Syracuse.

PENCILMAKERS — St. Thomas Aquinas.

PENITENT DRUNKARDS — St. Martin of Tours.

PENITENT WOMEN — St. Margaret of Cortona.

PHILOSOPHERS — St. Catherine of Alexandria.

PHYSICIANS — St. Blaise.

PILGRIMS — St. Alexis.

PIONEERS — St. Joseph, husband of Mary.

PLAGUE SUFFERERS — St. Roche of Montpellier.

PLASTERERS — St. Bartholomew.

PORK BUTCHERS — St. Anthony, abbot.

POTTERS — St. Fiacre of Breuil, St. Goar.

PRINTERS — St. John, apostle, St. Genesius.

PRISONERS — St. Leonard of Limoges, St. Sebastian.

PUBLISHERS — St. John, apostle.

ROPEMAKERS — St. Catherine of Alexandria, St. Paul, apostle.

SADDLERS — St. Catherine of Alexandria, St. Lucy of Syracuse.

SAILORS — St. Andrew, apostle, St. Christopher, St. Erasmus of Gaets, St. Nicholas.

SCHOLARS — St. Gregory the Great, St. Jerome the Great.

SCHOOLBOYS — St. Laurence.

SCHOOLCHILDREN — St. Benedict.

SCHOOLMASTERS — St. Cassian of Imola.

SCHOOLMISTRESSES — St. Ursula.

SCHOOLS OF LEARNING — St. Catherine of Alexandria.

SCRIBES — St. Lucy of Syracuse.

SCULPTORS — St. John, apostle, St. Luke, apostle.

SEAFARERS — St. Cuthbert.

SEEDSMEN — St. Marcel.

SERVANT GIRLS — St. Lucy of Syracuse.

SHEPHERDS — St. Cuthbert.

SHOEMAKERS — St. Crispin, St. Bartholomew.

SILVERSMITHS — St. Dunstan, St. Eligius.

SINGERS — St. Gregory the Great.

SISTERS OF MERCY — St. Elisabeth of Hungary.

SOLDIERS — St. Maurice.

SPAIN — St. Isadore.

SPINNERS — St. Margaret of Cortina.

SPINSTERS — St. Catherine of Alexandria.

STUDENTS — St. Catherine of Alexandria.

SURGEONS — St. Lambert of Maestricht.

SURGERY — Sts. Comas and Damian.

TAILORS — St. Bartholomew, St. Boniface, St. Casimor, St. John the Baptist, St. Lucy of Syracuse.

TANNERS — St. Bartholomew.

TAPESTRY WEAVERS — St. Francis of Assisi.

TEACHERS — St. Gregory the Great.

THEOLOGIANS — St. Thomas Didymus, apostle.

TILEMAKERS — St. Fiacre of Breuil.

TRAVELERS — St. Christopher, St. Joseph, husband of Mary, St. Julian, hospitator, St. Raphael, archangel.

TRELLISMAKERS — St. Fiacre of Breuil.

TRUSSMAKERS — St. Lambert of Maestricht.

UNDERTAKERS — St. Joseph of Arimathea.

VINEGROWERS — St. Bartholomew.

VINTNERS AND VINEDRESSERS — St. Urban, St. Vincent of Saragossa.

WASHERWOMEN — St. Laurence.

WAX-CHANDLERS — St. Blaise.

WAX REFINERS — St. Ambrose.

WEAVERS — St. Blaise, St. Lucy of Syracuse.

WILD ANIMALS — St. Blaise.

WOMEN IN CHILDBIRTH — St. Margaret of Cortona.

WOOLCOMBERS — St. Blaise.

WOOL WEAVERS — St. Bernadino of Siena.

WRITERS — St. John, apostle.

YOUNG GIRLS — St. Agatha.

EMBLEMATIC STATE FLOWERS, BIRDS, AND TREES OF U. S. A.

In 1782 the bald eagle became the emblematic national bird of the United States. (See p. 22:9.) Colorado was the first state to make an emblematic floral adoption, and since 1889 one state after another has chosen a favorite flower, bird, tree, or animal to become a symbol of the people — some by legislative adoption, some by yielding to the choice of children of the schools, and many through the urgency of the women of the Federated Clubs of the different states. One needs but read histories of the states for the interesting stories attending the adoptions. (For excellent color representations of the state flowers, see the Plate of State Flowers in Webster's *New International Dictionary*, 1961.)

EMBLEMATIC STATE FLOWERS

State	Flower
Alabama	Camellia, (Goldenrod, 1927)
Alaska	Forget-me-not
Arizona	Saguaro Cactus
Arkansas	Apple Blossom
California	Golden Poppy
Colorado	Columbine
Connecticut	Mountain Laurel
Delaware	Peach Blossom
District of Columbia	American Beauty Rose
Florida	Orange Blossom
Georgia	Cherokee Rose
Hawaii	Red Hibiscus
Idaho	Mock Orange (Syringa)
Illinois	Violet
Indiana	Peony (1957)
Iowa	Wild Rose
Kansas	Sunflower
Kentucky	Goldenrod
Louisiana	Magnolia
Maine	Pine Cone and Tassel
Maryland	Black-eyed Susan
Massachusetts	Mayflower (Trailing Arbutis)
Michigan	Apple Blossom
Minnesota	Lady's-Slipper (Moccasin Flower)
Mississippi	Magnolia
Missouri	Hawthorn
Montana	Bitterroot
Nebraska	Goldenrod
Nevada	Sagebrush
New Hampshire	Purple Lilac
New Jersey	Violet
New Mexico	Yucca
New York	Rose
North Carolina	Dogwood

State	Flower
North Dakota	Wild Prairie Rose
Ohio	Red Carnation
Oklahoma	Mistletoe
Oregon	Oregon or Holly Grape
Pennsylvania	Mountain Laurel
Rhode Island	Violet
South Carolina	Carolina Jessamine
South Dakota	Pasqueflower
Tennessee	Iris (Passion Flower)
Texas	Bluebonnet (Lupine)
Utah	Sego Lily
Vermont	Red Clover
Virginia	Dogwood
Washington	Rhododendron
West Virginia	Rhododendron
Wisconsin	Bird's Foot Violet
Wyoming	Indian Paint Brush

EMBLEMATIC STATE BIRDS

State	Bird
Alabama	Yellowhammer
Alaska	Willow Ptarmigan
Arizona	Cactus Wren
Arkansas	Mockingbird
California	California Quail
Colorado	Lark Bunting
Connecticut	Robin
Delaware	Blue Hen Chicken
District of Columbia	Wood Thrush
Florida	Mockingbird
Georgia	Brown Thrasher
Hawaii	
Idaho	Mountain Bluebird
Illinois	Cardinal
Indiana	Cardinal

State	Bird
Iowa	Gold Finch
Kansas	Western Meadowlark
Kentucky	Cardinal
Louisiana	Brown Pelican
Maine	Chickadee
Maryland	Baltimore Oriole
Massachusetts	Black-capped Chickadee
Michigan	Robin
Minnesota	Scarlet Tanager
Mississippi	Mockingbird
Missouri	Bluebird
Montana	Western Meadowlark
Nebraska	Western Meadowlark
Nevada	Mountain Bluebird
New Hampshire	Purple Finch
New Jersey	Eastern Goldfinch
New Mexico	Chaparral (Road Runner)
New York	Eastern Bluebird
North Carolina	Cardinal
North Dakota	Western Meadowlark
Ohio	Cardinal
Oklahoma	Scissor-tailed Flycatcher
Oregon	Western Meadowlark
Pennsylvania	Ruffed Grouse
Rhode Island	Rhode Island Red
South Carolina	Carolina Wren
South Dakota	Ring-necked Pheasant
Tennessee	Mockingbird
Texas	Western Mockingbird
Utah	California Gull
Vermont	Hermit Thrush
Virginia	Cardinal
Washington	Willow Goldfinch
West Virginia	Cardinal
Wisconsin	Robin
Wyoming	Western Meadowlark

EMBLEMATIC STATE TREES

Of those states which have an adopted or chosen emblematic tree, the selection for some was made because of its traditional symbolic implications, but for most states the choice was made because of the fact that that special tree was able to thrive best in the environment of the region in which the choice was made. These states have a chosen tree:

State	Tree
Alabama	Southern Pine
Arizona	Palo Verde
Arkansas	Pine
California	California Redwood
Colorado	Blue Spruce
Connecticut	White Oak
Deleware	American Holly
Florida	Sabal Palmetto
Georgia	Live Oak
Hawaii	Kukui or Candlenut
Idaho	White Pine
Illinois	Oak
Indiana	Tulip Tree
Kansas	Cottonwood
Kentucky	Tulip Tree
Louisiana	Southern Magnolia (unofficial)
Maine	White Pine
Maryland	White Oak
Massachusetts	American Elm
Minnesota	Red or Norway Pine
Mississippi	Magnolia Grandiflora
Missouri	Flowering Dogwood
Montana	Ponderosa or Western Pine
Nebraska	American Elm
Nevada	Single-leaf Pinon
New Hampshire	White or Paper Birch
New Jersey	Red Oak
New Mexico	Pinon or Nut Pine

State	Tree
New York	Sugar Maple
North Dakota	American Elm
Ohio	Buckeye
Oklahoma	Redbud
Oregon	Douglas Fir
Pennsylvania	Hemlock
Rhode Island	Maple (unofficial)
South Carolina	Palmetto
South Dakota	Black Hills Spruce
Tennessee	Tulip Poplar
Texas	Pecan
Utah	Blue Spruce
Vermont	Sugar Maple
Washington	Western Hemlock
West Virginia	Sugar Maple
Wisconsin	Sugar Maple
Wyoming	Cottonwood

INDEX OF ILLUSTRATIONS

BIBLIOGRAPHY

As stated in *The Preface,* source material for this study, *Symbols —
Our Universal Language,* has been diversely scattered. Upon examination
of bibliographies on the subject of symbols, one notes a preponderance of
titles dealing with symbolisms of the church. This is to be expected, for
it is in that special field of interest that most books dealing with symbols
alone have been published. Yet, were I, in providing this selective list of
references of my research, to include the many, many books written in
English on various subjects which have incidentally contributed valuable
information on origin, meaning, and use of symbolical terms, the number
would be beyond comprehension. I have included only a few.

The values of general reference works in my search for information
are not to be overlooked. The factual articles on symbolisms, the bibliographies, and often illustrations served as an excellent starting point, and
might well be examined by those persons who are interested in following
one particular phase of symbol study. This brief list is merely representative:

The Encyclopedia Americana
The Americana Corporation, New York, 1962.

The Encyclopedia Britannica
Encyclopedia Britannica, Inc. Chicago, 1961.

The World's Great Religions
Time Incorporated, New York, 1957.

The Catholic Encyclopedia
The Gilmary Society, New York, 1951.

Standard Dictionary of Folklore, Mythology and Legend
Funk and Wagnalls Company, New York, 1949.

The Universal Jewish Encyclopedia
Jewish Encyclopedia. Inc. New York, 1939.

Hastings Encyclopedia of Religion and Ethics
Edinburgh, 1925.

A SELECTIVE REFERENCE LIST

Appleton, Le Roy H. and Stephen Bridges, *Symbolism in Liturgical Art.* New York, Charles Scribner's Sons, 1959.

Audsley, William and G. A., *A Handbook of Christian Symbolism.* London, Day, 1865.

Bailey, Henry Turner and Ethel Pool, *Symbolism for Artists, Creative and Appreciative.* Worcester, Massachusetts, The Davis Press, 1925.

Branston, Brian, *Gods of the North.* New York, The Vanguard Press, 1955.

Bulfinch, Thomas, *The Age of Fable.* New York, The Heritage Press, 1942.

Burdick, Marjorie J., *Church Symbolism.* Boston, Chapman and Grimes, 1940.

Cole, Herbert, *Heraldry and Floral Forms as Used in Decoration.* New York, E. P. Dutton and Company, 1922.

Conway, J. Gregory, *Flowers East-West.* New York, Alfred A. Knopf, 1939.

Cook, A. B., Zeus — *A Study in Ancient Religion.* New York, Cambridge University Press, 1914.

D'alviella, Count Goblet, *The Migration of Symbols*, with Introduction by Sir George Birdwood. New York, University Books, Inc., 1956.

De Bles, Major A., *How to Distinguish the Saints in Art.* New York, Art Culture Publications, 1925.

Earle, Olive L., *State Birds and Flowers.* New York, William Morrow and Company, 1951.

Evans, E. P., *Animal Symbolism in Ecclesiastical Architecture.* New York, 1951.

Ferguson, George, *Signs and Symbols in Christian Art.* New York, Oxford University Press, 1954.

Ferry, Ervin S., *Symbolism in Flower Arrangement.* New York, The Macmillan Company, 1958.

Fleming, Daniel J., *Christian Symbolism in a World Community.* New York, The Friendship Press, 1940.

Fox-Davies, Arthur Charles, *A Complete Guide to Heraldry.* New York, Thomas Nelson and Sons Ltd., 1956.

Frazer, James G., *The Golden Bough*. New York, The Macmillan Company, 1951.

Fritz, Dorothy B., *The Use of Symbolism in Christian Education*. Philadelphia, The Westminster Press, 1961.

Goldsmith, Elizabeth, *Sacred Symbols in Art*. New York, J. P. Putnam's Sons, 1912.

........................*Ancient Pagan Symbols*. New York, J. P. Putnam's Sons, 1929.

Griffith, Helen S., *The Sign Language of Our Faith*. Washington, D. C., Saint Alban's Press, 1939.

Guerber, H. A., *Myths of Greece and Rome*. New York, American Book Company, 1893.

...................*Myths of the Norsemen*. London, George G. Harrap and Company, 1908.

Haight, Elizabeth, *Aspects of Symbolism in the Latin Anthology and in Classical and Renaissance Art*. New York, Longmans, Green and Company, 1952.

Johnson, F. Ernest, *Religious Symbolism*. New York, Distributed by Harper and Brothers, 1955.

Kerney, C., *The Gods of the Greeks*. London and New York, Thames and Hudson, 1951.

King, Elizabeth W., *Seals of Our Nation, States and Territories*, National Geographic Magazine, Vol. XC, July, 1946.

Knapp, Sister Justina, *Christian Symbols and How to Use Them*. Milwaukee, The Bruce Publishing Company, 1935.

Knight, Richard Payne, *The Symbolic Language of Ancient Art and Mythology*. London, J. W. Bouton, 1876.

Koch, Rudolf, *The Book of Signs*. New York, The Dover Publications, 1955.

Kunkle, Howard R., *Symbols and Terms of the Church*. Philadelphia, The Muhlenberg Press, 1938.

Langer, Susanna K., *Feeling and Form*. New York, Charles Scribner's Sons, 1953.

Lehner, Ernst, *Symbols, Signs, and Signets.* Cleveland and New York, The World Publishing Company, 1951.

Marcus, Margaret Fairbanks, *Period Flower Arrangement.* New York, M. Barrows and Company, 1952.

Muller, Wilhelm Max, *Egyptian Mythology.* Boston, Marshall Jones Company, 1918.

Murray, Alexander, *Manual of Mythology.* New York, Tudor Publishing Company, 1954.

Norris, Herbert, *Church Vestments, Their Origin and Development.* London, J. M. Dent and Sons, 1949.

Parmelee, Alice, *All the Birds of the Bible, Their Stories, Identification and Meaning.* New York, Harper and Brothers, 1959.

Rest, Friedrich, *Our Christian Symbols.* Philadelphia, The Christian Educational Press, 1954.

Roeder, Helen, *Saints and Their Attributes.* Chicago, Henry Regnery Company, 1956.

Schwab, Gustav, *Gods and Heroes.* New York, H. Wolff and Company, 1946.

Shankle, George Earlie, *State Names, Flags, Seals, Songs, Birds, Flowers, and Other Symbols.* New York, The H. W. Wilson Company, Revised Edition, 1951..

Smith, E. Baldwin, *Architectural Symbolism of Imperial Rome and the Middle Ages.* Princeton, New Jersey, The Princeton University Press, 1956.

Stafford, Thomas Albert, *Christian Symbolism in the Evangelical Churches.* New York and Nashville, The Abingdon Press, 1942.

Tredwell, Winifred Reed, *Chinese Art and Motives Interpreted.* New York, J. G. Putnam's Sons, 1915.

Troyer, Johannes, *The Cross as Symbol and Ornament.* Philadelphia, The Westminster Press, 1961.

Twining, Louisa, *Symbols and Emblems of Early and Mediaeval Christian Art.* London, John Murray, 1885.

Van Treeck, Carl and Aloysius Croft, *Symbols in the Church*. Milwaukee, The Bruce Publishing Company, 1956.

Webber, F. R., *Church Symbolism*. Cleveland, J. H. Jansen Company, 1938.

Weinstein, Michael, *The World of Jewel Stones*. New York, Sheridan House, 1958.

Whitehead, A. N., *Symbolism, Its Meaning and Effect*. New York, The Macmillan Company, 1927.

Whittick, Arnold, *Symbols and Signs and Their Meaning*. Newton, Massachusetts, Charles T. Branford Company, 1960.

Wilson, Frank E., *An Outline of Christian Symbolism*, Milwaukee, Morehouse-Gorham Company, 1933.

Zimmer, Heinrich Robert, *Myths and Symbols in Indian Art and Civilization*. (Edited by Joseph Campbell.) New York, H. Wolff and Company, 1947.

Grateful acknowledgment is extended to the following for use of material from their recently published books:

Reprinted by permission from *The Use of Symbolism in Christian Education* by Dorothy B. Fritz, 1961, W. L. Jenkins, The Westminster Press:

P. 16. Illustrative drawing of ICHTHUS.

P. 17. Drawing of the lamb.

Pps. 28, 29. Drawings of the emblems of Matthew, Mark, Luke, John.

Pps. 36, 37. Excerpts of "Symbolisms of the Church Year," appearing under the headword, *year*.

To Mr. Arnold Whittick, *Symbols and Signs*, 1961, Charles T. Branford Company, Newton, Massachusetts:

Scattered portions of Chapter XI, "Traditional and Familiar Symbols," valuable descriptive matters of history and meanings of traditional symbolisms.

To Mr. George Ferguson, *Signs and Symbols in Christian Art*, 1959, Oxford University Press, New York:

P. 3. Illustrative drawings of the crane.

P. 11. Drawings of the swallow, stork.

P. 17. Drawings of laurel, lily, lily of the valley.

P. 21. Drawing of the violet.

From section X, scattered details on the lives of saints.